Effective Platform Product Management

An effortless strategy and execution guide for product managers who want to scale their platform business model and grow their customer base

Tabassum Memon

BIRMINGHAM—MUMBAI

Effective Platform Product Management

Group Product Manager: Aaron Lazar

Publishing Product Manager: Kushal Dave

Senior Editor: Ruvika Rao

Content Development Editor: Rosal Colaco

Technical Editor: Karan Solanki

Copy Editor: Safis Editing

Project Coordinator: Deeksha Thakkar

Proofreader: Safis Editing

Indexer: Sejal Dsilva

Production Designer: Joshua Misquitta

First published: October 2021

Production reference: 2170522

Published by Packt Publishing Ltd.

Livery Place

35 Livery Street

Birmingham

B3 2PB, UK.

ISBN 978-1-80181-135-4

www.packt.com

To my mother; you were the strongest person I have ever met in my life. Thanks for all the sacrifices you made for me and for teaching me the importance of hard work. This book will always have bittersweet memories for me. I lost you the day I started working on its proposal. I hope you will be proud as you look down on me.

– Tabassum Memon

Contributors

About the author

Tabassum Memon is an expert product strategist who believes in lean product development and the platform-first approach. Currently, she is working as a CPO for Classroom Hunt, a company she founded. She has helped a lot of companies transform from product to platform thinking. During her 14-year product management and consulting career, she has worked with senior product leaders and executives of large enterprises in migrating from product to platform, defining product and platform strategies.

Acknowledgments

Rome was not built in a day, and neither was this book. This book is the result of the hard work and collaboration of a lot of people. Some of them were directly involved, while some have supported me in my journey, and I would like to thank each one of them.

Thanks to everyone on the Packt team who helped me so much. Special thanks to Rosal, Ruvika, Deeksha, and Kushal for editing and coordinating the publishing of this book.

I would also like to thank Pramod Sadalage and Sunil Mundra for helping me with the book's proposal.

To my technical reviewer, Mangalam Nandakumar, who thoroughly reviewed the book and caught things that I would have never imagined and thought about. Thanks for all the valuable feedback that improved the book.

I wish to thank Ananad Vishwanath and Kalyanasis Banerjee for helping and guiding me in different parts of my career and trusting me to take the responsibilities that helped me to learn and grow professionally.

A very special thanks to Max Griffiths for always motivating and encouraging me, and especially for having those intriguing discussions about platforms that triggered my interest in this area.

Finally, I would like to thank Ryan Murray for taking my interest in platforms to the next level, and for always guiding and mentoring me. Thanks a lot for believing in me, inspiring me, and supporting me in my journey. This book wouldn't have been possible without you; thank you so much.

About the reviewer

Mangalam Nandakumar has over 17 years of experience in product management and software delivery. She is an entrepreneur and has founded two start-ups. She started her career as a programmer and soon transitioned to business analysis and product management.

She co-founded her start-up, AIDAIO, in 2014, to enable businesses to enhance their customer engagement strategies. AIDAIO was shortlisted as one of the Top 10 Promising Start-Ups by CII in 2015. She was instrumental in establishing organization-level initiatives to coach and guide women to speak at conferences. She ran an art school and has conducted art workshops as well as exhibited and sold her artwork. She lives in Bengaluru, India, and enjoys playing and watching movies with her son.

Table of Contents

3

Research and Validation

4

Building a Platform Strategy

Section 2: Building the Platform

5
Defining the MVP and Creating a Platform Roadmap

6
Launching the Platform

7
Creating a Platform Operating Model

Section 3: Measuring the Performance of the Platform

8
Metrics to Measure the Platform Outcome

9
Ongoing Backlog Prioritization

10
Moving from Linear Products to Platforms

Other Books You May Enjoy

Index

Preface

In the last few years, platform business models have revolutionized various industries, such as retail, media, and travel. With the rise of platforms and increased use of technology, consumers nowadays want multiple options available digitally. They like to search, explore, compare, and choose between different options within a single uninterrupted user experience. Providing such an experience is difficult and indeed almost impossible using linear models. Hence, more and more businesses will have to adapt the platform-first approach. There is a shift needed at all levels and in every function of an organization. Right from strategy to execution, everyone will have to adopt the platform way of thinking.

Some organizations have already started moving in this direction. Executives have begun realizing the need and benefits of the platform. However, the challenge is building the right platform strategy and the execution of that strategy. One function of the organization that is most important in creating this strategy and helping in its execution is product management. Ironically, this is one function that is far from grasping the importance of platforms and of building the right strategy for them. Product managers still think in terms of linear products and forget to build the strategy and roadmaps that cater to the platform's needs.

This book will address this critical pillar of platform development, that is, product management. It will cover the difference between traditional product management and product management for platforms while explaining the importance and benefits of the platform. It will help and guide business executives and product managers in building the right platform strategy, defining the MVP, and ongoing prioritization. This book will also cover the steps and guidelines for organizations and especially product managers when transitioning from linear products to platforms. It will help them in the journey of this transformation. This book will answer all the essential questions of product management for building successful and scalable platforms.

Who this book is for

If you're a product manager, product owner, product director, or a business executive working on a platform strategy and its day-to-day execution, then this book is for you. It will also be useful for change managers and program managers tasked with transitioning from products to platforms. You won't need any prior knowledge of platform strategy or platform transitioning before you get started, since the book covers all the basics – but taking notes to reflect on your journey as you work through the practical examples in this book is recommended.

What this book covers

Chapter 1, Fundamentals of Platform Business Models, covers what a platform is in general and how that concept applies to digital platforms and the platform business model. It will cover the fundamentals of the platform business model by explaining the characteristics and components of a digital platform that are needed to support the platform model. This chapter will also describe all the benefits of the platform model. At the end of this chapter, you will have a good understanding of what a platform business model is, why it is important, and how it can be supported by the right digital platform.

Chapter 2, Differences between Linear Products and Platforms, explains why you have to adopt different techniques and mindsets for platform product management. The chapter will start by explaining how platforms are different from linear products and then explain how product managers should think differently in terms of the different methods that need to be applied when building platforms. This chapter will cover a real-world use case to explain the difference between a linear product and a platform. This chapter covers the *breadth* of the product life cycle, while each of the following chapters explores the *depth* of each step of that life cycle.

Chapter 3, Research and Validation, covers how to gather user insights and validate the platform use case. Doing research and gathering data for the concept validation of a platform is different from the process for a traditional product. Hence, this chapter will explain to you how to do the initial research and collect the right data. This chapter will include a case study on validating the concept of a platform.

Chapter 4, Building a Platform Strategy, explains how the business vision defines the business strategy and the business strategy defines the platform strategy. You will learn how important it is to have the right platform strategy to meet your business vision. This chapter will cover different types of platform strategies and the components of a good platform strategy. This chapter will continue the case study to build the platform strategy after the concept is validated.

Chapter 5, Defining the MVP and Creating a Platform Roadmap, explains how to translate a platform strategy to a long-term platform roadmap. In this chapter, you will learn how to create an end-to-end user journey for the platform and define the platform capabilities. You will learn how to carve out the MVP by prioritizing and ranking those capabilities. The case study will continue with creating the platform roadmap and defining the platform MVP.

Chapter 6, Launching the Platform, explains how to launch a platform, the factors that need to be considered before launching a platform, the elements of a successful launch, and what strategies must be implemented for the successful launch of a platform. By the end of this chapter, you will know how to create an effective marketing plan before the launch of a platform and how to execute the launch strategy successfully and enable its growth. The case study will continue with the launch of the platform.

Chapter 7, Creating a Platform Operating Model, covers how to create an operating model for the platform that can translate a platform strategy to successful execution. This chapter will explain what the most efficient team structure is, where the accountability and responsibilities lie, the ways of working, and how to govern the platform execution. The case study will cover efficient team structure and a successful governance model for platforms.

Chapter 8, Metrics to Measure the Platform Outcome, teaches you how to measure the outcome of a platform after it is launched and the governance structure is in place. This chapter will cover different metrics that should be collected to measure the success or failure of a platform. This chapter will also cover how to analyze the results after metrics data collection.

Chapter 9, Ongoing Backlog Prioritization, looks at how to keep backlog prioritization going. This chapter will cover how platform backlog prioritization is different from traditional product backlog prioritization, along with the challenges to face and mistakes to avoid during prioritization. The case study will further expand to cover ongoing platform backlog prioritization.

Chapter 10, Moving from Linear Products to Platforms, explains the transition from products to platforms. You will learn how to validate the viability of the platform business model for existing linear businesses. You will see what factors are to be considered before transitioning and how to start the transition. In this chapter, you will see the different phases of the transition of a linear enterprise product to a platform in the form of a case study.

To get the most out of this book

Some familiarity with basic product management concepts such as the product life cycle, MVP, feature prioritization, and product metrics will be useful.

Download the color images

We also provide a PDF file that has color images of the screenshots and diagrams used in this book. You can download it here: `https://static.packt-cdn.com/downloads/9781801811354_ColorImages.pdf`.

Conventions used

There are a number of text conventions used throughout this book.

Bold: Indicates a new term, an important word, or words that you see onscreen. For instance, words in menus or dialog boxes appear in **bold**. Here is an example: "As we discussed, during the initial startup phase, we should not have a separate **Governance** team, and executives should take up the responsibilities of the **Governance** team."

> **Tips or important notes**
> Appear like this.

Get in touch

Feedback from our readers is always welcome.

General feedback: If you have questions about any aspect of this book, email us at `customercare@packtpub.com` and mention the book title in the subject of your message.

Errata: Although we have taken every care to ensure the accuracy of our content, mistakes do happen. If you have found a mistake in this book, we would be grateful if you would report this to us. Please visit www.packtpub.com/support/errata and fill in the form.

Piracy: If you come across any illegal copies of our works in any form on the internet, we would be grateful if you would provide us with the location address or website name. Please contact us at `copyright@packt.com` with a link to the material.

If you are interested in becoming an author: If there is a topic that you have expertise in and you are interested in either writing or contributing to a book, please visit `authors.packtpub.com`.

Share your thoughts

Once you've read *Effective Platform Product Management*, we'd love to hear your thoughts! Scan the QR code below to go straight to the Amazon review page for this book and share your feedback.

https://packt.link/r/1-801-81135-0

Your review is important to us and the tech community and will help us make sure we're delivering excellent quality content.

Section 1: Building the Right Strategy for the Platform Business Model

In this section, we'll make sure that you understand the difference between the traditional linear business model and the platform business model, along with looking at the fundamentals of a digital platform. You will learn how product management aspects and techniques are executed differently for traditional linear products versus digital platforms. You will also learn how to validate the viability of the platform business model by applying the appropriate research. Finally, you will learn how to build a robust platform strategy for a successful sustainable platform.

This section comprises the following chapters:

- *Chapter 1, Fundamentals of Platform Business Models*
- *Chapter 2, Differences between Linear Products and Platforms*
- *Chapter 3, Research and Validation*
- *Chapter 4, Building a Platform Strategy*

1
Fundamentals of Platform Business Models

In the last decade or so, platform business models have revolutionized various industries, such as retail, entertainment, media, and travel. Companies such as Amazon, Spotify, and Airbnb have changed how businesses reach out to their consumers and how consumers use the products. One thing all these companies have in common is a platform business model that allows multiple producers to connect to their consumers. This multidimensional model is the biggest differentiator for these companies, giving them an edge over traditional linear business models catering to limited consumer segments or demographics. So, because of the rise of such platforms, more and more businesses are adapting to a *platform-first approach*.

But before we dive deeper into platform business models, it is essential to understand what the term *platform* means in general and how that concept applies to digital businesses. Hence, in this chapter, we will cover the following topics:

- What is a platform?
- Understanding platform business models
- Types of platforms

- Platform revenue models

- Benefits of a platform business model

- Building the right digital platform for a platform business model

What is a platform?

As per *Encyclopedia.com*'s definition, the literal meaning of the word *platform* is *a raised level surface on which people or things can stand* (`https://www.encyclopedia.com/ science-and-technology/computers-and-electrical-engineering/ computers-and-computing/platform`). It makes sense as a broader concept that a platform is an avenue for people or things to carry out crucial tasks. The word *platform* has different meanings in different industries and fields—for example, in the railway industry, construction, public speaking, and so on.

But one common thing in all the definitions of a platform is that a platform enables some core activities to occur. This brings me to the most precise and simple definition I have read of a platform: a platform is something that allows something else to happen. A platform is something that is foundational, enables people to undertake core activities, and helps connect different entities together. In terms of a platform in a public speaking context, a speaker can connect to the audience through a platform. Similarly, a train can connect to passengers via a platform, and a construction worker undertakes their core activities through a platform.

This analogy can also be applied to digital businesses, whereby a platform enables the core activities of the business and connects different entities; for example, in e-commerce platforms, sellers and consumers connect with each other, and the platform enables them to accomplish the core activity of selling and consuming goods. Similarly, in an audio-streaming platform, artists and listeners come together to share and listen to music. Similarly, in a payment-processing platform, banks or credit card companies connect with vendors to enable seamless money transfer.

A critical feature of a platform is that it allows a web of multiple channels to connect and perform core activities, not just two parties that connect linearly. For example, once a platform is built in an auditorium, all the speakers using the auditorium can address the crowd from one platform; we do not have to build a different stage (platform) for every speaker.

Another example here is a railway platform that, once built, is used by all the trains and passengers traveling to and from that station. The same is true for the digital world; multiple sellers can sell on an e-commerce platform, and many artists can upload their music on an audio-streaming platform. We will explore this multidimensional approach and a platform's network effect in more detail while discussing the characteristics of a platform business model.

Understanding platform business models

As mentioned earlier in this chapter, we have seen a tremendous shift and disruption in various industries in the last few decades. Traditionally, huge brick-and-mortar stores were synonymous with retail business, but today, the world's second-largest retailer does not have a single physical store. Companies such as Amazon, Spotify, Netflix, and so on have changed the business landscape. These companies took the very traditional concept of a platform and translated it into the digital world.

For example, Amazon is no different from the older-style marketplace where sellers display their products and buyers come to browse and buy products they are interested in. Netflix is no different from a video library where you bring home any video media with a small subscription fee. The traditional platform concept aided by technology is the secret sauce for the success of today's businesses. Imagine a marketplace where a buyer from Australia can buy goods from sellers in the US or a user from China can rent a movie from a video library in Europe.

This broader reach is possible because of platforms. It could be argued here that producers creating their own digital presence in the form of websites can still get a global reach. This is true, but this model is neither scalable nor cost-effective.

Let's look at an example here of a new designer who wants to launch their new line of clothing; if they create their own online boutique rather than leveraging an existing platform, they won't be able to optimize it or get it right as it is not their core capability. Secondly, they will divert from their competency of designing clothes.

On the other hand, a fashion retail platform already has all the foundations in place. They are an expert in customer acquisition, **Search Engine Optimization** (**SEO**), and other digital aspects that will take years for the new designer to build, and even then, they might not get it right. This model is a win-win for all parties, in the following ways:

- **Designers**: Designers can reach out to consumers worldwide without spending a lot of time and effort on doing this. They can focus on creativity and design to provide more options for consumers to choose from.

- **Fashion retail platform**: The platform can showcase and sell the work of different creative designers. They don't have to worry about designing, manufacturing, or producing. Their job is to connect the designers to consumers. Their success depends on how well they can scale and how many designers and consumers they can connect. The more consumers they can connect to the designers, the more revenue they generate for themselves and for the designers.

- **Consumers**: Consumers get access to designs from multiple designers across the globe. They can search, explore, compare, and choose between different options within a single uninterrupted **User Experience** (**UX**). Getting access to a variety of options in a single uninterrupted UX is not possible in the linear business world.

This example describes how a platform business model is beneficial to all the players involved. The majority of platforms have three primary parties: producers, consumers, and the platform owner, but there are few platforms—such as payment-processing platforms—where you will find additional entities such as a bank or credit card processor, which are referred to as intermediaries.

Characteristics of a platform business model

So far, we have seen the general definition of a platform and how it applies to platform businesses in the digital world. As we go further into understanding platform business models and digital platforms, let's look at some of the characteristics that define these models. There are, for sure, lots and lots of different features and characteristics of a platform, but in my opinion, the following three are the key characteristics or the essential elements of any platform business:

- Multidimensional

- Network effect

- Plug-and-play mechanism

Multidimensional

We briefly looked at the characteristics of a platform business earlier in this chapter: the platform does not just let two entities connect linearly but allows a web of multiple entities to create and deliver value.

In a traditional linear business model, there is only one producer who delivers value to a handful of consumers. At the same time, a platform model allows multiple producers to serve and provide value to multiple consumers—for example, an author of a book has their own website selling their own books versus Amazon selling books from multiple authors. The following diagram shows the one-dimensional flow in a linear product model as compared to the multidimensional flow in a platform model:

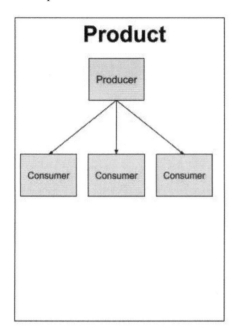 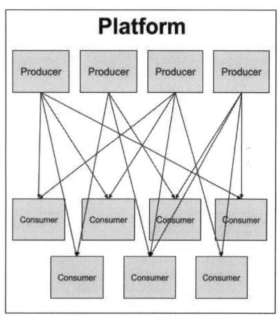

Figure 1.1 – Linear product and multidimensional platform

The preceding diagram depicts how consumers can choose to buy from any producer on the platform, whereas the consumer is restricted to only one producer in the linear product model. In the platform model, the flow of products is coming from multiple directions.

This nonlinear and multidimensional approach is what made companies such as Amazon, Netflix, and Spotify so different and set them apart from the competition. Amazon doesn't sell products from just one manufacturer, but it allows any seller to use its platform to sell. Similarly, Netflix streams content from hundreds of production houses from dozens of countries. Spotify is not restricted to just one artist but gives listeners access to multiple artists. Creating this multidimensional connection between producers and consumers is a crucial aspect of a platform business model.

Network effect

If we extend the multidimensional characteristic of a platform business, we get something called a **network effect**. The ability to connect multiple producers to consumers creates a network between all the entities of the platform. A network effect is something that increases the value of one entity as the number of participants increases in another entity.

For example, when a new seller joins a marketplace, all the buyers benefit from the new seller; similarly, when a new buyer enters the marketplace, all the sellers enjoy the benefit of this. Also, the higher number of participants in one group attracts more participants from another group. For example, as the Spotify user base keeps growing, more and more artists join Spotify to provide various music choices, which in effect attracts more users. The network effect is thus the cycle that is created by the platform business model. The platform is at the center of these entities, facilitating their connection and growth, as depicted in the diagram here:

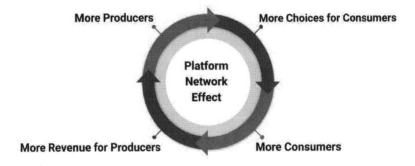

Figure 1.2 – Platform network effect

The network effect is the most crucial aspect in the success of a platform business. Platform business models cannot sustain and grow with just one entity. For example, there is no use in increasing the number of buyers when there are limited sellers on an e-commerce platform; the buyers will start dropping as they are not getting a big enough choice of products.

Similarly, if there are fewer buyers on the platform, this will not be profitable for the sellers, and hence they will move out of the platform. None of the entities can exist without the other. Growth and increase in one entity will lead to the development and growth of another, leading to the platform's growth. Therefore, a strong network effect is key in the success of any platform business.

Plug-and-play mechanism

As we saw earlier, a platform's success depends on how well it can connect and not on how well it can sell. One thing that facilitates the seamless connection between producers and consumers at a massive scale is the *plug-and-play nature* of platforms. The success of a platform depends on how easy it is for producers and consumers to join the platform. A linear business focuses on making consumer onboarding easier, but in the case of a platform, it is equally—or maybe more—essential to make producer onboarding easier and seamless so that they can launch and test their ideas or products quickly. The easier and quicker it is for producers to join, the more and more they will be attracted to the platform, bringing in more consumers and creating a strong network effect.

The plug-and-play mechanism is what disrupted the smartphone market a decade ago. Android and iOS were not significantly different in offering feature sets than some of their competitors, but their App Store/Play Store revolutionized the market. Any external developer can develop an app and create value using these platforms, and this plug-and-play mechanism is what differentiated them from their competitors.

The plug-and-play nature of a platform business enables its scalability and extensibility—for example, an e-commerce platform can quickly onboard new sellers and easily introduce new categories, and expand into new services. If the foundation of the platform is designed right, the possibilities are endless. If the producer onboarding to the platform is tedious and has lots of steps, or deals with complex configurations, producers might create something of their own. One of the crucial benefits of a platform for producers is to launch and test quickly. If producers cannot do that, they are unlikely to join the platform, reducing the number of choices to consumers and leading to a reduced number of consumers, hence hampering the platform's growth and sustainability.

To summarize, these three characteristics are the key to defining a platform business model's success. To be successful, a platform should connect entities in a multidimensional way to deliver value, scale to create a strong network effect, and enable easy onboarding via a plug-and-play mechanism.

Types of platforms

Different entities that a platform connects to deliver value are producers and consumers of products or services; as in our previous example, the designer launching the new clothing is a producer, and the person buying the clothes is a consumer. Hence, when building a platform strategy or creating a platform, it is essential to understand that there are two types of users: **consumers** and **producers**.

Designing a platform with both types of users in mind is necessary. However, there are specific platforms where the producers are also the consumers. The approach and design of these kinds of platforms where producers and consumers are the same will be different from that of a platform where producers and consumers have two separate personas. To understand this concept in detail, let's look at some common types of platforms, as follows:

- **Marketplace**: This is the most common and easy-to-understand platform type. Here, buyers and sellers (producers and consumers) are two different entities and they connect using the platform. Buyers get to explore various products, compare them, and make an informed decision about the purchase. Sellers can demonstrate their products to all potential and interested buyers. Amazon, eBay, Alibaba, Walmart Marketplace, and so on are some of the well-known platforms in this space.

- **Social media**: Everyone is familiar with social media platforms nowadays. They are where people connect, share ideas, and socialize virtually. Facebook, Twitter, and LinkedIn are some examples of popular social media platforms. Social media platforms are one type of platform where producers and consumers are the same. On these platforms, a user shifts between being a producer and a consumer within the same session and in a few minutes. For example, when a user is writing a tweet, they are the producer, but they are the consumer when they are reading someone else's tweet.

- **Search engines**: When I say *search engine platforms*, it is not just the Googles and Bings of the world, but it could be a search engine for a very specific category. For example, Zillow is a real-estate search engine where buyers/renters can search for properties, and Indeed is a search engine where candidates search for job openings. There are two entities in the specific search-platform category—on Zillow, there are homeowners and renters, and on Indeed, there are recruiters and job seekers. But information search engines that are category-agnostic, such as Google and Bing, only have consumers; there are no specific producers of that information.

- **Content and entertainment**: For entertainment and content platforms, content creators are producers, and users streaming and watching the content are consumers. On some of these platforms, content creation is restricted to artists and experts and is controlled by the platform owners—for example, Netflix or Spotify. But there are platforms where content creation is open to everyone and anyone—for example, on YouTube, which can also be categorized as a social media platform.

- **Knowledge and information sharing**: Knowledge and information sharing platforms are similar to social media platforms in that the producers and consumers are the same. Some common examples of such knowledge and information sharing platforms are Stack Overflow, Coursera, Quora, and Yelp. When a user asks a question or replies to a question on Stack Overflow, they are a producer, but when they are browsing and reading solutions, they are a consumer. Similarly, on Yelp, when a user is adding a review, they are a producer, but when they are browsing and reading reviews, they are a consumer.

- **Service-oriented**: Service-oriented platforms are the ones where a platform enables the aggregation of **Service Providers** (**SPs**) and connects them to the consumers. SPs are the producers in this scenario. Classic examples of this type of platform are Uber, Airbnb, DoorDash, and so on. These platforms crowdsource the SPs and connect them to the right consumers. Platforms such as DoorDash have an additional layer; they connect three entities instead of two, as seen in most platform types. They connect restaurants, dashers (drivers), and consumers for the seamless completion of food delivery.

- **Transaction and payments**: All financial platforms such as PayPal fall under this category. They facilitate the completion of a transaction by processing the payment. Most of them operate at a commission or transaction fee; we will cover this in the *Platform revenue models* section. Similar to DoorDash, transaction platforms have three layers or connect three entities—buyers, merchants, and banks.

- **Communication**: Direct messaging and chatting platforms such as WhatsApp, Slack, Skype, and so on are popular and familiar examples of communication platforms. Producer and consumer roles and responsibilities in communication platforms are similar to those of social media platforms. The same user acts as a producer or a consumer, depending on their action.

- **Infrastructure**: Infrastructure platforms provide hardware and computing resources to organizations. Infrastructure platforms take care of hosting, storage, networking, and other essential hardware and software needed to create and deploy any application. Cloud computing platforms such as **Amazon Web Services** (**AWS**) and Azure are the most popular and dominant players in this space.

- **Development**: All the operating systems are categorized as development platforms; some are controlled and closed, such as Windows and Apple App Store, whereas some are open source, such as Android and Linux.

  Apart from the operating systems, platforms built to access data via **Application Programming Interfaces** (**APIs**) or platforms that enable different software development aspects are also classified as development platforms.

Platform revenue models

As we have seen, there are multiple entities involved in the platform ecosystem: producers, consumers, platform owners, and, in some cases such as payment platforms, intermediaries such as banks. The platform ecosystem must be beneficial to all parties, hence picking a suitable revenue model for the platform business is crucial.

A platform ecosystem is like a network of these entities, and it only works when all the entities are present in the ecosystem and are doing what they are supposed to do. Therefore, for any platform's success, all the entities must benefit from it, which is only possible if the platform is operating with a suitable revenue model. Hence, choosing the optimized revenue model for all the entities is key in a platform business model's success.

Types of revenue models

Understanding different revenue models is essential before deciding which is the best revenue model for enabling all the entities involved in the platform ecosystem to function at an optimal level. The following are some standard and popular revenue models for platform businesses; let's look at them in detail:

- **Subscription**: A subscription model is where consumers pay a fixed amount of a monthly or yearly subscription fee and can access all the products and services offered by the business. This model is prevalent for content and entertainment platforms such as Netflix and Spotify. Consumers get access to all the content on the platform by paying a subscription fee. This model also works for knowledge and information sharing platforms.

  Producers on these platforms are usually paid a royalty on how much their content is consumed or a fixed amount for each piece of content that they create. A subscription model works best on content platforms as the content, once created, does not incur any additional cost based on its consumption. For example, the production costs of a movie that streams on Netflix do not increase as the number of viewers keeps increasing exponentially. Hence, a subscription model is the most suitable model for content platforms, but this model is not advisable and is not suitable for marketplaces or service-oriented platforms.

- **Advertising**: An advertising model is the reverse of a subscription model. In a subscription model, consumers pay a fee and producers get royalties, while in an advertising model, consumers do not have to pay anything but the platform charges producers to promote and provide featured placement of their content, products, and services. This model is suitable for and works best with social media and communication platforms such as Facebook, Twitter, LinkedIn, Skype, and so on. Some information-sharing platforms such as Stack Overflow also run on an advertising business model.

  This model works when the content is not premium and the content creator is not charging anything—for example, people tweeting on Twitter don't get paid for tweets, or people replying to Stack Overflow questions do not charge anything. When content is free, consumers don't have to pay, but the platform's cost and the profit for the platform owner are derived by promoting and sponsoring certain content, products, and services.

- **Pay-as-you-go**: Pay-as-you-go revenue models charge the consumer for the goods and services they are using. The price will depend on the size and cost of the goods or services consumed. A major part of the price goes to the producer, and the platform owner charges some service fee, transaction fee, or commission. These fees are sometimes a fixed amount but can also be a percentage of the total price or a combination of the two.

  This revenue model is suitable for marketplaces and service-oriented platforms such as Amazon, eBay, Uber, Airbnb, and so on. Most of the development and infrastructure platforms such as AWS also follow the same model; consumers pay for the services and resources they are using. This model is suitable when the cost of goods and services varies hugely and depends on its value. For example, one consumer buying a book and another purchasing a TV set on Amazon cannot pay the same subscription fee; they will have to pay differently for different products. Similarly, an Uber ride for a 3-mile journey will have a different cost from a 15-mile trip. Hence, in a pay-as-you-go model, consumers are paying as they are consuming.

- **Pay-per-listing**: A pay-per-listing model also charges the producers instead of consumers, as we saw with an advertising model. This model is quite prevalent on search engines, especially search engines of a specific category—for example, a job site will charge recruiters for job listings but won't charge anything to job seekers. Some search engines also offer free listings in the general search results but only charge for premium placements, such as at the top of search results or strategic locations where the listing is very prominent and users tend to click more. Some search engines extend a pay-per-listing model to a pay-per-click model, where producers are only charged when users click on their listing.

- **Hybrid**: Most platforms nowadays follow a hybrid revenue model where they combine two or three revenue models, such as advertising and subscription or advertising and pay-as-you-go. Search engines such as Google display advertisements and charge for a premium or sponsored listing. LinkedIn has a premium membership model but also earns revenue from advertisements.

  Amazon operates with a majority of or almost all revenue models; for example, it offers Prime membership at a subscription fee, earns a commission/fee on every purchase, offers sponsored products, and displays other advertisements and promotions. In most hybrid revenue models, the advertising model is usually combined with one other model. It does not directly impact the consumer but provides an additional revenue stream for platform owners from producers who are ready to pay a little extra.

We looked at the different types of platforms and the role of different entities such as producers, consumers, and platform owners in each of those platform types. We also looked at the different revenue models. This combination of platform types and various revenue models will help us understand how to choose a suitable model for any platform business.

Choosing the right revenue model

Selecting the right revenue model depends on two key factors, as outlined here:

- **Direct cost of product/service/content**: While deciding on a platform revenue model, it is essential to understand the cost structure of the product/service or content that the platform is offering. *Is the cost of production one-time, irrespective of quantities consumed, or does it multiply with the number of quantities?* When the production cost is one-time and does not increase exponentially with the consumption, a subscription revenue model is best suited. For example, songs produced once can be streamed millions of times on Spotify without incurring additional cost, or the cost of content created for Netflix does not increase with the number of times it is streamed. Hence, charging a subscription fee in exchange for access to the content is feasible for the platform owner. Consumers get unlimited access to the content on the platform for a fixed fee irrespective of how many hours' worth of content they are streaming.

Imagine a pay-as-you-go model here, where consumers had to pay for every video they watched. They would be very selective on what they watched, which would create very stiff competition between content creators. Netflix would have been even more selective in choosing the content they provided, but with a subscription model, Netflix can take a risk and give a chance to new content creators. Today, Netflix can afford to have a few average shows in their pile.

Similarly, when the cost of the goods or service or content increases exponentially with the quantity consumed, a pay-as-you-go model is most sustainable. For example, there is a cost associated with every ride on Uber, and there is a cost price for each **Stock-Keeping Unit (SKU)** of every product sold on Amazon. Hence, to cover the cost and generate profit for the producer and the platform owner, a subscription business model would not be feasible or sustainable in the long run. The price will depend on the goods or services that consumers are buying. The price will cover the product's cost, profit for the producer, and a fee for the platform owner. There are different options for platform owners to charge a fee such as a fixed amount per transaction, percentage of the transaction amount, or a combination of the two.

- **Charge from the producer**: Another factor to consider while deciding a platform's revenue model is how much the producer of the goods or services is charging. If the producer provides the goods or services or content for free, it is advisable to offer them for free to consumers. The cost of running the platform and the platform owner's profit can be generated through advertisement revenue.

  Most platforms falling into this category are social media or knowledge and information sharing platforms. If a producer provides content for free or at a meager cost, such as Stack Overflow or Twitter, platform owners do not charge the consumers but earn their revenue from advertisement. But if the content provider is charging a fee, the content becomes premium and a subscription model is best suited for such platforms, such as LinkedIn Learning.

Apart from the two critical factors mentioned here, there are few other things such as *access cost of the goods and service*, *market demand*, *the operating cost of the platform*, and so on that will play a minor role in selecting the platform's revenue model, but most of these factors are more relevant in choosing a price point rather than the revenue model itself. These factors will decide how much to charge rather than what structure should be used to charge.

The following table summarizes the preceding discussion on revenue-model selection:

Offering production cost	Revenue model	Example
Production cost per unit	Pay-as-you-go	Uber
One-time production cost	Subscription	Netflix
No or very low production cost	Advertising or pay per listing	Google Search

> **Important note:**
> Please note that a hybrid revenue model is not mentioned in the preceding table as a combination of any two or more models will be applicable for some of the platforms. Combining an advertising model with any other model is particularly common and widespread.

Benefits of a platform business model

We have discussed the different types of platforms and their revenue models, but why we should have a platform business or move from a linear business to a platform model is an important point to address.

Here are some benefits having a platform business model brings to consumers, producers, and platform owners, which will help you understand why platform businesses are disrupting the market and why small businesses want to leverage the platforms to grow their businesses. These benefits explain how a platform business model is advantageous for all the parties involved:

- **Reduced cost**: A platform business model benefits from economies of scale. Imagine a scenario where each seller is creating their own website and building an e-commerce foundation; the cost of everything will multiply. But that is not the case for platforms. Even with an increase in the number of sellers on the platform, the cost to build the foundation remains the same, distributing and reducing the overall cost of the products or services. Whereas, in a case where each seller has their own e-commerce presence, the cost of building and maintaining the website increases the overall cost of the product or service that they are offering.

- **Increased customer base**: It is easy for platforms to scale and grow their reach compared to individual producers. They have a robust foundation that helps them to expand into new categories, new geographies, and so on. More scale and better reach mean an increased customer base. As platforms offer various categories under a single experience, the traffic on the platforms is exponentially higher than on the website of an individual seller.

  This is like a mall versus a small showroom on the corner of a street. As malls offer everything from dresses to washing machines under one roof, the number of people visiting malls is way higher than for a small showroom, and all the sellers in the mall benefit from the higher footfall. There is always a correlation between the number of people visiting and the number of people buying.

- **Increased revenue**: Increased revenue is the result of an increased customer base. As the platform has already acquired many customers and is constantly acquiring more due to extensive choices and low cost, the producers' revenue increases with the increased customer base. As mentioned earlier, increased traffic always leads to increased revenue, be it a physical store or a digital platform.

- **Increased profit for producers**: Reduced cost and increased revenue means increased profit for producers. The cost of building and maintaining a digital presence is relatively high, but in the case of a platform model, this cost is distributed among thousands of different producers, in the form of commission or fees. This significantly brings down the operating cost for the producers, increasing their profit margins. Reduced costs and increased revenue due to an increased user base lead to higher profit margins.

- **Distribution of ownership and responsibility**: In a platform model, each entity is responsible for its own areas of expertise. Platform owners are experts in building a digital presence, customer acquisition, SEO, and so on. Hence, they focus on and build a robust foundation that can be easily maintained and expanded.

  Producers are more creative heads; they focus on offering different and specialized varieties to consumers. In some cases, intermediaries such as banks or drivers/dashers (DoorDash) own their specialized job. This distribution of ownership and responsibilities makes platform models highly scalable and guarantees quality, as different parties undertaking different tasks are experts in their respective fields.

- **Lower risk**: Distribution of ownership reduces business risk—the risk of failure and risk of investment. As we have seen, the distribution of ownership guarantees quality; it also distributes the risk and reduces the chances of failure. As each entity is an expert in its respective area, the chances of failure are fewer.

  I am not saying that there are zero chances of failure, but they are low for sure. This distribution also reduces the risk of investment. Let's look at the same designer example that we saw earlier: if our designer has to launch a new clothing line and build an e-commerce website, their investment will be enormous. If their clothing line doesn't work, the loss is considerable. But with a platform model, they can avoid investing large amounts in building a website. Hence, this targeted ownership and distribution of responsibilities leads to lower risks.

- **Variety of choices for consumers**: As the number of producers is significantly higher on platforms, consumers have ample options. The increased number of producers on platforms also leads to increased competition, indirectly bringing in more—and better—choices for consumers. Due to platform models, the options within a category have increased, and the number of offered categories has also multiplied. Several products, a variety of services, and a wide range of content are at users' disposal today, all thanks to platforms.

- **Lower prices for consumers**: Reduced costs, increased revenue, and stiff competition have brought down prices significantly. It is challenging—and almost impossible—to create a monopoly. Because of the choices and the variety that the platforms are offering, consumers can compare and find the best prices not just by sitting on their couch but without even visiting another website.

- **Faster and reduced time to market**: Platform models are best for experimenting with a new idea or a product. Let's again look at the same example of a designer who wants to launch a new clothing line. It will be swift to launch it via an existing platform and test the waters. The designer can get faster feedback if their designs are working or if they need minor modification or to scrap a particular design. If they were building an e-commerce website themself, this would have taken way more time to launch, but the feedback cycle post-launch would also have been slower because of low traffic generation.

Building the right digital platform for a platform business model

As discussed earlier, a platform business model is not a new concept; traditional marketplaces, libraries with subscription fees, or art exhibitions all follow platform business models. What is new is the power of technology added to a conventional platform business model. We saw earlier how a platform business model powered by technology enables global reach—for example, a marketplace where a buyer from Australia can buy goods from sellers in the US or a user from China can rent a movie from a video library in Europe. Platforms also facilitate scale and remove the constraint of limited physical resources such as space, workforce, and so on.

For example, an art exhibition can only accommodate a limited number of artists in a gallery and a marketplace can only fit a certain number of sellers, but digital platforms eliminate this limitation. Hence, to have a successful platform business, it is crucial to build the right digital platform, which brings us to the crux of this book. This book will focus on how to build the right digital platform to run a successful platform business. Before we move on to the depth of a digital platform strategy and the day-to-day execution of that strategy, let's look at what comprises a digital platform and the critical factors that should be considered while building one.

Factors to consider while building a digital platform

Here is a list of major factors to keep in mind while building a digital platform:

- **Easily scalable and expandable**: To reap all the benefits of a platform model, a digital platform must be highly scalable. The platform should technically and operationally support scalability in terms of the number of participants (producers, consumers, and intermediaries), the number of products and services, the number of categories, and the number of transactions processed.

  A successful digital platform should be able to quickly expand geographically and demographically. It should also be able to expand to new categories and new verticals. A good example here is Uber first expanding to multiple cities globally and then expanding to new business verticals, from ridesharing to food delivery via Uber Eats. The Uber platform's core aim was to match drivers to riders for ridesharing, which they expanded to food delivery by adding restaurants to the mix.

Now, all three entities—restaurants, drivers, and consumers—get benefits from the Uber platform. This expansion to the new vertical was only possible because Uber had a robust and highly scalable foundation of a digital platform. As we saw earlier, a successful platform business is one that can create a strong network effect, and to create a strong network effect for the platform business, a highly scalable digital platform is essential.

- **Independent**: A digital platform must be a separate entity. It should operate as a third party connecting different producers, consumers, and intermediaries. The platform is neither a producer nor a consumer. In some cases, platform owners can double up as one of the entities (producer or intermediary). When the platform is immensely successful or when a linear business has transformed to a platform model, this scenario becomes more common, but in these cases, the responsibility of the platform owner must be separated.

  To give an example here, Amazon sells its products on Amazon Marketplace; in this case, Amazon must be treated as two different entities: a seller and a marketplace owner. Clear demarcation of ownership and responsibilities between all the parties involved is crucial so that each of them works within their areas of expertise and reduces the risk of errors.

- **Flexible**: We are living in a very volatile world these days. Markets are very dynamic and businesses should adapt to changing market situations, and digital platforms are no different. A flexible platform that can respond to changing market conditions and adjust to the given situation will thrive.

  Netflix is a perfect example of responding to evolving markets and changing consumer behavior. They understood the market requirement and introduced their streaming service at the right time. However, they continued their original **Digital Video Disc** (**DVD**) rental service as well. Flexibility, adaptability, and responding to change are essential for any business but they are a must for digital platforms, as the foundation of their business model is to work with the volatility of the demand side (consumers) and the supply side (producers).

- **Open to all**: For any platform to be successful, it must create a strong network effect, and to create a strong network effect, it is essential to let as many consumers and producers as possible get onboarded on the platform. Platform owners should have checks for quality control and compliance, but apart from that, they should let all producers and intermediaries utilize the platform capabilities to offer their products and services. This also leads to making the platform onboarding easier. The higher the restrictions, the fewer the participants joining the platform. Hence, for a digital platform to succeed, it must create an inclusive and open environment for all.

Components of a digital platform

We looked at the different factors that must be considered while building a digital platform. But now, let's look at what digital platform consists of. These days, the term *digital platform* has become a new buzzword. Companies are wrongly using *digital platform* as a synonym for either their **Information Technology (IT)** transformation or revamping their architecture without understanding what an **End-to-End (E2E)** digital platform is or what comprises a digital platform.

There are mainly three components to any digital platform: **customer experience**, **business** (I also like to call it core), and **infrastructure**, as illustrated in the following screenshot:

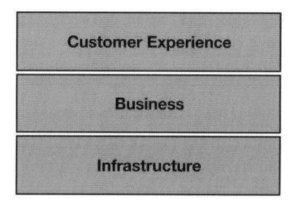

Figure 1.3 – Components of a digital platform

Each of these components can have sub-components, depending on the type of platform business or its size, but every sub-component can be categorized in one of these three major components. These components play an essential role in defining the platform strategy and creating platform roadmaps, and it is thus crucial to understand them. We will discuss each of these components while discussing platform strategy and roadmaps later in the book. But before that, let's understand what these components are, as follows:

- **Customer experience**: Customer experience—or the interaction component—is where users can interact with the system; for example, websites, mobile apps, smart TV apps, and so on. These experiences are not just restricted to the platform's consumer side but also include interactions from the producer side—for example, an Uber app catering to both riders and drivers. The user identity will decide the specifics of the interaction and experience, but the overall layer is the same.

- **Business/core**: This is the heart and brain of a digital platform. This component comprises all the business or core services—for example, product catalog, promotion, fulfillment, and so on in the case of an e-commerce platform, or subscription, content, and personalization in the case of a content platform. These services perform most of the business functions and expose the end result to the customer experience layer in the form of APIs. How the interaction between these two layers happens is a technical architectural decision, but as a business or a product person, a clear understanding and deep knowledge of this layer is very important in order to define a platform strategy and create a platform roadmap.

- **Infrastructure**: Infrastructure components provide hardware and computing resources to the rest of the platform. We have seen that infrastructure platforms take care of hosting, storage, networking, and other essential hardware and software requirements, making them an infrastructure layer for other platforms.

  For example, AWS is a platform that provides hardware, databases, **Virtual Machines** (**VMs**), and other essential deployment and development resources to other platform businesses such as Netflix, Facebook, and so on. In this example, resources provided by AWS become the infrastructure layer for platforms such as Netflix and Facebook. Their core services—such as personalization, content, and so on—become the business layer, and the mobile apps, Roku app, website, and so on become the experience layer.

Summary

In this chapter, we learned how platform businesses have revolutionized their respective industries by creating a solid network of producers and consumers who connect via a platform and deliver value.

We looked at how platform businesses are beneficial for all parties involved and why traditional linear businesses need to shift to a platform model and adapt a *platform-first approach*. We looked at different types of platforms and what roles producers, consumers, and platform owners play in each of these different types of platforms, and why it is essential to have separation of ownership between these parties.

We discussed how building the right digital platform plays an essential role in an overall platform business model's success. In today's world, a platform business's success depends on a highly scalable, flexible, and independent digital platform.

In the next chapter, we will go deeper into understanding the difference between traditional linear products and platforms and how product management is different for them. We will look at a case study of one business case solved with two different approaches: a standalone linear product and a digital platform.

2
Differences between Linear Products and Platforms

In the previous chapter, we understood the basics of a platform business model and how building the right digital platform is crucial for any platform business. The next step would be to go deeper into understanding the product management aspects of a digital platform. But before going into the weeds of platform product management, it is essential to know how digital platforms are different from traditional linear products at a fundamental level.

This chapter will cover the different stages of the product life cycle and explain the difference between traditional product management and platform product management at each stage. This chapter will cover the breadth of the product life cycle, highlighting the differences between the two approaches. The depth of each of the topics will be discussed and explored in the next chapters of the book.

In this chapter, we will see the overall difference between linear products and digital platforms and why we, as product managers, must adapt to different techniques and mindsets for platform product management. Product managers must wear a *platform thinking hat* when designing and building digital platforms. Traditional product management methods will have to be altered to fit the platform approach. Hence, to understand these methods, this chapter will cover the following topics:

- Linear product versus digital platform
- Traditional product management and platform product management
- Case study

By the end of this chapter, you will have a perfect understanding of the modifications that have to be made to traditional product management methods to fit platform product management. This understanding will play a vital role as we go deeper into applying different aspects of product management to digital platforms.

Linear product versus digital platform

In the previous chapter, while discussing the characteristics of platform business models, we looked at how the foundation of a digital platform is multidimensional, whereas traditional products are linear. If we expand this concept further, we will see that four major distinguishing factors set digital platforms apart, as outlined here:

- Entity versus mediator
- No ownership of products or content
- Users on both sides
- Accumulation of producers

Entity versus mediator

In terms of linear products, producers directly communicate or connect with consumers, but digital platforms are **mediators**. They act as a middleman and bind all parties involved in delivering value, such as producers, consumers, and intermediaries such as banks and dashers, who all communicate through the platform to complete a transaction. For example, if a user is ordering food from a restaurant's website, the restaurant is the producer who is also delivering the order. If the user is ordering it on DoorDash, DoorDash is just the mediator enabling the delivery, but not the producer. Hence, digital platforms are facilitators that connect producers and consumers.

No ownership of products or content

Platform owners do not own any products or inventory of any kind unless they are doubling up as producers as well. The producers own the inventory, and the platform only enables them to showcase it or sell it through the platform. For example, Airbnb does not own any property, Uber does not own cars, and Facebook does not have to generate content.

Users on both sides

Linear products only consider consumers as their customers—for example, guests booking rooms on Hilton Hotels' website. Whereas, digital platforms have users on both sides of the spectrum—for example, guests and homeowners on Airbnb. They are not only serving the consumers but also the producers. Multi-sided customers are a crucial difference between linear products and digital platforms, which impacts the overall business strategy, the selection of a revenue model, the roadmap, and feature prioritization for digital platforms.

Accumulation of producers

In the linear product world, producers are scattered, but digital platforms accumulate producers in one place. This aggregation of producers creates healthy competition, leading to better choices and reduced prices for consumers, which leads to more consumers opting for the platform and further attracting more producers. This strong network effect is one of the most significant disrupting factors for a digital platform.

The following two diagrams reflect the aforementioned four distinguishing factors between linear products and digital platforms. Here's the first diagram:

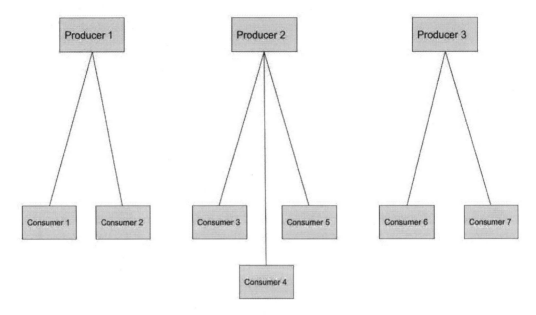

Figure 2.1 – Linear products

The preceding diagram depicts how producers directly connect to consumers, limiting their reach to a more extensive consumer base, and rather than accumulating in one place, producers are scattered, which limits choices for consumers.

On the other hand, the following diagram shows that a digital platform serves users on both sides, and these users (the producers and the consumers) do not connect directly, but the digital platform acts as a mediator between them and helps them connect. Producers are accumulated on the platform, giving more choices to consumers and increasing producers' reach to a larger consumer base:

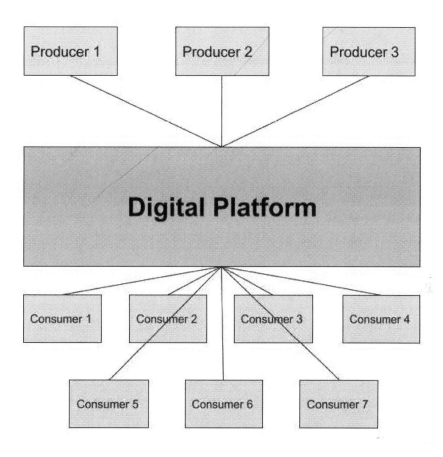

Figure 2.2 – Digital platform

Understanding the differences between linear products and digital platforms is essential before understanding how the technique and style of product management differ for digital platforms in each stage of the product life cycle. As we have seen the difference between linear products and digital platforms, we will now go deeper into determining the differences between product management for linear products and product management for digital platforms in the next section.

Traditional product management and platform product management

Product Management 101 tells us that every product goes through four stages: introduction, growth, maturity, and decline. But I believe that no one should plan for the decline stage. It might happen due to circumstances beyond our control, but the plan should be to *revamp* and *restart* in that case.

I also believe that there is one more stage before the introduction phase. A lot of time and effort goes into research, building hypotheses, and validating those hypotheses, and all this happens before introducing the product. Some people call it part of the introduction phase, but I like to call it **pre-introduction**. Hence, when you are planning, you should plan for the following four stages of a product:

- Pre-introduction
- Introduction
- Growth
- Maturity

Let's look at these four stages from a platform product management lens and see what the differences in each of these stages are when building a digital platform versus a linear product.

Pre-introduction

The **pre-introduction** phase involves ideation, research, problem definition, and validating the solution. I like to divide the pre-introduction phase into conceptualization and validation, as follows:

- **Conceptualization**: The conceptualization or idea-generation phase generally comprises three steps: problem identification, user definition, and solutions. The difference between linear products and digital platforms in this stage is that there are users on both sides of a digital platform. Hence, the problem and the solution should focus on both user types—producers and consumers. This acts in contrast to linear products, where problems and solutions revolve around one side: the consumers.

Digital platforms combine the concerns of producers and consumers and try to offer a common solution. For example, in the pre-platform world, the problem statement would have been that users cannot find hotels or rooms in small towns or remote vacation locations. So, the solution here (if there is enough capital and no existing hotels) is to build a small hotel or vacation cabins and create an online booking website. Another solution is to create an online presence for an existing hotel if a hotel already exists in that town.

But digital platforms will look at this problem from two sides, one where there is no easy way to find rooms in small towns for guests, and second, where there are homeowners who have spare rooms or unoccupied houses sitting idle. So, the solution here is to connect the homeowners and the guests, whereby both parties can mutually benefit. Identifying problems that are hampering both parties—producers and consumers—and offering suitable and beneficial solutions is what is needed from platform product managers.

- **Validation**: After we have identified the problem and the possible solutions, we have a concept in place. Now, the next step is to validate that concept. The validation stage usually consists of validating three things, as follows:

  - **Validating the problem**: Validation of the problem involves making sure that the identified problem exists and we are not trying to solve something that doesn't exist. In the case of digital platforms, this step is twofold: firstly, ensure that the problem exists, and secondly, validate that it exists at both ends of the spectrum.

  - **Validating the size of the problem**: Validating the size of the problem means knowing how extensive the user base is. This becomes a little tricky in digital platforms because the platform's success depends on a strong network effect, which is only possible if the platform has a good number of users from both sides. If there are plenty of producers and fewer consumers, digital platforms are not going to survive, and the same is true in the reverse scenario where consumers are many but producers are few. Therefore, a problem for which the user base is balanced on both sides is the most suitable candidate for a platform-based solution. Hence, it is crucial for platform product managers to validate the size of the market on both sides.

- **Validating the viability of the solution**: Validating that the solution can be sustained and can grow is one of the essential steps before product introduction. In this step, product managers usually analyze whether the solution is feasible with the given resources, can generate enough **return on investment (ROI)**, and can be sustained with minimum operating costs. But in the case of digital platforms, the viability is not just for the platforms to sustain and generate ROI for platform owners, but it also includes making enough profit for the producers. Along with financial viability, the solution should also be validated for technical feasibility. Technical feasibility will determine whether the proposed solution is realistic and achievable with the given financial and technical resources, and it will help in finding out the most efficient technologies that must be selected for long-term success. Technical feasibility validation must be done by architects or technical counterparts, with input from product managers. To summarize, in the validation step, product managers should validate that the identified problem exists for both the entities—producers and consumers—that it has a balanced user base on both sides, and that the solution is viable financially and technically for platform owners and producers.

Introduction

After conceptualization and validation, product managers start working on development with the team and also start planning activities for the launch. This is the most crucial phase for product managers as they are working with multiple teams, internally for development and release, and externally for marketing and launch. Hence, there are two parts to the introduction phase, as outlined here:

- **Development**: After the problem and solution are validated, the next step is development. In the development phase, product managers define features, carve out the **Minimum Viable Product (MVP)**, create a roadmap, and work with the team to deliver the MVP. Platform product managers go through similar steps, but the technique of defining features and prioritizing the MVP is different. One important thing to keep in mind while defining a digital-platform MVP is that it should cover the **End-to-End (E2E)** user flow for all the parties involved in the platform. We will discuss creating a platform roadmap and defining an MVP in detail in the upcoming chapters.

- **Launch**: Product managers start preparing for the launch while the team is developing. Creating a marketing plan, defining a go-to-market strategy, and identifying **Key Performance Indicators (KPIs)** are essential steps in this phase, as explained in more detail here:

- **Marketing plan**: Marketing plans for digital platforms should focus on the platform offering rather than on the product or the service. For example, a digital marketplace should market that the sellers can showcase and sell their products on the platform, and the buyers get various options to choose from products offered by multiple sellers, rather than marketing specific products.

- **Go-to-market strategy**: A go-to-market strategy consists of a pricing strategy, target audience, region of the launch, and so on. The difference between the go-to-market strategy for a linear product and digital platforms is that the target audience should consist of a proportionate number of producers and consumers. The pricing strategy for a revenue model should be beneficial to producers and sustainable for platform owners.

- **KPIs**: As iterated multiple times, the success of a digital platform depends on a robust network effect that involves the existence of all parties. Hence, it is critical to identify KPIs and metrics that can track data across all entities and not just consumers. The success criteria should focus on users on both sides of the spectrum.

As a product manager of a digital platform, you should create a marketing plan that attracts all parties of a platform, define a go-to-market strategy focusing on penetration in both producer and consumer segments, and identify KPIs to track the success of a platform as a whole rather than one group or entity.

Growth

Post MVP, product managers should focus on tracking usage and analyzing various metrics. These metrics and data are needed to understand the market fitment and enable growth. The growth phase is divided into two steps, as follows:

- **Market satisfaction**: Market satisfaction means establishing whether a product is solving the problem that it is supposed to solve and is the right fit. Finding the market fit is usually done by tracking the progress of the product, growth in the number of users, and overall usage of the product. In digital platforms, satisfaction must be tracked for all the entities involved in the platform—that is, consumers, producers, intermediaries, and digital-platform owners.

  If one entity is satisfied and sees a growth in the user base, but the other entities are not benefiting from the platform and don't see a fit, continuing the growth of the first entity will become impossible. Product managers of digital platforms must be well aware that all the entities co-exist and contribute to the platform's growth. Finding satisfaction and fitment for all is a must.

- **Expansion**: In this stage, product managers focus on increasing customer acquisition and improving engagement. To achieve this, they work on prioritizing the right features. The key to the right prioritization is understanding the market trend and keeping fingers on users' pulses. This technique for expansion is similar in the case of digital platforms, but it is convoluted and tricky because of the complexities of multiple entities involved and the creation of a network effect. We will cover this in detail in the ongoing backlog prioritization chapter later in the book.

Maturity

After a product has expanded and reached its peak, it is essential to sustain that peak and maintain market saturation.

Market peak sustainability is the step to maintain the peak, keep an eye on the competition, pivot, and revamp if needed. Product managers play a very crucial role here. Decisions such as revamping the existing product, expanding the product to a new business line, or spinning new products are made during this phase. Product managers are a vital part of this decision-making process.

Expanding to a new category or pivoting to a new business line are options that platform product managers should explore before a total revamp and reboot or termination. The foundation of a digital platform enables easy expansion to new business lines and categories—for example, Ola Cabs (a ridesharing platform in India) expanding to OlaMoney as a payment-processing platform, or DoorDash expanding from food delivery to pet supplies and other deliveries.

Case study

We have looked at the differences between linear products and digital platforms and how product management differs for them in each step of the product life cycle. Let's now apply that to a practical case study. We will see one business use case with two different approaches, one as a standalone linear product and another as a digital platform.

For the purpose of this case study, we will assume that our organization, **Barter Solutions**, specializes in building e-commerce solutions for specific categories catering mainly to the US, with a dominant presence around coastal areas. We want to expand into a new category in a city where we have a good presence, such as **San Francisco (SFO)**, **Los Angeles (LA)**, **New York City (NYC)**, Boston, or Washington D.C. We are product managers for Barter Solutions, and we own and are responsible for expansion into this new category. In this case study, we will look at the launch of this new category with two different approaches.

Standalone linear product

This is the first approach, whereby Barter Solutions will build a standalone solution to expand their footprint to a new category. As product managers for Barter Solutions, we must introduce a solution for this new category that will help users solve their problems and that is also profitable for our business.

Pre-introduction

We will start with the research, ideation, and validation that forms the pre-introduction phase of the product. As we discussed, the pre-introduction phase has two steps—conceptualization and validation. Let's see how we will approach our product in these two steps, as follows:

- **Conceptualization**: Assume we came up with a list of problem statements, and based on the factors (such as can it be solved by technology, current solutions available in the market, and emerging trends), we narrowed this down to a problem concerning the well-to-do shopper class, where they cannot conveniently explore and shop for their favorite designer brand. The solution we shortlisted is to create a website for the most popular designer and later pitch it to other designers to have their own similar websites. Other ideas and solutions that were brainstormed should go to the idea backlog.

- **Validation**: We have shortlisted the concept; now, let's look at some validating factors. For concept validation, I like to assign an impact and score to each element. The impact is measured as *high*, *medium*, or *low*, and the scores are *5 for high*, *3 for medium*, and *2 for low*. In our case, the problem is of medium impact. There is no easy way for fashion enthusiasts to explore and shop for the latest designer products, but there aren't many fashion enthusiasts. The market size is low as fashion enthusiasts or fans for expensive designer brands are fewer in number.

Also, we are looking at the market size only from the shoppers' perspective, hence a low impact. The viability of the solution is medium as the problem is relatively significant; the user base is affluent shoppers, which means higher cart values and higher transaction amounts and fees, leading to a decent revenue and ROI. You can see these elements with their respective impact and score in the following table:

Element	Impact	Score
The problem	Medium	3
Size of the problem	Low	2
Viability of solution	Medium	3

Based on the calculation from the preceding table, the total score is 8. I like to prioritize the idea with a total score of 9 and above, as it would be either significantly high in one of the elements or equal on all three of them, making it suitable to pursue. I usually consider 8 as an edge case, where I would analyze a few other factors such as competition, the shelf life of the solution, past and current trends, and emerging technologies. Anything that is 7 or lower is a high risk. Assume we analyzed some other factors, and the conclusion is in favor of proceeding with this idea.

Introduction

We have defined the problem and identified and validated the solution, so now, let's get into the introduction phase, which consists of development and launch, as follows:

- **Development**: During the development phase, a significant part of a product manager's role is to come up with features and define an MVP. For determining the MVP, we will select all the types of users or personas that will use our website and complete the E2E user journey. In our case, the user type or the persona is the shopper. The bare-minimum E2E flow for the shopper is browsing or searching for a product, selecting a product, providing the necessary details, and checking out.

  But to enable this flow, we will have to add merchandise to the system, accept the payment, and fulfill the order. These tasks can either be done by the designer as one of the users or can be carried out in the background, and don't need an elaborate **user interface** (**UI**). As we only have one designer, it is acceptable for the MVP to be a little raw from the designer side and for the tasks to be completed in the background. Features that were not included in the MVP should go to the backlog.

- **Launch**: The marketing plan and go-to-market strategy will target only the shoppers' user base. The target region will be decided by the designer based on where there are a significant number of well-to-do shoppers. For example, in this case, we can start with LA and then target NYC next. There is no revenue-model selection here. The designer will charge for the individual products based on the cost and profit margins. Barter Solutions would have charged the designer a one-time cost to develop the website and then charge a monthly or yearly fee for maintenance.

Growth

Our product is developed and launched for one designer, so the next step is to validate whether it is a fit and then work on it is expansion, as follows:

- **Market satisfaction**: To establish whether the website is satisfying its users and is the right fit for the market, following metrics must be tracked:

  - *The total number of shoppers using the website*

  - *The total time each shopper is spending on the website*

  - *Conversion rate*

  - *The total revenue*

  - *The profit generated from the website*

  These metrics are important for determining the performance of the website and the products in different aspects. For example, the total number of shoppers will help us determine the reach and awareness of the brand, if the marketing efforts are working, and whether any improvements are needed. Time spent on the website will determine whether the website is engaging and easy to use. The conversion rate will help us determine whether the products are useful and liked by users. The total revenue and profit will help us determine how the website is doing financially. Without collecting and analyzing this data, we won't be able to measure the success or failure of the business. Hence, evaluating the performance of the website and the business as a whole and taking corrective actions if tracking any of these metrics is crucial.

- **Expansion**: Based on the data that was collected from all the metrics, the designer will have to decide on the next steps. Suppose the numbers are too low and are showing a decline. In that case, it is essential to analyze the trend and decide if it is due to the brand and the products or if it is due to the online **User Experience (UX)** and behavior. The product design team should fix the former, but if it is the latter, then after the consultation and approval from the designer, as a product manager for the website, we should prioritize features that will improve the UX.

  If the numbers are decent and show an upward trend, we should prioritize features that will increase user engagement and attract more shoppers, such as providing style tips, recommending products to accessorize the look, and personalized recommendations based on shoppers' preferences and shopping history. The downside here is that as the products available are from a single designer, it will be difficult to attract shoppers who prefer other designers or are loyal to other brands.

Maturity

If our product reaches its peak and we have captured the maximum market that we could, with no possibility of further exponential expansion, in such a case we should plan to maintain the peak, as follows:

- **Market peak sustainability**: Once the website has peaked, product managers should focus on improving customer engagement to retain their customers. With the help of the latest technology trends, product managers can prioritize features such as virtual trial rooms or the use of **Artificial Intelligence (AI)** to offer personalized services, which may give them a competitive advantage in terms of advanced functionalities.

  But the challenge here is that there is a very limited number of shoppers that you can attract with these new features. The majority are interested in specific products or brands that might not be available on the website. If there is a need to revamp and reboot, the feature backlog must be referred to for a smaller pivot, and the idea backlog must be referred to for a significant overhaul.

  The following diagram shows stand alone websites replicated for different designers where core capabilities must be developed for each website:

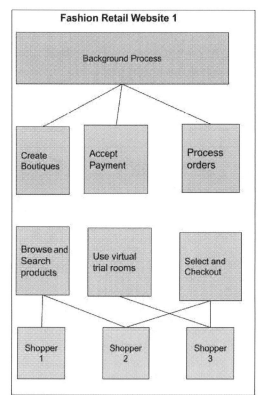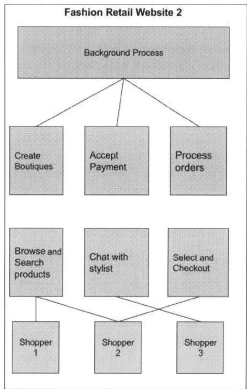

Figure 2.3 – Fashion retail standalone websites

As you can see, this is not a scalable and efficient model. Also, not all the features are available on every website, so if a shopper has to use a specific feature, they will have to stick with a particular designer or vice versa. Designers are scattered, which distributes the shoppers. Most of the actions that are needed from the designers are a background process, either manual or automated. As there is only one designer, these actions don't require customizations or configurations and can be carried out in the background without sophisticated interfaces.

Digital platform

This is the second approach, where we as product managers have decided to build a digital platform to expand to new categories. A platform approach will enable all the producers to leverage the capabilities of the digital platform, and they can easily opt in and opt out of the platform. Let's look at the E2E journey of this platform and understand how it is different from the standalone product approach.

Pre-introduction

Similar to the standalone website approach, we will start with the pre-introduction phase for our fashion retail platform. The pre-introduction phase will again consist of conceptualization and validation, as outlined here:

- **Conceptualization**: The assumption here is that we looked at different problems from the producer and consumer sides and narrowed these down to two related problem statements. One is that well-to-do shoppers cannot find and shop for their favorite designer brands, and the other is that there is no easy way for designers to reach out to these affluent shoppers. Hence, the shortlisted solution combines these two problems and offers a common solution for building a fashion retail platform. Other brainstormed ideas and solutions should go to the idea backlog, which will be helpful while expanding the platform to new categories and new business lines.

- **Validation**: After the concept finalization, let's look at factors to validate that concept. In the case of the platform, the problem has a medium impact, as the problem is the same as the one seen in the standalone website scenario. Hence, with a medium impact, the score for the problem is 3. Here, the size of the problem is medium as the user base is made up of shoppers plus designers. This doesn't mean that the size of the platform market will always be larger because it has users on two sides.

  Platforms do have more users, but what we are looking at during the validation phase is the proportion of users on both sides. If the proportion is skewed, the impact and score will be low, so let's call it market proportion instead of market size. And assuming that we have designers and shoppers in a decent proportion with a medium impact, the score will be 3.

The viability of the solution is high as the problem is relatively significant, and the revenue is huge because of affluent shoppers, the scalability of the platform to multiple designers, and a larger consumer base. As the impact is high, the score will be 5, as shown in the following table:

Validation	Impact	Score
The problem	Medium	3
Market proportion	Medium	3
Viability of solution	High	5

The calculation from the preceding table suggests that it is a viable and sustainable idea, and it is safe to proceed with the development of the solution.

Introduction

After the problem definition and solution validation, now is the time to understand how the introduction phase for our fashion retail platform will be different from the standalone website, as follows:

- **Development**: For defining an MVP for the platform, we must equally focus on both the user types—designers and shoppers. Designers should be able to create their boutiques and add merchandise. The user flow for shoppers will be similar, except that they can search and buy products from any designer. Hence, a critical feature for a platform MVP is to support multiple designers in a single flow or on the same interface.

- **Launch**: The marketing plan and go-to-market strategy will target both designers and shoppers. The target region will be decided based on the availability of designers and affluent shoppers in the right proportion. As NYC is the fashion capital of North America with headquarters of major fashion brands and top fashion-designing institutes, it is home to many established and upcoming designers as compared to LA. Hence, it makes more sense to start with NYC in the platform case and then move on to LA. The platform revenue model must be decided here. As we are developing a marketplace and there is a production cost for every unit, a pay-as-you-go model is the most suitable one.

Growth

Now that our platform is launched, we should focus on its growth. For the growth of the platform, it is important to see whether it is satisfying the market and its expansion strategy. Let's look at these two steps from the platform perspective, as follows:

- **Market satisfaction**: The market satisfaction of the platform is determined by an increase in the number and usage from both sides of the users. Along with tracking all the metrics for the shoppers, it is essential to track metrics for the designers. As well as the total number of active designers, the percentage increase in the number of designers and the total number of products/**Stock-Keeping Units** (**SKUs**) offered by the designers should be looked at. Numbers from both sides should show an upward trend. A decline in numbers from any side is not a good sign.

- **Expansion**: The prioritization of features for growth will depend on the metrics data collected. If the numbers are showing a decline in the metrics of one user type, it could be that the other user type has not grown as expected. If there were a decent number of designers to start with but the number of shoppers did not increase as per expectations, the number of designers would also drop. Hence, it is essential to see the numbers from both sides holistically when making changes to features or introducing new features.

Maturity

After expansion, let's now look at maintaining market saturation and sustaining the peak for our retail platform and understand how it is different from a standalone website approach, as follows:

- **Market peak sustainability**: Here, the possibilities are endless. Innovative features with the latest technology can be built to attract more shoppers, and the chances are that they will come and stay as they can shop from any designer on the platform. Innovation and the latest technology can be used not just to improve the shopper experience, but also to enhance the designer experience.

  Features such as automated pricing, AI-based fulfillment centers, and offering personalized products based on **machine learning** (**ML**) algorithms can significantly improve designer acquisition. Once this category has reached a saturation point, product managers should look at expansion into new categories such as home decor, pet grooming supplies, gourmet food, and personalized gifts.

  The following diagram shows a fashion retail platform where the core capabilities, once developed, can be leveraged by all the designers:

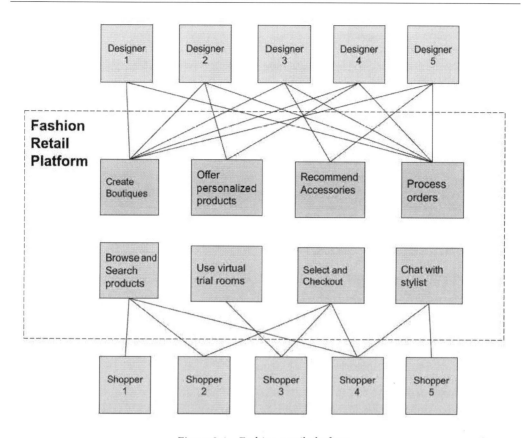

Figure 2.4 – Fashion retail platform

In the digital platform scenario, it is very simple to onboard new designers. All the features are available to all the designers, which gives shoppers a lot of choices and doesn't restrict them to a particular designer. As designers are also the customers of the digital platform, and there are multiple of them, the features used by designers must be customizable, configurable, and have an easy-to-use interface.

Conclusion

In the two scenarios of this case study, we have seen that the overall product life cycle for linear products and platforms remains the same, but each stage of the life cycle is executed differently. In this case study, the linear product example is similar to Oracle ATG, which specializes in providing e-commerce software to individual retailers, whereby each one of them does their own customizations and deploys their own instances.

Similarly, in our example, each designer will have to optimize for search engines, create their merchandise in the system, add their customizations, and deploy on their own infrastructure. Conversely, in the case of a platform, any designer can add their products and start selling without the upfront cost and spending time on configuration. They can quickly test the market and get early feedback about their products, and this will encourage more designers to join the platform. As seen in the previous chapter, this aggregation of designers (producers) on the platform will be beneficial for consumers, helping them in getting more choices and better prices.

A platform approach is also beneficial for companies providing software solutions—in this case, Barter Solutions, as they are developing a platform that many designers can use without additional cost. As there is no upfront cost for designers to join the platform, convincing them to join and partner with them is easy compared to individually selling them software with a steep price and involving lengthy customization.

There is no lock-in period, and designers can opt in and opt out as they deem fit. This easy onboarding and plug-and-play mechanism will attract more designers, bringing in more transaction fees and commissions. The drawback here for the platform owners is that the ROI is slow as their revenues come in small amounts compared to selling the entire software upfront, but if operated correctly, it becomes profitable in the long run and is sustainable for a much longer duration.

But these benefits come with different thinking and approaches. We cannot apply traditional product management techniques to a platform. Platform product managers should always consider the multidimensional nature of platforms and work toward designing a platform for the entire ecosystem. Product managers are always asked to put themselves in customers' shoes, but in the case of platforms, they should put themselves in multiple shoes simultaneously.

Summary

In this chapter, we learned that a digital platform acts as a glue that ties all the entities together to deliver value. We saw that digital platforms are mediators that enable a connection between producers and consumers whereas, in linear products, producers directly communicate with the consumers. This direct connection doesn't let the linear products scale, limiting their user base and consumer reach. We looked at how producers are scattered in the linear world, whereas digital platforms aggregate and accumulate them in one place, creating a healthy competition. This competition offers better choices and lower prices to consumers. Linear products limit options for consumers and restrict more extensive reach for producers, whereas digital platforms are built on this very foundation of creating strong network effects.

We understood that linear products and digital platforms are fundamentally different, and hence the exact same product management techniques cannot be applied to both. As platform product managers, we should wear a *platform thinking hat* when planning and designing digital platforms. Creating a strategy and building a platform for all the entities is the biggest differentiator of platform product management. Therefore, in each phase and every step of the product life cycle, we should focus on users on both sides of the platform and create features and strategies that will serve them all.

In the next chapter, we will cover gathering user insights and validating the platform use case in depth. Doing research and collecting data for concept validation of a digital platform is different from doing this for a linear product. Hence, in the next chapter, we will understand how to do the initial research and collect the right data to validate the concept of a digital platform.

3
Research and Validation

In the previous chapter, we understood the difference between linear products and digital platforms and how product management differs for each of them. Now that we have seen how traditional product management techniques must be modified to fit the platform, we can go into the specifics of product management for digital platforms. We will start from the first step of initial research and work our way up to digital platforms' sustainability and day-to-day operations.

Conducting research and gathering insights are essential in any product's journey, and digital platforms are no different. Even though the stage is the same, the techniques and specific data collected and analyzed are very particular in digital platforms. After *research* comes the *validation* phase, where we must validate that the concept of a particular digital platform is feasible and viable. This chapter will explain and explore each step of the research and validation phase in depth. We will discuss the following topics in this chapter:

- Defining the problem
- Identifying the solution
- Validating the concept
- Case study

After this chapter, we will know how to do the initial research and what data needs to be collected and analyzed while defining the problem statement and the solutions for a digital platform. This is the first phase in the digital platform's life cycle and a stepping stone for the overall platform product management.

Defining the problem

If we are building a digital platform, or any product for that matter, we are trying to solve a problem. So, it is very crucial to understand what problem we are trying to solve. Many product managers or business executives often miss this step of defining the problem and directly jump to the solution.

We cannot provide a solution unless we understand what the problem is, and to understand the problem, we must first know our users. If there is a perception that a problem exists and that problem can be solved in a digital platform space, we should validate whether the problem is a good candidate for the platform use case or can be solved by the linear product.

As a result, it is crucial that we look at the problem from the platform users' perspectives, which are present on two different sides. Therefore, we should know about the users from both sides of the platform. To define a good and accurate problem statement, we should know precisely who the producers and the consumers are.

Identifying pairs of producers and consumers

For the growth and sustainability of digital platforms, it is crucial that the platform is solving pain points from both sides. Problems must be appealing and solutions must be beneficial, to both producers and consumers. To identify such problems, it is essential first to identify the pairs of producers and consumers. Some well-known examples of producer and consumer pairs are as follows:

- Buyers and sellers
- Drivers and riders
- Artists and listeners
- Homeowners and guests
- Content writers and readers

If we are proceeding with a problem in the buyer's space, we should understand their counterparts (that is, the sellers) and know if they exist in the adequate proportion. Once you have shortlisted a pair, go deeper in understanding their current and future needs, challenges, and pain points. The best way to capture this data is to create an empathy map.

Creating an empathy map

An **empathy map** is a visual representation of user research. It is a powerful technique to summarize all the details about the user and consume those details throughout the product life cycle. It is a solid tool to communicate user behavior, needs, and pain points with a wider audience. As product managers or business owners, we all have heard that creating empathy maps is the first step in any design thinking ideation phase. This approach or method applies to digital platforms as well. There are quite a few empathy map templates available, but I prefer the following:

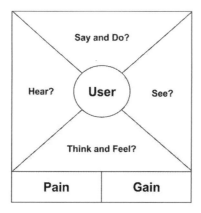

Figure 3.1 – Empathy map template

The data is categorized or collected in four different sections in this template, keeping the user at the center. This data is either gathered by interviews, surveys, or study groups. Once the information is collected, group them in the following sections, as depicted in the diagram:

- **Say and Do**: This section contains user behaviors and actions. In this section, you should also record direct quotes from users if you hear them in the interviews or study groups.

- **Think and Feel**: Put yourself in the user's shoes and consider what the user might think and feel. Read between the lines to understand their emotions and thought processes. When conducting the interviews or study groups, focus on their body language and tone. Take note whether they sound confused or excited about something.

- **Hear**: This section should cover things that users grasp from their social circle, workplace, and so on. If they mention stuff like *one of their friends said this* or *a colleague always talks about this* then record this in the **Hear** quadrant.

- **See**: Like the **Hear** section, this section should cover things that people see in their surroundings. Here, their surroundings are more extensive. It may also include influencers, celebrities, or someone they admire.

- **Pain and Gain**: After recording or categorizing findings in these four quadrants, summarize or list down the pains and gains. Pain is something that users are frustrated with or upset about. It could be something that exists but is not usable, does not provide desired value, or it could be entirely missing. Gain is something that the users are pleased about.

In the case of digital platforms, create one empathy map for each role or user type. For example, in a payment processing platform, we should have one empathy map each for buyers, merchants, and banks. Creating separate empathy maps will enable us to think from each user's perspective and help us to design a platform that is suitable and valuable for all of them.

Drafting problem statements

After we have shortlisted our pair of users and created empathy maps to record their needs and pain points, we should start framing the problem statements. Problem statements should focus on the users and empathy maps can be used to focus on the user's pain points. Emphasize the challenges and the future needs of users to draft the problem statement. The following are some valuable techniques that can be used to prepare a problem statement:

- **Organize and order**: In this technique, the pain points identified in the empathy maps are shifted to find patterns and trends. After finding the patterns, organize similar items in groups. Give each group a theme and try to come up with one meaningful problem statement for each theme. After you have grouped the pain points into themes and have identified a problem statement for each theme, rank them in the order of severity of the problem and the value to the user.

- **What, where, and why**: Drilling down in the research by asking the right questions helps in arriving at the problem statement. Usually, *who, what, where*, and *why* questions enable us to shortlist and frame the correct problem statement. We have already covered the *who* part in the user identification and the empathy phase. The remaining questions are what, why, and where:

- **What**: From the empathy map, try to find out what the problems are. We have already identified some pain points. See if there are any patterns or trends – *what is the user trying to accomplish, and what are their barriers?*

- **Where**: Asking and understanding where the problem is. This is with respect to the user journey or user experience. Going more deeply in the flow will let us know where things are broken and where exactly the problem is.

- **Why**: For every problem or pain point, ask why it is worth solving and why it matters – *what value will solving this pain point bring?*

- **Questioning the status quo**: This is a unique technique of identifying problems. Sometimes, people get so used to the norm that they do not even see the problem. In this technique, we should question the current behavior and challenge the status quo. Think of the alternative for every step and ask, *what if… ?* All significant innovations in technology and business were the result of challenging the status quo.

  As in the famous example of the **Ford Motor Company**, where people were demanding faster horses, Henry Ford actually understood the real pain point and the problem hidden behind their demand. In this example, people truly wanted a faster means of transport, and everyone was caught up with making horses faster. But he challenged the current status quo and started manufacturing cars.

  This example tells us that we should ask users about their pain points but derive the problem from their pains. The problem, in this example, was not that those horses were slow. In fact, horses might have reached their peak speed and couldn't have gone any faster. But the pain point of slower transport still existed. Hence, the problem statement here is that *people cannot commute from one place to another at the speed that they want.*

  Challenging the status quo always brings the best ideas out. Use this technique to dig deeper into user pain points and explore the exact problem behind the user's pain.

After creating the empathy maps for each of the user roles that will be involved in the platform, use one of the preceding techniques to define and rank problem statements. Sometimes, it is good to combine a couple of techniques. For example, organize the pain points into themes and then do what, where, and why for each theme. Creating and ranking problem statements must be done for each entity involved in the digital platform as we have already created empathy maps for each of them.

Combining producer and consumer problems

After we have identified and ranked problem statements for each user role, it is time to combine and holistically look at the problem statements from the platform perspective. Problem statements from each role should combine to form a common problem that a digital platform can solve. For example, the diner cannot go out to eat or pick up food due to busy schedules and time constraints. Restaurants cannot reach out to a large number of diners to take orders for food delivery. We can combine these two problems in a way that a digital platform can solve.

The problems might not be at the top of the order for both the entities, but when combined, the value added to solve this problem is enormous. Hence, after the problems for producers and consumers are connected, reassign the severity and the value. It might change the ranking of the problems. If the problem statement doesn't cut across the producer and consumer, it might not be a good candidate for the platform use case. And as mentioned earlier, here we are validating whether our problem statement is viable for a platform or can be solved by a linear product.

Sometimes, while holistically looking at the problems, we might figure out that another entity is required for the digital platform to be effective. In the same diner and restaurant example, if we go a little deeper, we might find out that if restaurants start getting huge orders, they might not have the infrastructure for delivery. Hence, a third entity – drivers, or delivery personnel – is needed here. This identification of the new entity can happen here or during the *solution* phase.

Identifying the solution

Identifying solutions is the next and most crucial step of the ideation phase for any product or platform. After we have identified a problem statement that is cutting across all the entities or user roles for our digital platform, we should dive into identifying solutions. And, in a similar way to the problem statement, we must also validate whether our solution is the right one for the platform. The holistic problem statement identified and shortlisted in the previous step should be the center of the solution phase. There are various techniques available that can be used to ideate solutions, so let us look at some of them in detail:

- **Brainstorming**: Brainstorming is the most common and popular technique for ideation. It is not just restricted to product ideas but can be used for any situation where there is a need to ponder different opinions and arrive at a solution. Here, a group of people should sit together and build ideas on top of each other until a final comprehensive solution is arrived at. In this technique, no idea is a bad idea. Just build on top of it to finally arrive at a solution. In the case of digital platforms, remember to focus on the holistic problem involving all the entities and user groups and not just one of them.

- **Metaphors**: This is the technique where the problem at hand is compared to a common situation in day-to-day life. Solutions are discussed by drawing metaphors between those situations and the problem statement, for example, comparing sharing a restaurant review online to teaching a class. To use this technique for digital platforms, I like to draw a table with the objects and terms from the problem statement against the metaphors from a typical situation. The table for our example of comparing online reviews to teaching a class would be:

Particulars	Problem Statement	Metaphor
Producer	Reviewer	Professor
Consumer	Readers	Students
Action/Task	Expressing views	Teaching

In this example, a professor uses college or a classroom as a platform to reach out to students and share their knowledge. In the same way, our reviewers need a digital platform to reach out to interested readers to share their views and opinions.

- **Mind mapping**: Mind mapping is an effective visual technique for any ideation exercise. It starts with a central phrase (in our case, the problem statement) in the middle, and then the elements related to the central phrase are extended out. Branches and sub-branches are used to drill down into a topic. In product ideation, mind maps are used to explore different solutions. The problem statement is in the center, and either solutions or abstract ideas are forked out of it:

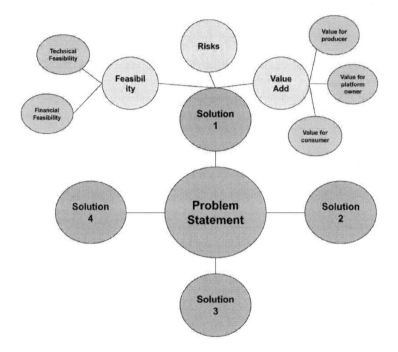

Figure 3.2 – Mind Map Example

This example shows different solutions branching out of the problem. Then, each solution has additional details that will help in choosing the best solution. Branches and sub-branches can be anything. It depends on what information is helpful at the time and what context is needed for further exploration.

- **Anti-problem**: This technique is based on turning or reversing the problem statement. Flip the problem over and seek the solution for this new anti-problem. For example, if the problem statement is *ordering and delivering food is very slow, how do we make it faster?* Reverse this problem to *ordering and delivering food is very fast, how do we make it slower?* The ideas generated in the reverse mode help to visualize the opposite scenario, making the real solution easier. This technique also helps in eliminating the ideas or solutions that might lead us in the wrong direction. In this technique, we explicitly think about things *not* to do. This technique really helps in bringing out the failure scenarios and edge cases.

- **Storyboarding**: This is another excellent visual technique, which helps in bringing vague ideas to life. In this technique, we take the user roles and create a story around them, specifically about how they would achieve the end goal of the problem statement. All the research and data collected during the empathy map creation will be used here, but instead of categorizing it into different types of actions, such as *see* and *do*, we arrange it in the form of a story:

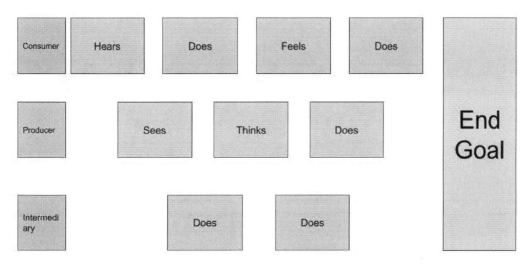

Figure 3.3 – Storyboard Example

As depicted in the storyboard example, put all the platform entities or user roles on the left side and the **End Goal** on the right, and start putting their thoughts, feelings, and actions in a sequence. Some of these we would have gathered during the empathy phase; some will evolve as we think through the solution while creating the story. If you want to challenge yourself, start from the end goal and work your way backward – this way, you will be thinking about what that user would have thought or felt before performing this action.

> **Important note:**
>
> Please note, this is not a user journey. Here, you are just telling a high-level story about a user trying to solve a problem. The user journey is much more detailed than this, which covers almost every action or process that happens in the system. Also, the user's feelings or thoughts are not captured in the user journey.

- **Moonshot idea**: The moonshot technique starts with coming up with an impossible way to solve the problem statement and then working downwards. When you are using this technique to generate solutions, put the problem statement at the bottom of the board and the moonshot idea at the top. Start replacing the impossible steps or impractical actions with more feasible solutions.

Keep repeating this till you have arrived at a possible, viable, and valuable solution. Do not forget to capture the solution at every step. The following diagram shows a sample of a moonshot idea board. It is how the board should look at the start of the exercise. As the exercise progresses, all the circles should get filled until we arrive at a solution that is next to the current state. Capturing all the steps helps for future reference. Some of the ideas from this board may go to the short-term and even long-term roadmap:

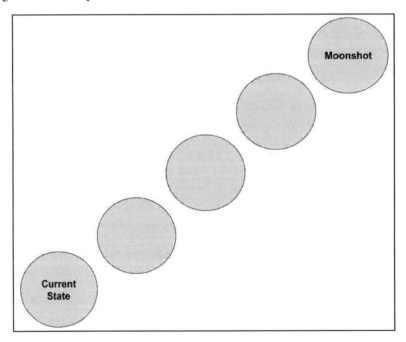

Figure 3.4 – Moonshot idea example

These are just some of the standard ideation techniques that can be used for identifying solutions. There are many other techniques that can be used, or you can use something new that you and your team are comfortable with. You can also combine a few of these techniques, for example, brainstorming and mind mapping, or metaphors and mind mapping, or a moonshot idea and storyboarding. Here are some more ideation techniques that you can use: https://innovationmanagement.se/2013/05/30/the-7-all-time-greatest-ideation-techniques/

It doesn't matter what method you use – the goal is to find a solution to the problem statement that is feasible, viable, and valuable to all the entities of the digital platform. If the solution cannot solve the holistic problem that is cutting across all the entities or add value for all the entities, then it is not a suitable solution for a digital platform.

Validating the concept

After defining the problem and narrowing down the solution, the next phase is to *validate* the problem and the solution, but the data must always back validation. Hence, doing the analysis and collecting the correct data is a crucial part of the validation phase. In this section, we will look at the different steps involved in the validation process. Along with validating the problem and the solution, we are also validating whether the problem is the right candidate for building the platform or can be solved by a linear product.

Concept validation steps

There are mainly four steps to validate the problem and the solution. It starts with specifying the objective and ends with validation, which includes the final decision. We will go through each of these steps in detail:

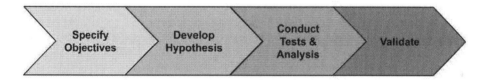

Figure 3.5 – Concept validation steps

Specifying objectives

In this step of validation, we should specify the validation objectives – that is, what needs to be validated. We have already covered that the objective of the digital platform validation phase is to make sure of the following:

- The problem exists for all the entities of the platform.
- The size of the problem is significant for all platform entities.
- The solution is viable for everyone involved in the platform.

The entire validation process should revolve around these objectives. Any analysis done (or tests conducted, or data collected) must be to fulfill one of these objectives.

Developing hypotheses

After specifying objectives for validation, the next step is to develop the hypothesis. Create a hypothesis to validate one or all of the objectives. The hypothesis must be testable, explicit, and distinct. For example, 40% of the diners who eat at the restaurants will write a review, and 80% of the diners will read the reviews before choosing the restaurants. These hypotheses mention accurate numbers and discrete user groups. It will test that the people want to read reviews about the restaurants before dining there and that there is a significant market share from both sides (producers and consumers).

Conducting analysis and tests

Once the hypothesis is developed, we should start conducting analysis and perform tests to validate the hypothesis. This is the longest step in the validation process. Remember that these tests and analyses are to validate the concept, which means they are conducted before the decision on the development has been taken. We have to use techniques such as talking to users, using prototypes for testing, or doing analysis on how competitors are performing. The following are some of the analyses and testing methods that can be conducted to validate the hypothesis for our concept validation:

1. **User feedback**: During the empathy phase, we would have carried out user research to understand their pain points and arrive at a problem statement. Now, to validate that problem statement, we should again reach out to the users to get their feedback on the problem and the solution. Collecting user feedback will give us insights into the severity of the problem and the potential interest in the solution. If a significant number of users agree with the problem statement but don't like the proposed solution, then the solution must be reconsidered. When collecting user feedback, make sure to involve all types of users, such as producers, consumers, and even intermediaries. Data from user feedback will help us validate the existence of the problem and the value of the solution to the users.

2. **Prototype testing**: In prototype testing, the design or mock-up of the solution is tested with potential users, and the feedback is then used to improve upon or completely change the solution. Prototypes can be as simple as a mock-up on a piece of paper or as sophisticated as low-fidelity wireframes. The goal here is to gather user feedback to validate the solution further. Prototype testing can be skipped if the data collected during user feedback is sufficient and we are happy with the results. Prototype testing gives an additional data point, so if you want to be extra sure, create a quick mock-up and get the user feedback. Remember to develop prototypes and get feedback for all the user roles, otherwise, the analysis will be one-sided.

3. **Competitor analysis**: As product managers or business owners, we should be aware of our competition. Doing a competitor analysis helps us identify where our idea or concept stands with respect to the competition, and what competitive advantage our concept has. Competitor data is crucial in understanding the size of the problem, what market share competitors currently have, and how much market share our idea will grab given our USP. It helps us to validate the hypothesis around the size of the problem and the viability of the solution. To do the competitor analysis, identify two or three major competitors and evaluate them under the following criteria:

    - Competition type
    - Their competitive advantage
    - Market share
    - Pricing strategy
    - Maturity level
    - Our competitive advantage

    You can include more evaluation criteria based on the product or the service, number of competitors, type of competitors, and so on. A detailed analysis report must be created while conducting the competitor analysis, exploring and detailing each evaluation criterion. But for a quick reference, we should also create a summary or a snapshot of the competitor analysis report, like the following:

Evaluation Criteria	Competitor 1	Competitor 2
Competition type	Direct	Indirect
Their competitive advantage	Brand exclusivity	Lower prices
Market share	45%	25%
Revenue model	Subscription	Advertisement
Maturity level	Advanced	Intermediate
Our competitive advantage	Easy user acquisition	Better profits for producers

4. **Cost and pricing analysis**: Cost and pricing analysis is essential to validate the feasibility and viability of the solution. As we are building a digital platform, its viability depends on all the entities' benefits and profitability. As part of this analysis, we should create a report on the following:

    -   The development cost for the platform

    -   Marketing and other operating expenses

    -   The suitable revenue model for the platform (as discussed in *Chapter 1, Fundamentals of Platform Business Models*)

    -   Price point (subscription fee, transaction amount, or advertisement charges)

    -   Revenue projection till breakeven

    This report will give us insights into the initial investment required to build the platform and will answer questions like: *When will we break even? What would be the profit margins and the growth rate after breaking even? Is this model beneficial to producers? Is this business sustainable in the long run?* Cost and pricing analysis is useful to validate the viability of the solution and whether the platform will be sustainable and profitable in the long run.

5. **SWOT analysis**: SWOT analysis is a very popular and strong analysis technique. It is used for identifying **Strengths**, **Weaknesses**, **Opportunities**, and **Threats** (**SWOTs**). It is used to identify SWOTs at the organization level, the team level, or even at a personal level. But it is equally applicable and helpful for new ideas or concept validation.

    In this case, the strengths and weaknesses of the concept are analyzed along with opportunities and threats. To conduct this exercise, a group of people responsible and accountable for the idea should be gathered and asked to add the SWOTs for the idea or the concept on the board. At the end of the SWOT analysis, we should have a report that looks like this:

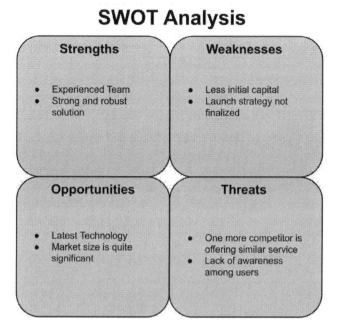

Figure 3.6 – SWOT analysis example

Data from all the other tests and analyses, such as user feedback, competitor analysis, pricing analysis, and so on, is used to capture strengths, weaknesses, opportunities, and threats. Hence, SWOT analysis acts as a summary of the analysis and testing stage of the validation process. As a result, it helps in validating the hypotheses around the size of the problem and the viability of the solution. Data from the SWOT analysis report becomes a crucial part of the final validation and decision-making process.

Validating the data

This is the final stage of the validation process. After all the analysis is done and tests are performed, it is time to collate and summarize all the data. Based on all the data collected and all the reports generated after various analyses and testing, business owners or executives conclude the validation by making a final go-no-go decision. Sometimes, the decision can be to modify a few things and then proceed, or to pivot, retest, and re-evaluate.

The go-no-go decision concludes the research and validation phase. We have learned how to do the initial research and collect the data for ideation and validation. Now, let us apply that understanding to a business case.

Case study

The case study that we will start in this chapter will continue throughout this book. As ideation and validation are the first phases of the product life cycle, here, we will begin with an example digital platform business case, developing and evolving it with each chapter.

Assume that we want to build a digital platform. We have already looked at some producer and consumer pairs and shortlisted educators and students as suitable candidates for our idea. We looked at some data like how digital learning is gaining importance after the pandemic has hit, and there are minimal options available for this group of users. Based on this analysis, we have the perception that there is a problem in the education space for students and educators. Hence, we decided to explore and research the idea of a digital platform for educators and students – let's call this platform **Escola**. Initially, we will scope our research and validation on the learning content for high school and undergraduate college students so that we can focus on a targeted group of educators and students. Also, this is the demographic of students that are most active on digital channels.

Today, we have so many platforms that connect different types of producers and consumers, such as **Uber** for drivers and riders, **Spotify** for artists and listeners, **Amazon** for buyers and sellers, and so on. But we don't have many platforms that connect students to educators. Escola will connect students to educators and will bridge the gap between them. Educators can share and impart knowledge, and students can learn through this platform. The business case of connecting students and educators is appealing – competition is low, and the market size for both students and educators is significant. Hence, this is potentially a good candidate for a digital platform. But to prove this, we should go deeper in exploring this idea. Therefore, let us now dive into the research and validation for this platform.

Making an empathy map for our case study

Now that we have identified the pair of users (that is, students and educators), we should now understand their current and future needs, pain points, and expectations. The assumption here is that we have spoken to some sample sets of users from both sides and collected this data. The following are some of the sample questions that we should ask the students group:

- *Do you actively seek resources to learn online?*
- *How do you find good content or the right educators to learn from?*
- *What do you do for digital learning? For example, what apps or websites do you use, groups do you follow, what activities online do you do, and so on?*
- *What are the challenges you face in the digital learning space?*

- *What would you like to see improve in the digital learning space in the next few years?*

- *What do you like the most about the current experience?*

- *What benefits and challenges do you see with digital learning becoming mainstream?*

After getting responses to these questions, either in interviews or surveys, we should summarize and synthesize the responses and create an empathy map for students. The following empathy map is created by assuming some standard responses from the students and, as mentioned earlier, our target for the student group is high school and undergraduate colleges interested in learning and educational content:

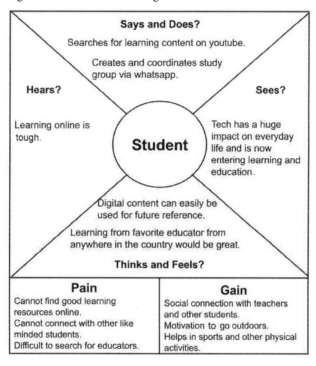

Figure 3.7 – Student empathy map

Now that we have created the empathy map for students, let's create one for the educators. But before that, let's look at some of the sample questions that we should ask the educators group:

- *Do you like teaching or sharing knowledge online?*

- *How often or frequently do you share content or teach online?*

- *What kind of content do you share digitally? For example, videos, articles, or papers?*

- *How do you reach out to interested students, and what platform/s do you use?*

- *Besides sharing content, what are the other activities you do to teach and share knowledge online?*

- *What are the challenges you face in the digital learning and teaching space?*

- *What would you like to see improve in this space in the next few years?*

- *What do you like the most about the current experience?*

- *What benefits and challenges do you see with digital learning becoming mainstream?*

After collecting the responses, let's summarize them and create an empathy map for educators. The following empathy map has some assumed standard responses from the sample set of educators teaching high school and undergraduate college students:

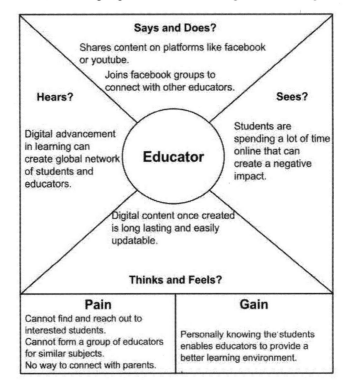

Figure 3.8 – Student empathy map 2

> **Important note:**
> Please note these empathy maps don't have a comprehensive list of items in all the quadrants or pain and gain sections. This is the summarized list of items repeated in multiple surveys and interviews by multiple users.

Designing problems

After creating empathy maps for students and educators, we should move on to design a problem statement. We will use the *organize and order* technique to formulate a problem statement.

Here is a list of problems for students:

Problem	Severity Rank	Value Rank	Cumulative Rank
Cannot search and find the right educators.	1	2	1
Cannot find good learning resources online.	2	1	1
Cannot connect with other students with similar interests.	3	4	3
Cannot create study groups.	4	5	5
Cannot connect with educators for 1-1 learning or advice.	5	3	4

Here's a list of problems for educators:

Problem	Severity Rank	Value Rank	Cumulative Rank
Cannot reach out to interested students.	2	2	2
No easy way to share content.	1	1	1
Cannot connect with other educators.	5	3	4
Cannot connect with parents.	4	5	5
No easy future reference of shared content.	3	4	3

All the problems are extracted from the empathy maps. The severity and the value rankings are assigned based on the user research done by talking to a sample set of students and educators. After organizing and ranking the problems for individual user roles, we should now create a holistic problem statement.

Creating a holistic problem statement

The top two ranking problems from both educators and students look to be connected and can be combined – not being able to find exemplary educators and not being able to reach out to students are complementary problems and can form one problem statement. Similarly, not finding good learning resources online and not being able to easily share content are connected problems. Therefore, these two problems are suitable for a digital platform.

If we look at other problems, such as "cannot connect with other students" or "cannot create study groups," these problems are specific only to students. Even connecting with other educators for 1-1 learning doesn't create value for educators or other students. Hence, these problems are not suitable for a digital platform use case. Similarly, if we look at some of the issues from educators, such as "connecting with other educators" or "reflecting on past shared content," they have nothing to do with students and therefore are not good candidates for digital platforms.

We saw that "not finding and connecting with other parties" and "no easy sharing or easy access to the learning content" are the two problems that are suitable candidates for building a digital platform. But if we look at these two problems, they are incomplete, or they are not end-to-end problems in themselves. For example, *what would educators and students do after finding each other?* The answer here is: *share knowledge or learning resources*. Hence, these two are parts of the same problem. Individually, they do not add value. Therefore, our combined holistic problem statement that cuts across educators and students would be *educators cannot reach out to interested students to share learning content and students cannot find the right educators to receive that content.*

Identifying a solution

We have our holistic problem statement, and now it is time to identify the solution. Assume we used the brainstorming technique to determine the solution and there were a few suggested results, so we looked at the following three:

1. Educators can create carefully structured and well-designed courses, and students can buy and learn from the courses they are interested in.

2. Students will subscribe to the platform and have access to all the courses. Courses are competently structured and skillfully designed.

3. Educators can share teaching videos, articles, presentations, and so on, and students can follow their favorite educators and can have access to all the content shared by their favorite educators. The content here is not a formally structured or designed course.

The first two solutions are premium digital learning platforms, and the last one is a social media platform dedicated to educators and students.

In the first two solutions, students will have to pay the upfront cost, and as a result, it will be difficult to penetrate the market and acquire a substantial number of students. Also, educators will have to spend a reasonable amount of time creating structured courses. Hence, having a decent repository of good courses will take some time. The third solution is a quick way to capture the market, both from the student and educator sides. But the drawback here is that there is nothing in it for educators. So, a suitable approach here would be to start with free content that educators can share to create their follower base, then, once they have a good number of followers, they can offer paid premium courses. In summary, start with *Solution 3* to capture the market and then move to a combination of *Solutions 1* and *3*.

Validation

As we decided to start with *Solution 3*, let's first validate the problem and that solution. Our objective here is to validate the problem, the size of the problem, and the viability and feasibility of the solution.

To validate these things, we will test the following hypothesis:

40% of educators will share learning content online, and 55% of students will follow one or more educators and consume their content. We chose this hypothesis as it will prove that the problem exists for a decent number of users, and capturing close to half the market share will create enough revenue to sustain the platform in the long run. To test this hypothesis, we will have to collect user feedback and perform prototype testing and competitor analysis. To test the viability of the solution, we will conduct a cost and pricing analysis. Finally, we will do a SWOT analysis to summarize our findings and conclude the validation:

- **User feedback and prototype testing**: Assume that we conducted interviews and sent out a survey to a sample of users from our targeted demographic (high school and undergraduate students and their educators) to get their feedback on the concept. Also, we did some prototype testing with another group of educators and students. The feedback from all the user feedback and prototype testing was positive for the majority of the users.

Both educators and students were excited about a dedicated platform. One concern in multiple responses was around the viability of an additional social media platform when quite a few already exist. But the majority were positive responses, demonstrating excitement about an education and learning platform that is free from political and social shenanigans. Around 70% of the students and 55% of the educators who were part of the user feedback group responded that they would use such a platform. Some additional resources on conducting the prototype testing can be found at `https://maze.co/blog/prototype-testing/`.

- **Competitor analysis**: We do not have any direct competitors for now as there is no dedicated social media platform for educators and students. We have indirect competition from **Facebook** (as a social media platform) and **YouTube** (as a content-sharing platform). **LinkedIn** is also a social media platform, but it is mainly used for building professional networks and job search and is therefore only a tertiary competitor.

There are learning platforms such as **Udemy** and **Lynda.com** (now LinkedIn) that are premium learning platforms targeting working professionals. These might become indirect competition if we go with the option of offering premium courses in the future. Hence, we did a detailed analysis of Facebook and YouTube as indirect competitors. The following is the summary report:

Evaluation criteria	Facebook	YouTube
Competition type	Indirect	Indirect
Their competitive advantage	Well established brand	Content creators get paid a small amount
Market share	65% of total social media	30% of total video sharing services
Revenue model	Advertisement	Advertisement
Maturity level	Advanced	Advanced
Our competitive advantage	Dedicated to a specific group	Dedicated to a specific group. Not restricted to just videos

- **Cost and pricing analysis**: To determine if the solution is viable, we will have to explore cost and revenue estimates and understand when we can break even. To find that out, we will have to first decide on our revenue model. In the first phase, as we are not paying anything to educators and not charging anything to students, we should opt for an advertising revenue model.

But an advertising revenue stream will not start before we have users on the platform. Advertisers will only be attracted once there is a significant user base. As a result, for six months we should focus on onboarding users. After six months, having increased the traffic and the active number of users on the platform, we should start on sponsored posts and advertised listings. To project the advertising revenue, I found this blog useful: `http://plantostart.com/how-calculate-advertising-revenue-startup/`

Apart from the revenue projection, we should also estimate the cost and expenses, which will include development and infrastructure costs, marketing, legal, compliance, and other miscellaneous expenses. Estimating all costs and expenses and projecting the revenue will give us an approximation of the break-even timeline.

> **Important note:**
> Please note, the numbers used in the graph are hypothetical and do not suggest the actual cost or revenue for such a digital platform.

The following graph explains our break-even point:

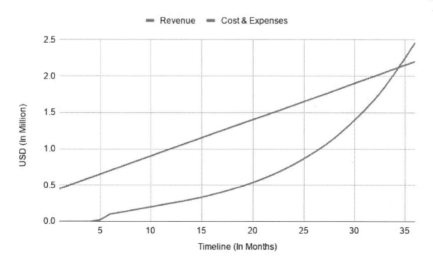

Figure 3.9 – Escola cost and revenue projection

As we can see that the **Cost & Expenses** don't start from zero, but there are some initial expenses, which include development and infrastructure costs, initial marketing and launch expenses, legal, and other miscellaneous charges. Post-launch there is a month-on-month operating and marketing cost.

As discussed earlier, for the first six months, we should not focus on **Revenue** but concentrate on grabbing the market and increasing the number of users on the platform. As the traffic on the platform increases, advertisers will be attracted. Initially, we should have a target timeframe to focus solely on increasing the number of users and continuously evaluating if we can hit the target by the set timeframe (in this case, six months).

From six months onwards and till the end of the year, we should target a minimum advertising revenue to get our foot in the water. After 12 months, we should target a 10% growth in revenue every month, which will take us to the break-even point around the 35th month, which is close to the third year. We will be profitable from the fourth year if we target the said growth rate and continue with the same model. If we add premium courses on the platform, then revenue generation will increase, and we will break even faster.

This is the first level of cost and revenue modeling to help us in the go-no-go decision. A detailed pricing strategy and financial projections are done in the next phase, where we will work on a comprehensive and thorough digital platform strategy.

- **SWOT analysis**: After finishing the user feedback, prototype testing, competitor analysis, and pricing strategy, now is the time to summarize all our validation with SWOT analysis. All the stakeholders will get together to do the SWOT analysis. The assumption here is that everyone has read all the analysis and testing reports and findings. The team will get together and create a SWOT analysis report.

The points added or discussed during SWOT analysis will be based on all the analysis results, the results of all the testing, the participants' research, and any instincts from their past experiences. This report will help us summarize all our findings and be a crucial aid for our final decision. Here is the sample of the SWOT analysis report:

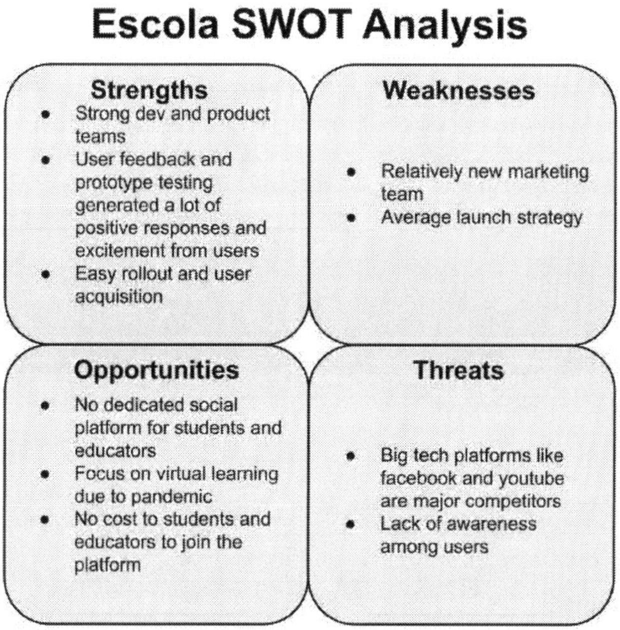

Escola SWOT Analysis

Strengths
- Strong dev and product teams
- User feedback and prototype testing generated a lot of positive responses and excitement from users
- Easy rollout and user acquisition

Weaknesses

- Relatively new marketing team
- Average launch strategy

Opportunities
- No dedicated social platform for students and educators
- Focus on virtual learning due to pandemic
- No cost to students and educators to join the platform

Threats

- Big tech platforms like facebook and youtube are major competitors
- Lack of awareness among users

Figure 3.10 – Escola SWOT analysis

We have results and reports of all our testing and analysis. We have also summarized our findings by conducting a SWOT analysis. As a result, now it is time to conclude our validation and make the final decision.

As the user feedback suggested that most users are excited about and will use the platform, and the pricing analysis suggested a break-even over three years, it is safe to proceed to the next phase. But there is some tough competition from well-established tech leaders, which will be a challenge. Plus, the SWOT analysis revealed that our marketing team is new, and our launch strategy is not very strong. Hence, grabbing the market share from the strong competitors will be very difficult.

Therefore, the conclusion here is that if we are moving ahead with the idea, we will have to pull all our resources together and put extra effort into marketing and creating user awareness. Our launch strategy must be very robust and impactful. We will have to constantly deliver features that will set us apart from these giant competitors and pave our way in grabbing the market.

Summary

In this chapter, we learned the end-to-end process of digital platform ideation and validation. We started with identifying the user, then moved on to formulating the problem statement and defining the solution, and, finally, validating the concept.

In the problem definition phase, we looked at some of the distinguishing factors with respect to digital platforms. For example, in digital platforms, user identification involves identifying the pairs of producers and consumers, and the problem statement should cut across that pair. It should be a holistic problem statement involving all the user types and roles. We also discussed how before arriving at the problem statement we can create empathy maps. For digital platforms, each user type or user role should have its own empathy map.

We looked at some of the established techniques available to identify the solution. While collecting ideas for a solution, we should always keep the holistic problem statement at the center and never lose sight of it. The identified solution should solve the problem for all the user roles and entities involved in the digital platform and add value to all of them. If it is not valuable for all the entities, it is not the right solution for a digital platform.

Finally, in the validation phase, we looked at the different steps of the validation process. We also understood what analysis must be conducted and the tests that must be performed to gather the correct data that will help us validate our concept. Reports generated during research and the data collected during tests must be used to decide whether to proceed with the digital platform.

In the next chapter, we will learn how to build a platform strategy. We will discuss the relationship between business vision, business strategy, and platform strategy, and understand how it is essential to have the right platform strategy to meet the business goals. We will learn the different components of a good platform strategy and look at the different types of platform strategies.

4
Building a Platform Strategy

In the previous chapter, we explored the first step of platform product management: research and validation of the concept. We understood that it is essential to define the exact problem before arriving at the solution and validating it. We explored different techniques for problem definition and identifying the solution.

We looked at the step-by-step guide to validate our problem and the specified solution. During the validation process, we explored some important types of tests and analyses, such as user feedback, prototype testing, competitor analysis, and pricing analysis, that must be conducted to decide whether to proceed with the identified problem and the solution.

After the research and validation, if we decide to proceed with the platform's development, the next step is to create a **platform strategy**. In order to define a strong platform strategy that will help introduce our platform to the market and enable its expansion, it is crucial to understand what a platform strategy is. It's also important to understand what goes into creating a robust and powerful platform strategy, its relation to business vision, and the business strategy. Therefore, to help us create a strong platform strategy, we will cover the following topics in this chapter:

- What is platform strategy?
- Defining the business vision

- Defining the business strategy
- Defining the platform strategy
- Case study

By the end of this chapter, we will understand the relationship between business vision, business strategy, and platform strategy. It will help us create a powerful platform strategy that will give our platform a solid entry into the market and enable it to grow and sustain prudently. A thought-through and well-crafted platform strategy will guide us through the day-to-day product management of our platform.

What is platform strategy?

The word *strategy* means an action plan to achieve an overall objective or goal, and this meaning also applies to the platform strategy. A **platform strategy** is an end-to-end plan to reach the final aim of the platform. It entails what you should do and how you should do it to achieve the ultimate goal of what your platform is meant for. It should provide an action plan from entry to sustainability at the peak. Hence, the platform strategy should answer the following questions:

- How would you enter the market?
- How would you grow?
- What should be done to sustain your goal?

For the platform strategy or the platform business model, these three questions should be answered in conjunction with the characteristics of the platform that we saw in *Chapter 1, Fundamentals of Platform Business Models*, which are as follows:

- It is multidimensional.
- It enables an easy plug-and-play mechanism.
- It creates strong network effects.

Entry to the market for platforms should include entry at both producers' and consumers' sides. The growth plan should make the producer and consumer onboarding easy and convenient. Sustainability should focus on creating strong network effects, as platforms cannot sustain in isolation. They must grow as a network of producers, consumers, and intermediaries. Hence, a robust platform strategy should plan the platform's entry, growth, and sustainability while meeting all its characteristics.

But answering these questions to create a platform strategy is impossible unless we know the business strategy. So, to understand and come up with the business strategy, we should know the business vision. Hence, a platform strategy cannot be defined on its own; it is derived from the business strategy, which is derived from the business vision. The following diagram illustrates the flow of steps for defining the platform strategy:

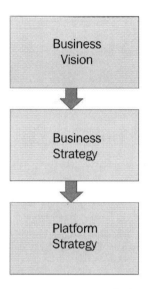

Figure 4.1 – Business vision to platform strategy

Drafting the platform strategy includes defining the business vision, defining the business strategy, and finally defining the platform strategy. We will look at all of these in detail, but to give you a very high-level example: if we must create a platform strategy for a ridesharing platform, we should start with its business vision, which will be something such as *make everyday travel easy for people.*

The business strategy of this ridesharing platform would be to connect the people who want to go from one place to another (riders) with people who have vehicles and spare time to offer the service (drivers). Based on the business vision and the business strategy, the platform strategy should cover how drivers and riders can be connected (entry), what would attract more of them to join (growth), and what would make them stay (sustainability).

Now that we have seen how the relationship between the business vision, business strategy, and the platform strategy works, let's look at each of them in detail.

Defining the business vision

The **business vision** is something that is the core of what your business is supposed to do. A rightly defined business vision provides an aim and the goal to the business. It gives a sense of direction and guides you on the right path. It is the first step in formulating any strategies or plans. Setting the right business vision will help in establishing the right direction for our platform. Defining the business vision is the first step toward defining the platform strategy. Once the business vision is specified, it enables the definition of the business strategy, which then helps in formulating the platform strategy.

Before going into the weeds of creating the platform strategy, we should understand how to define the business vision.

Steps for defining the business vision

Business vision should clearly mention the business's objective and where you see your business a few years down the line. It must be precise and straightforward and should provide a sense of direction. Avoid keeping it very generic and ambiguous, such as becoming the best at something or the most trusted name in some category.

You can define your business vision the way you want; as long as it clearly defines the objective of your business and provides a direction, it should be good. The following are the steps or guidelines you can refer to if you need a starting point in defining your business vision:

1. **Mention the output and the objective**: Your business vision should clearly mention what output your business is delivering or what its objective is. This is the simple part, and most businesses get it right. Avoid keeping it open-ended, such as being the most trusted partner for people. This is an extreme example; no one defines a vision like this, but the point here is that your vision should tell people what your business is.

   In the earlier mentioned example, we defined a very high-level business vision for a ridesharing platform to *make everyday travel easy for people*. This business vision is very ambiguous, but it mentions the output of the business, which is helping people with travel. Anyone reading this vision will know that the company is in the travel industry and its objective is to help people with everyday travel.

2. **Call out the exclusivity**: After mentioning the output of the business, the next important thing is to call out the exclusivity of your business: what makes you better than others and why people should choose you over your competitors. Exclusivity must be particular and specific. Stay away from phrases such as the best in class, most trusted, or most suitable. Mention why you are the best in class or what makes you the most suitable.

   Let's look at our example of a business objective for a ridesharing platform. It says *make travel easy*, which is not very specific; easy can mean different things to different people in different situations. We must clearly mention what we are changing or what improvements we are bringing. Let's refine our example and remove the word *easy* and mention the specifics, such as cheaper, faster, or anything that will make us stand out. Hence, our updated business vision should be to *make everyday travel faster and cheaper for people.*

3. **Target the specific user group**: Along with mentioning the business output and the uniqueness, it is essential to target a specific group of people, a particular community, or a confined set of users. Instead of calling out to people or the world, direct your business vision to a targeted audience. If possible, bring in the specificity in the business output as well, such as listening to music instead of entertainment.

   Now, if we look again at our example, we mentioned our output as travel, which is broad. As a ridesharing platform, we specifically target people commuting daily to work, school, or fitness centers. Hence, we should replace the word *travel* with *commute*. Changing travel to commute targets a particular group and precise output. If we want to further refine this business vision, we should replace the word *people* with something specific. We have already mentioned the commute; hence, it implies that we are talking about shorter distances and local commutes. Thus, we can replace the word *people* with *the local community*. Therefore, our updated business vision should be to *make everyday commutes faster and cheaper for local communities.*

The following diagram summarizes the steps of defining the business vision:

Mention the output

Example: Make everyday travel
easy for people

Call out the exclusivity

Example: Make everyday travel
faster and cheaper for people

**Target the specific user
group**

Example: Make everyday
commutes faster and cheaper for
local communities

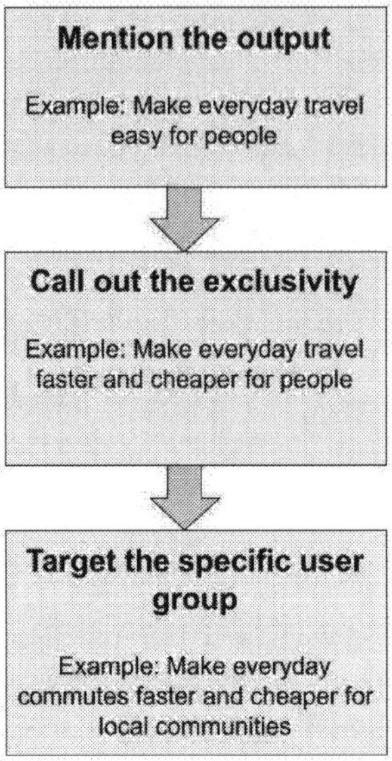

Figure 4.2 – Steps for defining the business vision

This business vision clearly defines the business objective and the output. It explicitly mentions what the benefits are and how it is better than its competitors. It also targets a particular community and set of users. This business vision also provides a direction to the company to make the local short-distance commutes faster and cheaper. How that would be achieved should be covered in the strategy.

After defining the business vision of our platform, we should be able to derive and define the business strategy based on the business vision.

Defining the business strategy

Defining the platform's business strategy is different from that of linear businesses because of the multi-sided nature of platforms. The business strategy depends on the type of platform, the current availability of producers and consumers, and potential growth in their numbers. The following are the types of business strategies that will be applicable in different scenarios:

- **Draw new consumers**: When there is an existing network of producers, but consumers are either non-existent or fulfill their requirements by other means, then this strategy of drawing new consumers is the most appropriate one. For example, before **Yelp**, people were trying to get reviews of restaurants by several different means, such as their social circle or expert advice.

Some people did not even realize they needed to find out about the restaurant before they dined there. But Yelp generated that demand and created a consumer base that wanted to read the reviews. If the number of producers is high and the number of consumers doesn't exist with that specific demand, but there is a potential to generate the demand and create a compelling consumer base, then this is the best strategy.

- **Generate a new category of producers**: This is the most tricky and innovative business strategy. Here, there is high demand from consumers, and their demands are met by traditional means, which are either inefficient or not scalable. Hence, there is a need to create a new category of producers to meet the increasing consumer demands effectively and efficiently.

  Identifying the need for this new category and building and scaling it to meet the demand is the most challenging and innovative part. The most famous examples of this strategy are **Uber** and **Airbnb**. They created a new category of producers in the form of drivers and homeowners even when taxi services and hotels existed to meet the transport and accommodation needs of the people.

- **Aggregate and connect**: If a proportionate number of producers and consumers are available, but they are scattered and cannot effectively connect, then the strategy to aggregate and connect is best, such as an e-commerce marketplace that aggregates the sellers and connects them to buyers.

  Before the existence of the platforms, the buyer's needs were met, but the approach was inefficient and not scalable. Hence, in this scenario, where producers and consumers are scattered, the strategy of aggregation and connection creates an efficient, scalable, and cost-effective ecosystem. **Amazon**, **Netflix**, and **Spotify** are popular and familiar examples of platforms implementing aggregation and connection strategies.

- **Target uncharted producers and consumers**: As the name suggests, this strategy targets an untapped market of producers and consumers that needs to be connected. When both producers and consumers exist but meet their needs in numerous other ways, and communicate in scattered and unorganized channels, this strategy must be implemented. Another criterion to choose this strategy is when the producers and the consumers are the same users. Whether they are producers or consumers depends on the action that they are performing. Social media platforms and knowledge-sharing platforms such as **Stack Overflow** are popular examples that follow this strategy.

- **Expand to the other side**: This strategy is best suited for existing linear businesses that want to move to a platform model. This existing business could cater to the producers or consumers and expand to the other side when they decide to move and extend to the platform model. For example, suppose you own a standalone e-commerce website and already have users on the consumer side. When you are transitioning to a platform model, you would want to grow your producer side.

  Similarly, if you have a B2C payment processing company, your existing user base consists of sellers, which is on the producer side, and when you want to transition to the platform model, the strategy should be to expand the consumer side. This strategy is most appropriate for transforming an existing business, which is a massive topic that we will cover in *Chapter 10*, *Moving from Linear Products to Platforms*.

The following table illustrates a summary of selecting the right business strategy for the platform business model in different scenarios:

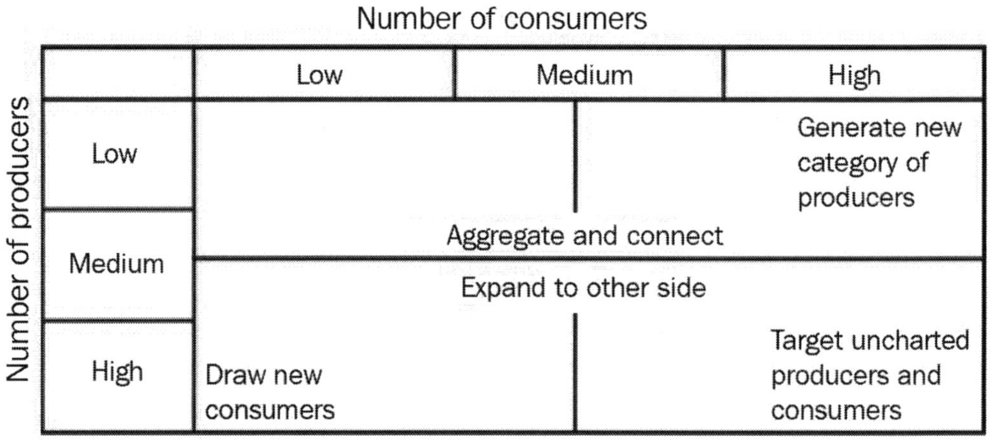

Number of consumers

	Low	Medium	High
Low			Generate new category of producers
Medium	Aggregate and connect		
	Expand to other side		
High	Draw new consumers		Target uncharted producers and consumers

Number of producers

Figure 4.3 – Business strategy selection criteria

The preceding table depicts that when **Number of producers** is high, but **Number of consumers** is almost non-existent, then generating new consumers works best. In an opposite scenario, where we have more consumers and fewer, inadequate producers, then developing a new producer category is most appropriate.

When the producers and consumers are both in high numbers, or they are the same users, the **Target uncharted producers and consumers** strategy where you attract them all is the most suitable one. If the producers and consumers are in the right proportions but are scattered, then **Aggregate and connect** is the right strategy. However, if you already have a significant user base on one side and the other side exists in the right proportion, then expanding your business to the other side is the correct approach.

Now that we have learned about defining the business vision and the business strategy, we can now create the platform strategy.

Defining the platform strategy

To create a **platform strategy**, we must understand what goes into creating a good platform strategy or the components that make up a strong strategy. But before that, we must know the different types of platform strategies and how to select the right one in conjunction with the business strategy. Therefore, let's first understand which platform strategy is best suited for the business strategy that is appropriate for our platform.

Types of platform strategy

Understanding the types of platform strategies is a continuation of understanding different business strategies. The business strategy of a platform will determine and derive its platform strategy. Hence, choosing the right platform strategy is dependent on which business strategy you have selected.

Building on top of the chosen business strategy and going deeper into the execution and application of that business strategy will lead us to define the platform strategy. So, let's explore and understand these platform strategies in detail:

1. **Target the expansion at the consumer side**: This platform strategy applies to the first business strategy of drawing new consumers. This strategy focuses on the platform's consumer side and aims to increase the number of consumers on the platform. The approach of this strategy is that once a significant user base is established on the consumer side, producers will pay to reach out and connect to this sizable and considerable number of consumers.

   To attract more consumers, capabilities built on these platforms and the revenue model must appeal to them. The launch strategy should be designed to penetrate and expand in the consumer market. Once a good number of consumers are actively using the platform, different revenue options such as targeted advertisements or pay per listing can be adopted. Building an extensive consumer network that will attract producers and create different paths for monetization is the key to this strategy. Search platforms such as **Zillow**, **realtor.com**, and **Trip Advisor** followed this strategy.

2. **Growth and easy onboarding of producers**: Growth and easy producer onboarding applies to the business strategy of generating a new category of producers. This strategy aims to increase the number of producers by making it easier and seamless for them to join the platform. Remember that these are not professional producers. For example, homeowners before Airbnb had never experienced renting a room, and car owners before Uber or Lyft had never done professional driving.

   Hence, it is imperative to make the experience hassle-free for these new producers. Effortless, straightforward joining, and simple usage of the platform, will bring in a higher number of producers. More producers will give better choices and offer competitive prices to consumers, attracting them to use the platform. Hence, the success of this strategy is to increase the number of producers on the platform to create efficient and cost-effective choices for consumers.

3. **Proportionately increase producers and consumers**: This platform strategy is applicable when the business strategy is to aggregate and connect. As we have seen, in the case of the aggregation and connection strategy, the number of producers and consumers is proportionate. Hence, it makes sense to proportionally increase them on the platform.

   This strategy should focus on both sides of the platform, concentrate on building the capabilities and features for both producers and consumers, and proportionately increase them to create a strong network effect. The revenue model should be attractive to both, and the launch strategy should equally focus on both sides. This strategy believes that *the stronger the network, the more successful the platform will be.*

4. **Focus on building an enormous user base**: Building an enormous user base falls under the business strategy of targeting uncharted producers and consumers. As discussed under that strategy, producers and consumers are the same users. Their actions determine which side they are on at that particular moment.

   For example, when sharing posts on **Facebook**, they are producers, and when reading them they are consumers. As the producers and the consumers are the same users, this strategy focuses on building an extensive network of these users on the platform. After attracting a large number of users, a repository of their behaviors and preferences can be created based on the patterns of their usage. This data can be used to monetize the platform by giving targeted access to the user group to the advertiser and the promoters.

5. **Complete the network**: Completing the network is applying the business strategy of expanding to the other side, which is implemented while transforming the existing linear business to the platform model. The approach here is to use the existing network of one side to attract the other side of the users.

Walmart Marketplace is a classic example of this strategy. Being the biggest retailer globally, they have a considerable consumer base and the infrastructure to cater to this humongous consumer group. They used this infrastructure and the massive network of buyers to attract the sellers to their platform. This strategy focuses on increasing the number of users on the new side until an excellent and sustainable proportion is achieved. Until then, the aim should be to attract the new side as much as possible by building capabilities valuable and beneficial for them, or creating revenue and pricing models that are alluring.

The following graph shows the targeted growth of producers and consumers while implementing different platform strategies:

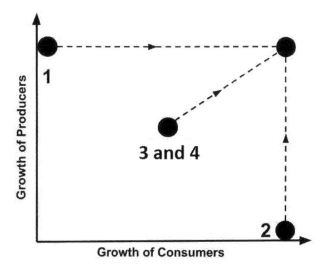

Figure 4.4 – Growth based on platform strategy

The preceding graph illustrates that producers are high in number in the first strategy, so growth should be targeted at the consumer side. At the same time, the second strategy is the opposite, where the number of consumers is high, and producers cannot meet demand efficiently and effectively, so growth should be targeted at the producer side.

In the third strategy, the focus should be to grow producers and consumers proportionally. As producers and consumers are the same users in the fourth strategy, increasing the user base will grow both equally. The last strategy is not shown on the graph. It would focus on increasing either producers or consumers, depending on what your existing business already has. The transformation and expansion to the platform business model will be exclusively covered in *Chapter 10, Moving from Linear Products to Platforms*, where we will explore this strategy in detail.

To help and facilitate the growth and expansion on either one or both sides of the platform, the end-to-end definition and the execution of the platform strategy are essential. To define and create this overarching strategy, we should understand the different components that make up a solid and robust platform strategy.

Components of a platform strategy

The components of platform strategy are like building blocks. Once we understand them individually, creating the strategy is like putting these blocks together to create a structure. The following diagram illustrates all the components of the platform strategy; let's look at them in detail:

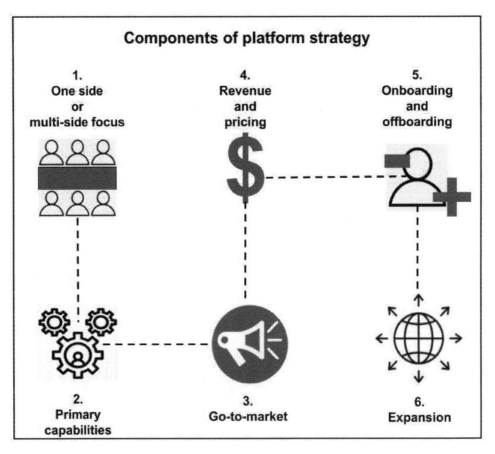

Figure 4.5 – Components of a platform strategy

The preceding diagram consists of the following components:

1. **One-side or multi-side focus**: This is the first step in defining the platform strategy, and it is selecting one of the combinations of the business and platform strategies. Based on the type of platform and the chosen business strategy, we should decide whether to focus platform growth on the producer side, the consumer side, or both.

   This is the most crucial and foundational step in defining the platform strategy. All the subsequent steps and components, such as building the capabilities, and deciding the revenue and pricing strategies will depend on which direction we want our platform to grow in. The following table summarizes the focus of the platform strategy based on the current state and the business strategy:

Current State	Business Strategy	Platform Strategy Focus
More producers and less or no consumers	Draw new consumers	Consumer side
More consumers and inadequate producers	Generate new producer category	Producer side
Proportionate but scattered producers and consumers	Aggregate and connect	Both sides proportionally
Unfocused users that are both producers and consumers	Target uncharted producers and consumers	Increase the total user base

2. **Primary capabilities**: Once we know the focus of our platform strategy, the next step is to define and strategize on the primary capabilities that the platform must offer. If the platform's focus is on the consumer side, the capabilities must attract more consumers to the platform and vice versa. But this doesn't mean that the other side should be neglected completely.

The essential capabilities, also referred to as primary capabilities, must be offered on both sides so that they can co-exist and deliver value. This means that the capabilities that enable the end-to-end flow of the platform's core offering should get the highest priority. However, the capabilities that aim at convenience, ease of use, and so on must be targeted for the focus side of the platform after the primary capabilities. For example, in a search platform such as realtor.com, where the focus of the platform strategy is on the consumer side, capabilities such as predictive search, intelligent sorting, and filtering must be prioritized after the primary capabilities and before any other capabilities to enhance the producer side.

Similarly, in a service-oriented platform, if the focus is on the producer side, capabilities such as adding availability, acceptance, declining the service, and multiple payment transfer options must be prioritized over the *nice-to-have* features on the consumer side.

3. **Go-to-market**: The go-to-market strategy usually consists of when, how, where, and for whom to launch the product, and it is part of the overall product strategy and plan. Platforms are no different, which means the go-to-market strategy must be part of the overall platform strategy. Hence, it is an essential component and step in defining the platform strategy.

    The launch effort must be targeted on the focus side of the platform. For example, search platforms of specific categories such as Trip Advisor or Yelp will not be rolled out to the producers during the launch, as all the features and capabilities will be targeted at consumers. But producers will be part of all the marketing communication and will be informed about the platform's launch. Producers will also be kept aware of the growth of the platform. In contrast, an e-commerce marketplace that focuses on growing both sides proportionally will be launched and equally marketed to buyers and sellers. Hence, the target side of the launch would depend on the type of platform and the focus side of the platform.

4. **Pricing and revenue**: In *Chapter 1, Fundamentals of Platform Business Models*, we discussed how to select the most suitable revenue model of the platform. In *Chapter 3, Research and Validation*, we looked at the pricing analysis of the platform to decide its viability. The pricing strategy for the platform is the combination of the following three elements:

    A. Revenue model

    B. Pricing analysis

    C. Growth focus of the platform (producer, consumer, or both)

    The platform's revenue model is decided based on the type of platform and whether the production cost of the goods, services, or content is one-time or not. The price point is decided based on the development cost of the platform, the platform's monthly marketing and operating cost, projected growth, and the expected break-even time frame.

Along with deciding the revenue model and the price point, a platform pricing strategy should also focus on how to attract producers or consumers through attractive monetary benefits, and what discounts and free services can be offered that will compel users to join the platform. These offers and promotions should be based on the growth strategy of the platform.

For example, if we want to attract more drivers to the ridesharing platform, offer the first few rides with no commission. And if the platform strategy is to focus on the consumer side, then provide discounted prices to buyers on an e-commerce marketplace. The following table illustrates the examples of the different offers that could be made on various platforms with varying models of revenue. Any offers, discounts, or free trials must go through a pricing analysis done by the financial team with input from product managers:

Revenue model	Examples of producer-side focus	Examples of consumer-side focus
Subscription	Premium price for content	Free trial subscriptions
Pay as you go	Low transaction fee or first few transactions with zero commission	Offers and discounts
Advertising	First few advertisements free	No cost
Pay per listing	Free placements	No cost

The following blog provides detailed analysis on pricing strategies for marketplaces and other types of platforms: `https://stories.platformdesigntoolkit.com/pricing-platforms-marketplaces-151ab67b130a`.

5. **Onboarding and offboarding**: Onboarding and offboarding decides how easy and convenient it is for producers and consumers to join and leave the platform. The onboarding and offboarding strategy depends on which side of the platform you are focusing more on. Consumer onboarding is more straightforward and has been sorted out for years with the traditional linear business.

But producer onboarding is tricky, especially if your business strategy is to generate a new category of producers. This becomes the most critical and crucial part of your platform strategy. The platform's success will depend on onboarding enough new producers to meet the demand efficiently and cost-effectively, which was not possible from the traditional producers.

Hence, their onboarding on the platform must be seamless and effortless, and financially beneficial. Capabilities, pricing structure, and the process should focus on making the life of the producers easier. Offboarding of producers from the platform must also be simpler. They should be able to leave the platform if they wish. They should get the option to either temporarily or permanently leave the platform. Creating unnecessary lock-ins will discourage them from joining.

6. **Expansion**: The expansion plan is the final component of the platform strategy. It depends on several factors, such as the growth focus of the platform, current competition, potential future competitors, pricing strategy, and the break-even time frame. For example, suppose the focus of the platform strategy is growth on the consumer side, and the pricing strategy suggests revenue growth of 10% every month. In that case, the number of consumers should increase at the same proportion on the platform.

   To achieve the expected number of consumers every month, we should expand in new geographies and new demographics, and offer new capabilities to attract users in existing regions and segments. The expansion plan should also consider whether to target a slower increase in the user base with an early monetization plan or an aggressive growth in the user base with a strategy of first capturing the market and later generating the revenue stream.

These components can be put together to build an overarching platform strategy, which will help us to launch our platform into the market and have a growth and sustainability plan in place.

Case study

Let's continue with the case study of our educational content sharing and learning platform, **Escola**. In the previous chapter, we researched to define the problem statement and identify the solution, and we also validated the viability and feasibility of our platform. The conclusion after different tests and analyses was to proceed to the next step for the Escola platform. Hence, in the next step, we will define the business vision, business strategy, and finally create the platform strategy for the Escola platform.

Business vision

To define the business vision, we must look at the problem statement that we are trying to solve and provide a direction to our company based on that problem. The problem that we were trying to solve through the Escola platform is that educators cannot reach out to interested students to share learning content, and students cannot find the right educators to receive that content.

Solving this problem will provide the business objective or output to our business vision. We are trying to help people connect, share, and learn. These are the three outputs that we can specify based on our problem statement. Hence, just based on the objective and the output, our business vision would be *connect people to easily share and learn*.

This vision is ambiguous and lacks specificity. It does not mention what value we are going to provide. As we learned during our research phase, educators could not find students, and their reach is limited. Similarly, students cannot approach or learn from any educators that they want. Hence, we should make the process more reachable and extensive. Also, sharing content is a tedious and time-consuming task; therefore, we should add value by making it simpler and faster.

If we must refine our business vision by adding our exclusivity, it would be *connect people to make sharing and learning unrestricted, extensible, scalable, and efficient*.

This vision clearly mentions the benefits and the values that this platform will bring. But it still lacks some specificity in terms of the target audience and the output. Adding the target audience, in this case, is easy as we have already specified educators and students in our problem statement. We can further refine the vision by adding the specific output of educators sharing educational content. Hence, our final business vision will be *connect educators and students to make learning and sharing of educational content unrestricted, extensible, scalable, and efficient*.

Here is a diagram that visualizes Escola's business vision:

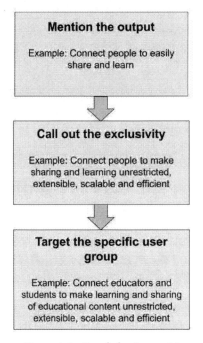

Figure 4.6 – Escola business vision

This business vision provides a goal and direction to connect the educators and students to improve the content-sharing experience. How to connect them and make the experience better should be covered in the strategy. Let's explore and discuss how we will create and define the business strategy and the platform strategy for Escola.

Business strategy

As our business vision is to connect educators and students, and provide them with extensive reach, our strategy should be to increase the number of users (educators and students) on the platform as much as possible and as fast as possible. We know that both producers and consumers – in this case, educators and students – exist in higher numbers, but no one has ever created anything targeting this user group.

They were using different methods to meet their needs and were communicating in unorganized channels. Hence, these are unchartered producers and consumers who need a platform targeting them, meeting all their demands, and solving their problems.

As seen earlier, when we are targeting an untapped market, the strategy should be to attract as many producers and consumers as possible and build a huge user base. Hence, our strategy for the Escola platform should be to onboard a sizable number of educators and students on the platform. This strategy of increasing the number of users on the platform also aligns with our business vision of connecting our educators and students and providing them with an extensible and scalable reach.

Platform strategy

We have defined the business vision for our platform, Escola. We have also identified the business strategy to target uncharted producers and consumers and create a sizable user base for our platform. Now, the next step is to draft the platform strategy. We will apply each component of the strategy to Escola and, finally, create a summary of our platform strategy:

1. **One-side or multi-side focus**: As our business strategy is to create a sizable user base by adding as many educators and students as possible to our platform, the focus of our platform must be on both sides. We should proportionally increase the number of educators and students.

2. **Primary capabilities**: As the focus of our strategy is on both sides of the platform, we should plan to build capabilities and features that are useful and appealing to both sides. We should target features that connect educators and students and make the content's sharing and learning experience easy for them. All the capabilities must be added to the platform roadmap in detail, and the strategy should mention, at a high level, what the primarily targeted capabilities are based on the focus of the platform strategy. Some of the capabilities that we should target for each of our user sides are as follows:

    A. **Students**: Personalization, streaming, and notifications

    B. **Educators**: Content creation, content management, connection, and engagement

3. **Go-to-market**: We should plan to market the platform's launch in the cities and towns that have a higher number of schools and colleges. We can launch across the country, but marketing should focus on seven cities with Ivy League colleges. These cities have educators and students from Ivy League colleges and have a considerable number of preparatory schools. Escola should be launched to both educators and students. The marketing should strategically plan to target educators in the first few weeks so that they join the platform, start creating content, and invite students.

4. **Onboarding**: As we are targeting an increase in the number of users on the platform rapidly, our onboarding should be seamless. Joining our platform would be a simple sign-up process with very few details. We should offer incentives such as gift vouchers and other monetary prizes to educators for sharing quality content for the first few months. We should personally invite famous and influential educators to join the platform. We should market these influential educators and the quality content on the platform to the students to attract them to join Escola.

5. **Expansion**: Our expansion strategy should target aggressive growth in the number of users. You should know that established social media platforms grew at an average rate of 50% to 70% in their initial years of launch. As our platform is not for everyone and focuses on a particular group of users, we should expect and target 30% to 40% monthly growth in users in the first year after the launch.

6. **Pricing and revenue**: We can make an assumption that the advertisement-revenue model is one of the most suitable revenue models for Escola, as we are not charging students anything to access the platform and are not paying anything to the educators for creating and sharing the content. But for the first year, our focus should be to capture the market by creating a sizable user base and not target any revenue.

   We should start the revenue stream through targeted advertisements from the second year. If our plan is to break even and recoup our investment in three years, then we should be aiming to start our revenue with 25% of the platform development and operating cost of the first year and target revenue growth of 10% every month. Our break-even period will change based on how much higher or lower our revenue growth is compared with the target. We can use this blog (`https://www.adspeed.com/Blog/How-much-charge-advertising-website-1104.html`) to get started on how to determine the charge of the advertisement on our platform. Please remember this only gives us the methods and techniques of calculation, not the exact pricing.

Based on the previous discussion on the different components of the platform strategy, we can summarize Escola's platform strategy in the following table. Please note these are some of the suitable options for the platform based on the assumptions we have made about Escola's business context and our current understanding. These options would differ based on the results of different research and analysis:

Component of the strategy	Details
Focus side	Both (educators and students).
Primary capabilities – students	Personalization. Streaming. Notifications.
Primary capabilities – educators	Content creation. Content management. Connection and engagement.
Go-to-market	Across the US, with a focus on seven cities with a high number of colleges and schools.
Onboarding	Special incentives and prices for educators to join and share content. Heavy marketing on campuses for students onboarding.
Expansion plan	Aggressive growth and increase in user base. The targeted increase in the number of users every month is 30% to 40%.
Revenue and pricing	No revenue stream for the first year; focus on capturing the market. From the second year onward, start with the advertising model. The projected starting revenue is 25% of the platform development and operating cost of the first year, with a 10% growth in revenue every month.

Summary

Our primary focus in this chapter was to learn how to build a successful platform strategy that can help us launch the platform, grow it, and sustain it during its peak. We learned that a platform strategy cannot be built in isolation; it is derived from the business strategy, which is derived from the business vision. Hence, to create a robust and powerful platform strategy, we should first define the business vision, define the business strategy, and then draft a platform strategy.

While defining the business vision, we understood that it must be precise and clearly state the company's direction. It should mention the business objective and the uniqueness of the business, and it must be specific. We looked at a sample business vision with a step-by-step guide to refine it. We learned that the business vision sets the agenda for the business strategy. A business vision answers *what the business is supposed to do*, whereas a business strategy answers *how it should be done.*

We explored and understood different business strategies that can be implemented for different business cases and scenarios. We looked at how we can extend these business strategies to choose and implement a specific platform strategy. Choosing the right platform strategy is the continuation and the expansion of selecting the business strategy. For example, if the business strategy is to generate a new category of producers, then the platform strategy should focus on onboarding more and more producers. Similarly, if the business strategy is to aggregate and connect producers and consumers, the platform strategy should aim to increase producers and consumers proportionally.

We also looked at different components of the platform strategy and how these components come together to build a solid and vigorous strategy. A well-crafted and thoughtfully designed platform strategy can prepare us to creatively launch a platform that can set us up in the right direction. Along with the launch and go-to-market strategy, a good platform strategy also contains growth and expansion plans and revenue projections that enable long-term sustainability.

From the next chapter onward, we will move into the execution and day-to-day operation of platform product management. We will understand how platform strategy can be translated into a platform roadmap. We will understand how to define capabilities and how to prioritize and organize them.

Section 2: Building the Platform

This section makes sure that you can translate a platform strategy into platform roadmaps and define the platform MVP, launch the platform, build an operating model, and have an execution plan in place. You will learn about everything from building a roadmap to the day-to-day execution of platform product management.

This section comprises the following chapters:

5
Defining the MVP and Creating a Platform Roadmap

In the previous chapter, we learned how to define the platform strategy. While understanding the process of creating a platform strategy, we learned that it could not be defined or produced in a vacuum. Platform strategy depends on the business strategy, which depends on the business vision. Hence, to create a strong platform strategy, we must first define our business vision, derive the business strategy from that vision, and formulate the platform strategy. We looked at different types of platform strategies and how to choose the right one based on our business strategy. We explored various components of a good platform strategy and how to put those components together to build a robust and long-lasting platform strategy that will enable our platform's launch, growth, and sustainability.

In the last two chapters, we covered the strategic part of the platform business model and digital platforms in general. After covering the strategic sections, now is the time to move to the tactical and execution part. Therefore, we will start with creating the platform roadmap based on our business and platform strategy in this chapter.

To create an actionable and realistic platform roadmap, it is crucial first to understand what a roadmap is and how it differs from a linear product roadmap. Once we know this difference, we will go in-depth about creating the platform roadmap, which consists of three phases: defining platform capabilities, defining the platform MVP, and finally creating the platform roadmap. To meet this agenda, we will explore and discuss the following topics in this chapter:

- Understanding the roadmap

- Defining platform capabilities

- Defining the platform MVP

- Creating the platform roadmap

- Case study

Following this chapter, given the business and platform strategy, we should be able to create a pragmatic and valuable platform roadmap to meet our business goals. The platform roadmap will consist of the MVP and the other milestones post-MVP. It is the first step of the execution phase of the platform product management, which will enable us to create a launch strategy for our MVP and maintain an ongoing platform backlog.

Understanding the roadmap

In the previous chapter, while understanding the business and the platform strategy, we discussed that strategy is a plan to achieve an overall objective or goal. A roadmap is one step beyond that. It is a plan for executing the strategy. A roadmap is a plan of action that specifies the objective or goal and the path to reach that objective, along with significant milestones.

At the strategic level, business vision tells us our business's goal, and the strategy tells us how we will achieve that goal, whereas at the execution level, the roadmap tells us what we are building, and the strategy tells us why we are building it. Let's look at the example of the ridesharing platform from the previous chapter:

Strategic level	Business vision	*What is the goal of our business?*	Make the everyday commute faster
	Strategy	*How are we going to achieve the goal?*	By connecting drivers and riders
Execution level	Roadmap	*What are we building?* (capability/feature)	Finding a nearby driver
	Strategy	*Why are we building the feature or capability?*	To connect drivers and riders

The roadmap is a link that connects the strategy to the execution. It communicates what we are building and relates it to the strategy to know why we are building it. It is a potent tool used by product managers to share the strategy with the execution team. It covers the *why* and *what* of the business proposal so that the team can decide the *how* part. A detailed roadmap also includes the *when* (timeline) and the group of *whats* (milestones). It gives a direction on how the product will evolve in alignment with the strategy and the vision.

The elements of a roadmap

For a roadmap to be practical, it should cover some essential elements and answer some critical questions. Thus, a well-crafted roadmap serves as a navigation tool for the team from the starting point to the destination while covering critical milestones. The following are some of the vital elements of a good roadmap:

- **Vision and strategy**: The roadmap connects the strategy to the execution. Hence, a good roadmap should include the vision and the strategy; each feature and every milestone must align with the overall business vision and the strategy. It is prevalent to forget the big picture when working on tactical items and short-term goals. Therefore, it is crucial for the roadmap to clearly specify the business vision and the strategy, and tie all the features and milestones back. The engineering team needs to know the big picture when designing the solution; it helps them think about the future and design a product that will evolve functionally and architecturally.

- **Themes**: Business strategy is broad and high-level. Along with the strategy, we need something in our roadmap that can be easily tracked and measured. Once we have specified the strategy, we should break it down into more minor and logical themes and add those themes to the roadmap. Each theme should be part of the broader strategy and business vision. A few examples of themes for our ridesharing platform could be driver onboarding, end-to-end booking for riders, payment processing, and so on. Themes are company-wide initiatives, such as in our ride-sharing platform, where improving driver onboarding could be one theme and payment-processing enhancement could be another.

- **Features**: Themes are further broken down into features. Features are the specific functionalities that accomplish a task or add value. Therefore, each theme will have its own set of features. In some cases, a theme might just have one feature when it is not large enough. For instance, improving the driver onboarding theme from the earlier example might just have one feature. In contrast, the payment-processing enhancement theme could have multiple features, such as credit card integration, PayPal integration, payment fulfillment, and so on.

- **Milestones**: Business vision defines the end goal. While we want to reach there finally, we cannot do that directly; we will have to achieve certain milestones on the way. Hence, we must divide our overall business goals into smaller milestones. Every milestone should be a step towards the end goal and business objectives. Some examples of milestones could be the beta launch, general availability, the partner API release, and so on.

- **Timeline**: Mentioning a timeline in the roadmap is always recommended. It helps in tracking whether we are on schedule or lagging behind. Timelines are associated with the milestones, such as the beta launch, the partner API release, and so on. Mentioning the timeline is crucial for launch strategy and ongoing marketing plans. All the communication to stakeholders and, most notably, to end users will be based on these timelines. We should avoid putting in the exact date; instead, set a timeframe, such as Q1, Q2, and so on. The timelines on the roadmap are always based on approximations.

All the aforementioned are some of the critical elements that are necessary to make the roadmap valuable and effective. There are a few additional things, such as metrics, business value, and so on, that some product managers like to include in the roadmap. Items included in the roadmap are highly dependent on the type of roadmap and the audience of the roadmap. For example, the roadmap for executives will differ from the roadmap for engineering teams, and roadmaps for internal teams will be different from roadmaps for external stakeholders.

The following is a sample roadmap displaying all the essential elements:

	Business Vision		
	Q1	Q2	Q3
Milestones	Milestone 1	Milestone 2	Milestone 3
Theme 1	Feature 1 / Feature 2 / Feature 3	Feature 4 / Feature 5	
Theme 2	Feature 1 / Feature 2 / Feature 3	Feature 4 / Feature 5	
Theme 3	Feature 1 / Feature 2 / Feature 3	Feature 4 / Feature 5	Feature 6 / Feature 7
	Business Strategy		

Figure 5.1 – A sample roadmap

Important note:

This is just a sample view to paint a high-level picture of what a roadmap looks like. We will go in-depth about creating the roadmap in the later sections of the chapter.

One important thing to remember about the roadmap is that it is a living document. It should be constantly updated and evolved along with the product. It is not a rigid or set-in-stone document that, once created, will never change.

Linear product roadmap versus platform roadmap

Now that we know what a roadmap is and the different elements or components that make up a useful and constructive roadmap, we should understand the difference between the linear product roadmap and the platform roadmap. There are many differences between the two, right from the vision and strategy specification to the breakdown of specific functionalities. Let's look at some of the key differences:

- **Features versus capabilities**: Sometimes, features and capabilities are used interchangeably when mentioning the quality of a product to fulfill a goal. The difference between the two is very subtle. The feature is an end-to-end flow to accomplish a task or add value, whereas a capability is the ability to achieve the desired result. For example, on maps, searching for directions is a feature. In this feature, the user puts the source and the destination locations, and the map displays the shortest route (the happy path).

Calculating and giving out the shortest route is a capability. This capability can be used for the direction search feature or any other features on the map, such as locating the closest pizza place or even a third-party app such as a delivery service. Platforms work with capabilities because of the involvement of multiple entities and the separation of different components, such as infrastructure, business, and experience. At the same time, linear products work with end-to-end features. Hence, it is essential to specify capabilities on a platform roadmap instead of features.

- **Customer-centric versus multi-entity-focused**: Roadmaps for linear products focus on the consumer side as consumers are the only or the primary customers for linear products. But because platforms are multisided, the roadmap for platforms should reflect their multidimensional nature. It means that platform capabilities that are added or prioritized on the roadmap must be helpful and valuable to all the entities.

  Furthermore, platform capabilities must be sequenced based on the focus strategy of the platform. For example, the strategy for our ridesharing platform is to focus on growing the number of producers by enabling easy onboarding. So, the capabilities around the easy onboarding of drivers must be the highest priority, whereas, in most linear products, consumer-centric features are given the highest priority. There is always a workaround identified for the producer-side features as there is only one producer (owner of the product/service).

- **A combination of multiple roadmaps**: The platform consists of different components, infrastructure, business, and customer experience. Each component has its own mini roadmap, and the platform roadmap ties them all together. All the roadmaps focus and revolve around the overall business goals and strategy. They have their own specific goals and strategy, but they should work towards meeting the overarching platform end goal. For example, all the components in our ride-sharing platform should work towards connecting riders and drivers to make the everyday commute faster.

  In this example, the goal of the customer experience component could be to create an intuitive user flow for an end-to-end ride, which indirectly aims to make the commute faster. The platform roadmap is a consolidation and aggregation of these multiple roadmaps. It stitches them together and presents a coherent view of how the platform will evolve and mature over time in alignment with the business vision and strategy.

These are some of the important differences that distinguish the platform roadmap from the linear product roadmap. Understanding these differences will help us in different phases and steps of roadmap creation, such as identifying capabilities, defining the MVP, and so on. So, let's move on to these steps and explore them in detail.

Defining platform capabilities

The most critical step of creating a roadmap is to identify and define features. As we are making the platform roadmap, we should start by defining capabilities. As we discussed, a capability is the ability to achieve an outcome. Hence, to identify different capabilities, we will have to start by creating an end-to-end user journey. A user journey will list down all the steps and actions that need to be taken to accomplish the goal. Completing those actions and steps will tell us what capabilities are required. Hence, to identify and list down the capabilities that our platform should possess, we will start by mapping an end-to-end user journey and then extract capabilities from it.

Mapping an end-to-end user journey

A **user journey** is a flow or end-to-end depiction of user actions to reach from one state to the other or from the current state to the end goal. These steps and actions are plotted together to create a user journey map. It is a very popular and effective tool to understand user behavior, pain points, new opportunities in the system, or an end-to-end guide to creating a new product from scratch. A user journey map can be created for different reasons during different stages of the product life cycle. We will focus on mapping the user journey for the end-to-end flow of a new product, starting from the current state to reaching the end goal with our new product. In linear products, the focus of the user journey has always been the consumer, but for the platform user journey, we should equally focus on all the entities, and the end goal of our user journey should be aligned with the overall platform goal.

The following diagram is a sample of a straightforward user journey map. Of course, the actual map will vary greatly depending on the type of user journey, the **End Goal**, the number of users, and the product's maturity.

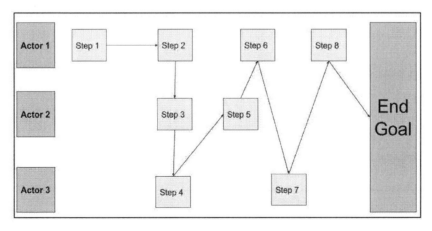

Figure 5.2 – A sample user journey

There are various types of user journey maps. Selecting the type of the map depends on the overall objective of the journey mapping exercise. For example, *are you creating the journey map to understand the current pain points in the usage of the product, or are you doing it to decide the product's future state, or do you want to understand the inner workings of your product?* Therefore, the type of journey map is selected based on the reason for the journey mapping exercise and the state of the product, for example:

- **Current state**: Current state journey maps are primarily used for already developed and matured products. These are used to understand the pain points in the current user experience, the missing features, and the areas of improvement.

- **Future state**: Future state journey maps are most suited for new products, where the reason and goal of the journey creation are to know what the future will be with this new product. However, this journey map is also used for introducing significantly new features in existing products.

- **Service blueprint map**: Service blueprints list out all the actions and steps from every system involved in the product ecosystem. They show the inner workings of all the systems and how they connect to accomplish specific actions.

These are the most used journey maps, but there are a few more types of user journey maps, such as an experience journey map, a day-in-a-life journey map, and a strategic journey map. Therefore, you should choose the most suitable journey map for your needs and situation.

Sometimes, you can also use multiple types of maps, such as the current state type to know the existing pain points and the future state type to understand how the new product will evolve after addressing the pain points and adding new opportunities. Combining a current state map or future state map with service blueprints is also very common. It gives you the user experience combined with the inner workings of the systems, which could help you find the reasons for the current pain points or understand the overall system landscape of the future product.

After selecting the type of journey map, we can start the user journey mapping exercise. The following steps will create a valuable and effective user journey map:

1. **Set the end goal for the overall journey**: Whenever starting a user journey, start with setting the overall goal of the journey. You must first decide the reason why you are creating the journey map. It will also help you select the type of journey map. The reason for the journey should then be tied to and aligned with the business objectives. It could be your business vision or part of it, or something different, depending on why you are creating the journey and in what phase of the product life cycle you're creating the user journey. For new products, it is usually the end of the user flow or a short-term goal that you want to achieve within a few months of the launch, or part of the end-to-end user flow.

    For example, if we look at our ridesharing platform example, the business objective is to make the everyday commute faster for local communities by connecting drivers and riders. In this example, to make the commute faster, we will have to enable the completion of the ride while keeping our uniqueness of connecting local car owners to riders. And the reason for journey mapping is to understand how this ridesharing platform will be shaped and the future state of the local commutes. So, the end goal for our user journey would be to know how to complete the end-to-end rides by allowing riders access to local car owners or drivers.

2. **Define actors**: Every user journey has different actors. Actors are different from personas. Sometimes people use them interchangeably, but these are two different concepts. Actors are all the users (various roles) and the systems that are interacting with the product, such as the buyer, supplier, merchandise manager, content management system, and so on for an e-commerce platform.

    Whereas personas are specific personalities and types of actors, buyers have multiple personas, such as college students, corporate employees, stay-home moms, and so on. Similarly, sellers have different personas, such as small-shop owners, midsized business owners, and so on. It is also possible that some of the actors only have one persona. Also, personas are only for users and not for systems. Hence, not all the actors will have different personas.

3. **Assign a goal for each actor**: As we have a goal for the overall user journey, each of our actors should also have a goal targeted at the end of the journey. Like the end goal of the overall journey, goals for each actor would depend on the reason for mapping the journey and the phase of the product. Also, not every actor will have an end goal, especially the system or non-human actors, who might not have a specific target. In the case of a platform, each entity, such as the producer, consumer, and intermediary, should have an end goal. For example, in our ride-sharing platform, the target for the rider would be to get from one place to another as fast as possible.

    Similarly, for drivers, the target could be to find as many riders and complete as many trips as possible in the shortest time. In the case of a food delivery platform, where there are three entities involved, the target of the diner could be to find a good restaurant and get the food delivered as fast as possible. For delivery personnel, the target could be to make as many deliveries as possible in the shortest time. For restaurants, it could be to ship as many food orders as possible.

4. **Define stages of the journey**: Every journey goes through different stages. For example, if you are traveling from one city to another, you will start by walking to a nearby subway or local transit stop. Then, you reach the airport using the local transit and fly to your destination city. Finally, you take a cab or any other local transit mode to reach your destination. Similarly, a user journey in the digital world goes through different stages. For example, for a retail or e-commerce platform, different stages of the user journey are discovery, selection, purchase, and fulfillment.

    Some of these might change based on the exact product or service that is offered by the platform. But the point here is that the user journey can be and should be broken down into logical stages, and then each stage should have its own steps. While mapping the user journey, you will realize that different actors play a prominent role in various stages. For example, buyers will be crucial in the discovery and selection phase, but the seller will be prominent in the fulfillment phase. In the case of a platform, this presence and prominence of a particular user role will also depend on the focus strategy of the platform.

5. **Identify touchpoints**: Touchpoints are the points at which users interact or communicate with the product. These are the different entry points of how users will reach the product. These can be internal and external to your system, such as search engine adverts, social media postings, email promotions, third-party integrations, and so on. Listing all the touchpoints is a crucial step of user journey mapping. You should be aware of where your users are going to interact with the application. It would be best to list all the touchpoints that you are aware of before mapping the user journey. But you will also discover a few touchpoints while you are in the process of mapping the journey. We should list touchpoints for all the entities, producers, consumers, and intermediaries for the platforms. For example, in our ridesharing platform, make sure to list down all the entry points for drivers and riders.

6. **Map the journey along with the focus of the strategy**: After doing all the groundwork of setting the goal, defining the actors and their targets, defining stages of the journey, and identifying all the touchpoints, it is time to map out the actual user journey. Start putting down each step of the end-to-end user flow. Do not segregate the journey based on the actors. Instead, follow it as the steps or process take place. The flow will move from one actor to another, and the journey will move from the starting point to the end goal. While mapping the journey, you might identify new touchpoints or even new actors, which is fine. One of the reasons for mapping the user journey is to find out the hidden elements that we might otherwise miss.

7. **Review and validate the journey against user goals and empathy maps**: Once the mapping is completed, review the journey for missing steps. The reviewing of the user journey will help in identifying gaps in the user flow. Revisit all the steps to see if moving from one step to the next is possible or a step in between is missing. While reviewing the user journey, make sure that each user is meeting their end goal and that we have considered their pain points and emotions while mapping their journey.

    Make necessary changes if things are missing or need adjustments, but make sure that all users are meeting their targets and their pain points are considered. Along with reviewing the journey against each user's target, we should also validate whether we are meeting the overall end goal of the user journey that was defined in the first step. Once the reviews and validations are done, the user journey is complete.

Always remember that the user journey map is a living document and must be regularly updated. During the product life cycle, the user journey will be and should be updated, based on discoveries, changing priorities, changes in external factors, and so on. Still, it should always align with the business vision and strategy.

The following diagram shows a sample user journey map with all the essential elements, such as its end goal and stages, various touchpoints, actors and their end goals, and a flow from start to finish. This journey map illustrates a platform user journey of a search-and-purchase experience, with stages such as discovery, purchase, and fulfillment, and touchpoints such as a website home page, search engines, and third-party sites.

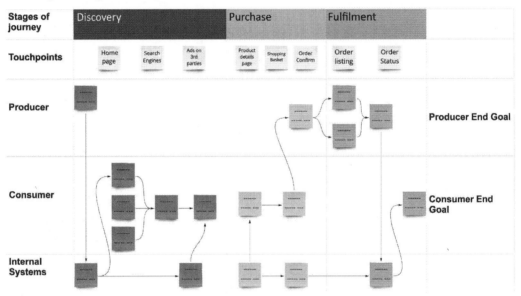

Figure 5.3 – The elements of a sample user journey

Now that we have understood how to create a user journey, the next step is to pull out capabilities from the user journey. Let's dive deeper into it.

Extracting capabilities from the user journey

After completing the end-to-end user journey, the next step is to extract the capabilities from the user journey. We briefly looked at what capability means while discussing the difference between features and capabilities; it is the ability to achieve the desired result. Hence, we should look at the steps in our user journey and identify what capability is required to accomplish each step. For example, showing the list of products is a capability that can be used for either search or browse features. Some of the capabilities will be very apparent, but some capabilities will be hidden, especially technical capabilities, which will usually be hidden behind the functional capabilities. For example, data encryption is a capability that is needed for security reasons. Hence, the platform capabilities can be divided into two, functional and technical capabilities. Let's look at them in detail:

- **Functional capabilities**: Functional capabilities enable the functional elements or features of the platform, such as searching, browsing, adding, removing, and so on. Functional capabilities will depend on the core business of your platform. To identify the functional capabilities, we as product managers should work with our technical partner to go through the user journey and see how each step can be accomplished. We might add one capability for every action for the first few steps, but we will have multiple steps being accomplished by one capability as we go further. One thing to keep in mind here is that the capability should cater to all the different touchpoints or entry points. For example, the capability of listing products must fulfill searching and browsing from all the entry points.

- **Technical capabilities**: Technical capabilities are also referred to as non-functional capabilities. These capabilities do not fulfill a functional requirement but enable the foundational operations of the platform, such as security, observability, data management, hosting and environment creation, API management, developer tooling, and so on. Identifying technical capabilities is trickier than identifying functional capabilities. Going through each step of the user journey and answering the question, *do we have all the foundations ready for accomplishing this step?* is the right way to start listing down the technical capabilities. Once the mapping with the user journey is done, we should validate for overarching technical capabilities such as security, observability, and so on. It is recommended for a technical person to derive and lead the technical capability identification part.

The following diagram illustrates how capabilities should be mapped to a user journey:

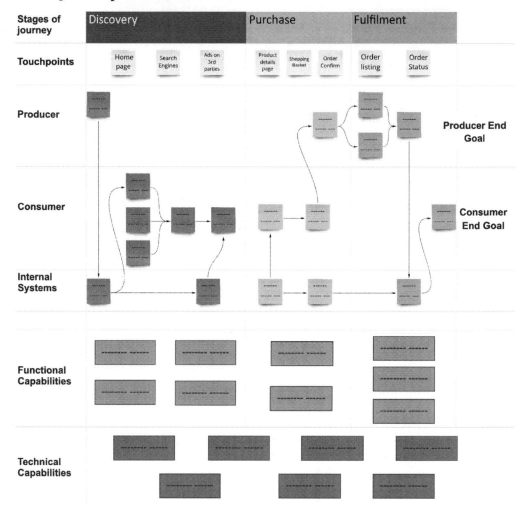

Figure 5.4 – Capabilities mapped to the user journey

The diagram suggests that while identifying the capabilities, you should try to list them in the stage of the journey at which they are most closely associated. For example, the listing of products will be in the **Discovery** stage, and the payment processing will be in the **Purchase** stage. **Technical Capabilities** are usually not tied to a stage but cut across the entire user journey.

Defining the platform MVP

Now that we have identified the capabilities, the next step is to carve out the platform MVP from those capabilities. And to slice out the MVP, we should prioritize the capabilities and identify the must-have capabilities to complete the end-to-end flow for all the entities.

Prioritizing capabilities

The prioritization of the functional capabilities will depend on the business strategy and the focus of the platform strategy. For example, adding capabilities to enhance the producer's experience versus the consumer's experience will depend on which side of the platform you want to grow. But the bare minimum capabilities required for the end-to-end functioning of the platform must be added on both sides. However, for technical capabilities, we should focus on building the platform's foundation first and then move on to make it scalable and extensible.

As a product manager, you must be aware of different prioritization techniques. We will discuss some of these techniques in detail in *Chapter 9, Ongoing Backlog Prioritization*. But for the MVP, I usually prefer the *MoSCoW* method. The *MoSCoW* prioritization technique is a very common and popular method that helps in categorizing features or capabilities into *must have*, *should have*, *could have*, and *won't have* buckets. The must-haves are essential capabilities required for the end-to-end functioning of the platform. Without these capabilities, either the platform won't function (technical capabilities) or the end-to-end user journey will not be feasible (functional capabilities).

The **Should Have** capabilities are important but not mandatory. These capabilities might provide a competitive advantage, but they are unnecessary for the users to complete the end-to-end journey. The platform can operate and function without these capabilities, but, if added, they provide good value. The **Could Have** capabilities are nice to have and might improve the experience and help in the long run, but they don't provide any significant value immediately.

The **Won't Have** capabilities are not crucial for the platform right now. However, they can be added in the later releases. These might be needed with scale or needed to make the journey more comprehensive or to target more user groups and so on, but they are not required in the current release or for the launch. The following diagram summarizes the **MoSCoW Prioritization** technique:

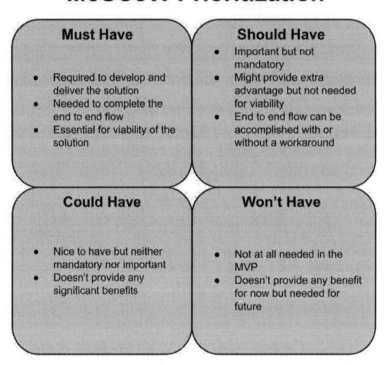

Figure 5.5 – MoSCoW prioritization

Using the MoSCoW technique, we should prioritize all the capabilities that we have identified so far. Then, we can add priority to the user journey or create another document. I usually prefer first making a list of the capabilities in a spreadsheet with a **Priority** column and then providing some identification mark on the journey map.

Adding capabilities with priority on a spreadsheet helps to sort and filter them when presenting and discussing them with the team. For example, you can quickly filter the list by must-haves and discuss the solution's viability or look at all the won't-haves and quickly verify whether we have left out anything important. The following table illustrates how to add priority for capabilities for our ridesharing platform example. It is just an illustrative sample set of capabilities. However, the actual list would be way more extensive:

Capability	Priority
Find all the nearby drivers	Must
Calculate the trip cost	Must
Schedule trip for later	Should
Add favorite location	Could
Add ratings	Won't

Make sure to include technical capabilities in the list as well for assigning the priorities. All the technical capabilities that enable the development, launch, and functioning of the platform must be part of the MVP.

Ranking touchpoints and experiences

Along with prioritizing the platform's capabilities, it is also important to rank and prioritize the touchpoints. As discussed earlier, touchpoints are the communication points for users to interact with the platform. Some touchpoints are external, such as search engines, promotions on other websites, or third-party systems, and some are internal to the platform. The internal touchpoints become the experience layer of the platform. External touchpoints like third-party systems usually communicate via an API.

Some teams and organizations create a web gateway layer for external systems to integrate with the platform APIs. But some teams do not differentiate between internal system calls or external integrations. The technical lead or architect should decide the integration mechanism, but as product managers, we should determine whether the third-party integrations are in scope for the MVP or later releases.

Platform experiences, sometimes also referred to as channels, are multilayered. The first layer is the channel itself, and the next layer is the touchpoints inside the channel, such as a website and different pages of the website, or an Android app and different screens within the app. To rank experiences, we should prioritize both layers. For example, if the website as a channel is prioritized for the MVP, we must further rank and prioritize different website pages. Similarly, if the Android app is a priority, then different screens within the app must be prioritized and ranked. But if a channel is out of scope, then the sublayers' ranking will not be applicable.

The following table illustrates the example of prioritizing multiple channels and different touchpoints within those channels. This is a sample set of channels and touchpoints for our ridesharing platform example:

Channel	Touchpoint	Priority
iOS	Ride search	Must
	Ride confirmation	Must
	Trip progress	Could
	Payment options	Should
	Add ratings	Won't
Android	Ride search	Must
	Ride confirmation	Should
	Trip progress	Could
	Payment options	Should
	Add ratings	Won't
Web		Won't

We have completed the first step of defining the MVP, prioritizing and ranking capabilities and touchpoints. The next step is to slice and map the end-to-end MVP from the user journey in conjunction with the assigned priorities.

Mapping the end-to-end MVP

We should relook at the user journey map for slicing and mapping the MVP based on the assigned priorities of all the functional and technical capabilities and touchpoints. To get a visual representation of the priorities, I like to add an indication against all the capabilities and the touchpoints on the user journey map, as follows:

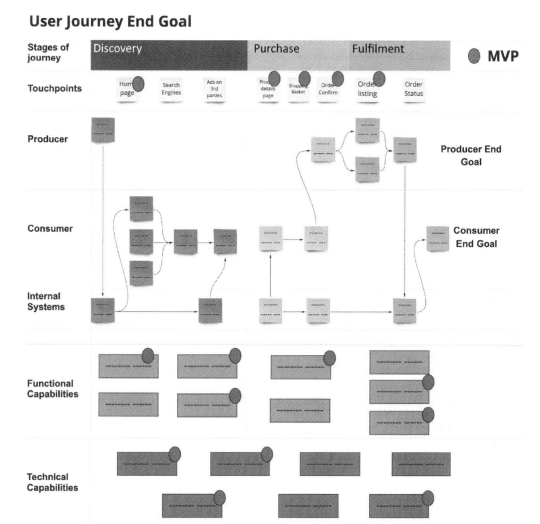

Figure 5.6 – The capabilities prioritized for MVP

We can escape the spreadsheet and add the priority indication on the user journey map directly, but I prefer having both as they have different benefits. The preceding diagram illustrates the visual representation of the MVP on the user journey map.

While adding the visual indication, we should go through the user journey step by step to identify the steps that will not be part of the MVP. As in our example of the ridesharing platform, we have kept the capability of adding ratings out of the MVP; hence, all the steps and actions related to ratings must be out of scope for the MVP. Similarly, we should also ensure that all the capabilities identified as a must for the MVP accomplish all the actions needed for the feasibility of end-to-end flow and the viability of the platform for the launch.

For example, in our ridesharing platform, the minimum requirement is that riders should complete the trip and make the payment, and drivers should finish that trip and receive the compensation. Hence, the capabilities prioritized for the MVP must accomplish these minimum tasks. While going through the capabilities in conjunction with the user journey, the priority of some of the capabilities might get reassigned. The objective here should be to identify the bare minimum capabilities that can accomplish the end-to-end flow of the feasible and viable platform for the launch.

This step completes the definition of the MVP. But if you want to have a crisp and precise representation of your MVP, you can create a user journey map that will be a subset of our original user journey, representing only the MVP user flow. It helps in quickly referring to the MVP or presenting a side-by-side comparison between the overall user journey and its subset prioritized for the MVP.

After defining the MVP, we can proceed to create the platform roadmap by organizing all the capabilities and experiences along with milestones and releases.

Creating the platform roadmap

Now that we have our MVP defined and a list of functionalities and capabilities that are not prioritized for the MVP but needed in the later releases, we can proceed to the next phase, which is creating the roadmap.

Defining milestones

To create the roadmap or organize our capabilities and experiences against a target, we should define a few milestones and approximate timelines. Usually, the MVP launch is the first milestone. Some businesses also do a beta launch, followed by a general availability release. The goal of milestones is to have some achievable targets that can be met quickly to test the waters and get some early feedback.

Apart from the MVP and the beta release, some other examples of milestones could be achieving X number of users or hitting Y number in revenue, or launching the product in multiple geographies, and so on. Milestones should be the subset of the overall business strategy and work towards meeting the overall business objectives. Milestones can be added without a timeline, but adding one helps track and give a targeted direction to the team. It also helps with the long-term planning and marketing of the platform. The following are some of the factors that must be considered when defining milestones:

- Milestones should align with the overall business objectives and goals.

- Milestones should provide value to users and the business.

- Milestones should help gather feedback and iterate upon it.

- Milestones should be targeted at a frequency that is achievable and valuable.

Once the milestones are identified and agreed upon by all the stakeholders, the technical team can provide the estimates to arrive at the timelines. These will be very high-level estimates to come up with a range of timelines, such as Q1, Q2, and so on. We do not want to get into a detailed estimation process currently. Based on these high-level estimates, we should calculate the approximate timelines for each milestone and then arrange all the capabilities and touchpoints on the roadmap across those timelines.

Organizing capabilities against milestones

After identifying the milestones and knowing the approximate timelines, the last step is to organize all the capabilities and touchpoints in a roadmap format. As discussed earlier, the platform roadmap combines the mini roadmaps, and these roadmaps consist of technical capabilities, functional capabilities, and touchpoints.

The technical capabilities form the infrastructure layer, the functional capabilities form the business layer, and the touchpoints form the experience layer of the platform. These three roadmaps together create a platform roadmap. All the other elements, such as milestones, themes, business vision, timeline, and so on, will remain the same as in any other product roadmap. The following diagram illustrates a sample platform roadmap with all three layers:

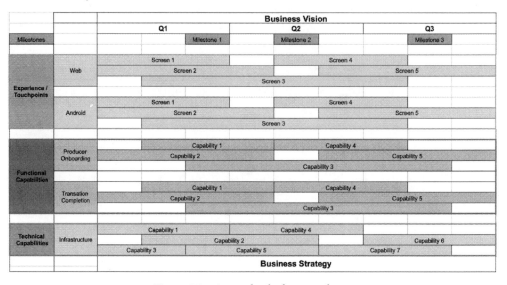

Figure 5.7 – A sample platform roadmap

This diagram shows three smaller roadmaps that cover different layers of the platform but are moving towards the same milestones and the same overall business objective. This platform roadmap view is strategic and milestone-based, usually created in the initial planning and MVP definition phase. Some other roadmap views, such as release-based, team-based, or portfolio roadmaps, are more detailed and intended for different purposes.

This was the final step of platform roadmap creation. Now we can apply all our learnings to a practical example and continue with our case study from the previous chapter.

Case study

In this chapter, we will define the MVP and create the roadmap for our educational content sharing and learning platform, **Escola**. But before we proceed with the MVP and the roadmap, let's revise a few things from the previous chapter that will be useful for us here:

- **Escola business vision**: Connect educators and students to make learning and the sharing of educational content unrestricted, extensible, scalable, and efficient.

- **Escola business strategy**: Target uncharted producers and consumers by increasing the total user base.

- **Escola focus of platform strategy**: Both sides (producers and consumers).

Now that we know the business vision and the strategy of our platform, we can start with the MVP and the platform roadmap. To define the MVP, we must start with mapping the user journey, identifying the capabilities, prioritizing those capabilities, and then slicing the MVP. So, let's first map the user journey for our platform.

Escola user journey map

To create the user journey map, let's define the following elements of a user journey map:

- **User journey end goal**: The end goal for the user journey should be in conjunction with our business vision. As our business vision is to connect educators and students to make learning and the sharing of educational content unrestricted, extensible, scalable, and efficient, the user journey should aim to connect educators and students to share and consume content.

- **Actors**: As described a few times, the actors for our user journey will be educators and students. Along with them, there will be some automated steps that will be carried out from within the system. Hence, we will add the internal system as one of the actors.

- **Actors' end goal**: We have defined the actors, so we should now define their end goals or targets. To keep things simple in this case study, we will define end goals only for human actors and not system actors. Here, the user journey end goal can be broken down into the educator end goal and the student end goal, which gives us this:

  A. **Educator goal**: Connect with students to share and impart knowledge.

  B. **Student goal**: Learn and gain knowledge from favorite educators.

- **Touchpoints**: Touchpoints here are different interaction points in the platform and, in some cases, landing from search engines. For example, when searching for a particular educator on Google, it might bring up the link to the profile page of the educator. Other touchpoints here are Android and iOS mobile apps, which I have not called out separately in the user journey map. The assumption is that every interaction point on the web also means the corresponding screen on the mobile app. For example, the educator profile page means all three channels: web, Android, and iOS.

After identifying all the elements of the user journey, the next step is to map and plot the step-by-step journey:

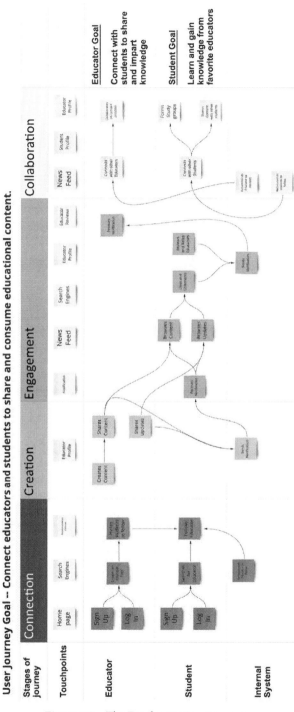

Figure 5.8 – The Escola user journey map

The preceding diagram covers the end-to-end user journey for educators and students, right from signing up the platform to sharing and consuming content or collaborating with other students and educators. This end-to-end user journey is divided into four stages:

- **Connection**: This is the stage where educators and students will join the platform, find each other, and connect.

- **Creation**: In this stage, educators will generate and share content and other updates. This stage involves heavy participation from educators, but students are not very active at this stage.

- **Engagement**: This is the stage of students' engagement with content and other materials shared by the educators. Contrary to the creation stage, students are very active at the engagement stage, but educators are not highly involved.

- **Collaboration**: In this stage, users collaborate with their peers in the same group. Educators connect and collaborate with other educators, and students connect with other students.

One thing to remember here is that our strategy is to increase the number of both educators and students to create a significantly large user base. Hence, our user journey is equally focused on educators and students.

After mapping the end-to-end user journey, we should now identify all the corresponding capabilities for our platform.

Escola capabilities

To identify the capabilities, we should go through each step of the user journey and determine the functional and technical capabilities required to accomplish those steps. For example, to sign up users on the platform, we will have to create the educators and the students, and authenticate and authorize them with their respective roles and the right level of permissions. Similarly, while logging in, we will have to authenticate and authorize the users to have the correct access and the proper permissions. Let's look at our user journey map and assign capabilities corresponding to each step of the journey:

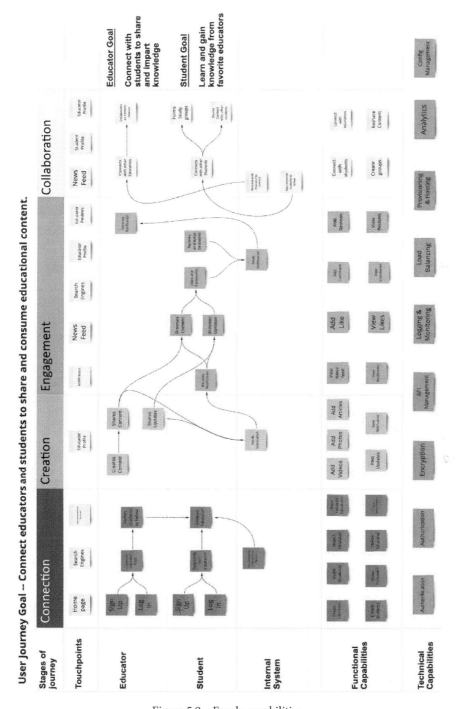

Figure 5.9 – Escola capabilities

The preceding diagram shows the functional and technical capabilities of our user journey. **Functional Capabilities** are assigned to the stage of the journey with which they are associated. Sometimes, a capability might fall under more than one stage. In that case, you can assign it to its closest association. **Technical Capabilities** are mostly overarching, but some might fall under a particular stage of the user journey. Also, sometimes there is a thin line between the technical and functional distribution of capabilities. For example, some product managers put authentication and authorization under **Functional Capabilities**, and some categorize them under **Technical Capabilities**. It should be fine to put such capabilities in either of the buckets if we have identified them and assigned them the proper priority.

Capabilities and experience prioritization

We have mapped the user journey with all the touchpoints and identified the capabilities required to accomplish all the steps of the user journey. We have also identified the technical capabilities necessary for the platform's development, building its foundation and its ongoing operations, such as API management, identity encryption, logging and monitoring, analytics, and so on. Each of these technical capabilities is explained in the following table, along with its prioritization. Now, it is time to prioritize all the capabilities and the experiences. We will use the MoSCoW technique for the prioritization of the MVP. This means that if a capability is assigned a *must* priority, it is required for the MVP, and if it is assigned a *won't* priority, then it is not needed for the MVP but could be implemented in later releases.

1. **Functional capabilities**: The priority for all the functional capabilities is assigned in the following table:

Capability	Priority	Comment
Create educator	Must	Creating educators and students is the foundation of our platform. Hence, it must be done for the MVP.
Create students	Must	
Search educators	Must	To follow the educator, students should be able to search them. Hence, searching educators is a must for the MVP.
Invite students	Should	Inviting students to follow educators is not a critical capability, as long as students can search and follow educators on their own. But this capability adds value from the educator's perspective. Hence, this capability should be developed for the MVP.

Capability	Priority	Comment
Follow educators	Must	To consume content from an educator, students should follow them. Hence, this capability is a must for the MVP.
Show followed educators	Could	Doesn't add an immediate significant value. Hence, it is nice to have the capability for the MVP.
Show recommendations	Won't	Showing recommendations of who to follow adds good value to the overall platform but can be left out of the MVP, as it is not critical for the end-to-user flow.
Add videos	Must	These capabilities are related to creating and sharing different types of content. Sharing content as an educator is one of the most important functionalities of our platform. Hence, these are a must for the MVP.
Add photos	Must	
Add articles	Must	
Post updates	Must	
Send notification	Should	Sending and receiving a notification when the favorite educator has shared something, or content has received a like or a comment, does not hamper or stall the end-to-end user flow but adds tremendous value, especially for students, who become aware of the updated content. Hence, these capabilities should be implemented for the MVP.
View notification	Should	
View newsfeed	Must	This capability is part of consuming content in a newsfeed as a student, which is the primary need of our platform. Hence, a must-have for the MVP.
Add likes	Must	These capabilities are required to create engagement between students and educators. They provide feedback to educators on how their content is performing. Without these capabilities, students and educators will be isolated and will not be able to share thoughts and appreciation. Hence, these capabilities are necessary to create a connection between the students and educators.
Add comments	Must	
View likes	Must	
View comments	Must	

Capability	Priority	Comment
Add reviews	Could	Adding and viewing reviews are the capabilities that will enhance the experience of the students, as they can read about an educator from other students before following them. But these capabilities are not vital for the platform from the get-go. To get valid reviews, educators should be on the platform for some time. Hence, these are nice to have for the MVP but are only required in later releases.
View reviews	Could	
Connect with students	Won't	These capabilities are needed for collaboration within the same group, such as students connecting with fellow students and educators collaborating with other educators. These are not critical for the functioning of the platform or the minimum end-to-end user flow. They do not add significant value for educators or students. Hence, they can be developed in later releases.
Connect with educators	Won't	
Create groups	Won't	
Reshare content	Won't	

Now that we have assigned the priorities to all the functional capabilities, let's move on to prioritizing technical capabilities for the Escola platform.

2. **Technical capabilities**: The priority of all the technical capabilities is assigned in the following table, which is an exemplary list of technical capabilities. There will be more such capabilities needed for our platform; your technical partner should lead the identification of those capabilities:

Capability	Priority	Comment
Authentication	Must	Authentication is the foundation of any secure web system. It ensures that only users who are supposed to use our platform should be allowed in.
Authorization	Must	Authorization provides the right level of access to different users. For example, educators can edit content but only content created by them, whereas students cannot edit content at all.
Encryption	Must	Encrypting the passwords and personally identifiable information of a user is a must to make the platform secure. It secures the data and important information of users from malicious usage from the outside world.

Capability	Priority	Comment
API management	Must	API management is needed for creating and publishing APIs. APIs are foundational to any platform. All the platform capabilities are exposed in the form of APIs. Hence, standardizing the API creation, monitoring its performance, and analyzing its usage is a must.
Provisioning and hosting	Must	Provisioning and hosting are the fundamental infrastructural requirements for developing and deploying any application.
Logging and monitoring	Must	Logging and monitoring are essential for ensuring application availability, monitoring performance, alerting in the event of downtime, and helping in analyzing and finding the root cause during failures.
Analytics	Must	Analytics is needed to collect and track key metrics. The usage of the MVP and its success or failure can only be determined with robust analytics. To get feedback on the MVP performance and determine the next steps, it is essential to collect data for analytics.
Load balancing	Should	Load balancing is required for scaling and optimization. It is not critical for the MVP but will be very valuable if added as early as possible.
Configuration management	Won't	Not critical immediately but needed as the platform grows and scales.

> **Important note:**
> Please remember that identification of all the capabilities must be done in association with the technical partner, who should derive and lead the technical capability part.

As we have assigned priorities to technical and functional capabilities, we should also assign priorities to the experience and touchpoints.

3. **Experience**: The priority of all the channels and touchpoints is assigned in the following table:

Channel	Touchpoint	Priority	Comment
Web	Home page	Must	This is a landing page for the users, from where they will log in or sign up. Hence, this is a must for the MVP.
	Educator profile	Must	This is the page from which educators will create and post content. As this is one of the most important functionalities of our platform, this page is a must for the MVP.
	Newsfeed	Must	This is the page from which students will read and consume content posted by the educators. Hence, this page is a must for the MVP.
	Notification center	Should	The notification center is the UI corresponding to the receiving notifications capability. As the capability should be implemented for the MVP, so should its UI.
	Recommendation carousel	Won't	As showing recommendations is out of scope for the MVP, its UI will also be out of scope.
	Review and ratings overlay	Could	Adding and viewing reviews and ratings could be developed from the MVP. Hence, its placeholder in the UI will have the same priority.
iOS		Won't	Developing the Android and iOS apps will be kept out of the MVP. The website will be responsive, so users can still use the platform from their phones. Specific mobile apps will be developed in later releases.
Android		Won't	

After assigning all the priorities, we should revisit our user journey to slice the MVP based on our prioritized list of capabilities.

Mapping the end-to-end Escola MVP

After all the prioritization, we should now plot and map the end-to-end MVP of our platform. We can start by adding the visual indications for capabilities and touchpoints, and then create the subset of our user journey representing only the MVP user flow.

The following diagram shows *must have* and *should have* capabilities and touchpoints for the Escola platform MVP:

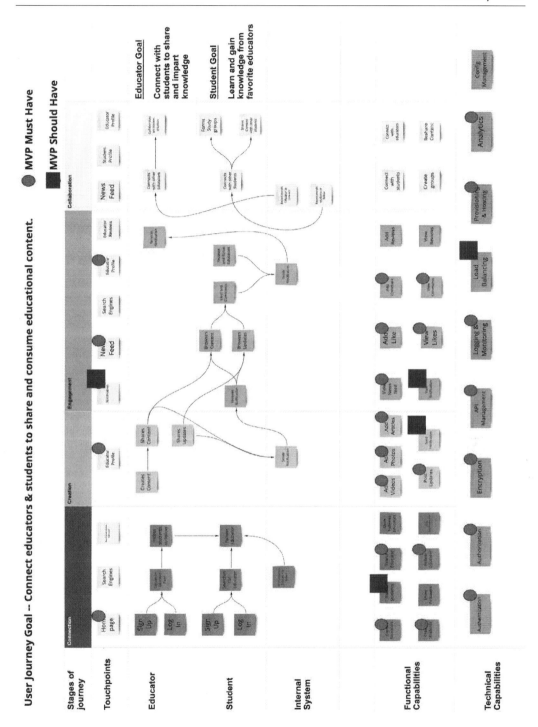

Figure 5.10 – The Escola MVP priorities

In this diagram, the capabilities and touchpoints required for the MVP (*must* and *should*) are indicated. The rest are all either nice to have or not required for the MVP. This visual representation gives us pretty much everything needed to present our MVP to the team and the stakeholders.

But if you want to make your presentation crisper and easily absorbable, you can go one step further and create a view of the user journey only representing the MVP. This way, you can present the comprehensive overall user journey and the MVP user journey side by side for comparison. The following diagram illustrates the MVP user journey for the Escola platform:

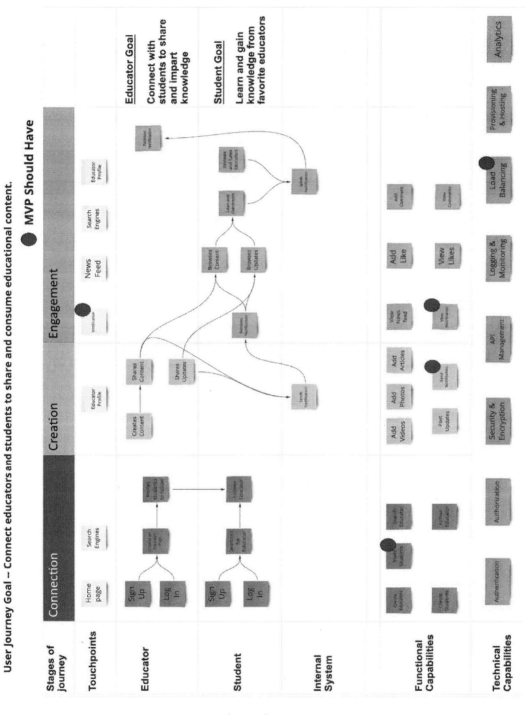

Figure 5.11 – The Escola MVP user journey

This user journey map represents the MVP flow, including the capabilities and touchpoints that are *should have* for the MVP. Indicating the *should have* priorities will help when something goes wrong and we need to deprioritize something from the MVP.

Now that we have our MVP defined and we have a list of functionalities and capabilities that are not prioritized for the MVP but needed in later releases, we can create the roadmap for our platform.

Creating a roadmap for Escola

Before we create the roadmap or arrange our capabilities and experiences in a roadmap format, we will have to define a few milestones and approximate timelines. Let's look at a few important milestones that we should target for our Escola platform:

- **MVP**: The first milestone will be the launch of our MVP, where we will release all the capabilities and functionalities that we have identified for the MVP.

- **Expansion in multiple cities**: In the platform strategy of Escola, we have decided that we will launch it across the country but focus our marketing effort only on seven cities during the MVP launch. Therefore, our next milestone should be to expand our focus to more cities. Expansion in more cities means attracting more users, which will need scalability-related technical capabilities. And to attract more users, we should add functional capabilities to enhance the educator and student experience. Hence, this milestone should focus on scalability and improving the experience for students and educators.

- **Mobile app launch**: For the launch, we only focused on the web with a responsive experience and kept the mobile apps out of scope. To attract more users and provide a well-rounded experience on all the channels, we must launch Escola on mobile platforms, such as Android and iOS. Therefore, launching mobile apps should be our next milestone.

- **Monetization**: Once we have established the user base from all the channels, we should focus on monetizing the platform. Hence, in the next milestone, we should target capabilities, such as showing sponsored recommendations, and so on.

After defining the milestones, we should get the high-level estimates and timelines from the technical team. Please remember that these are planning-level estimates to get an idea of the timeframe for the launch and a couple more milestones. Once we have the timelines, we can organize all the capabilities and experiences on a roadmap in the following format:

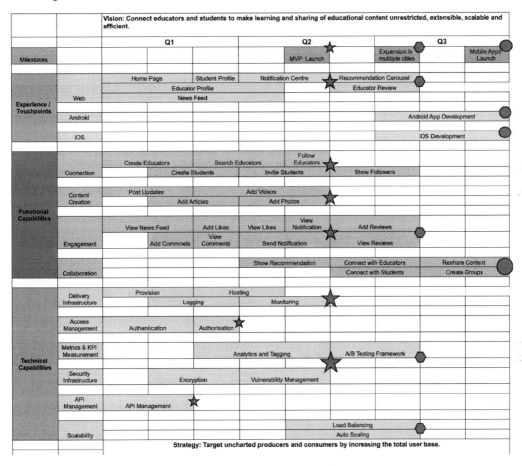

Figure 5.12 – The Escola platform roadmap

This diagram indicates the completion of all the MVP capabilities and functionalities by the middle of Q2. The *should have* capabilities for the MVP like notification and inviting the students are at the end, so these capabilities can be pushed to the next milestone if something goes wrong. Our second milestone is to expand in more cities; hence, improving the platform's scalability is a must. We should also target enhancements, such as reviews and recommendations, that will improve the experience and attract more users.

Different shapes on the timeline represent milestone releases: *star* is release one, *hexagon* is release two, and *circle* is release three. Everything in the feature row until the *star* will be released with milestone one. For example, **Connection** features up to **Follow Educators** and **Invite Students** are part of the milestone one release, and the rest will be released in later milestones. For milestones one and two, we have detailed visibility, but for milestone three, which is the mobile app launch, we have very high-level visibility, which is fine because as we get closer to the milestone, we can expand its capabilities and add them to the roadmap.

Similarly, the fourth milestone of monetization has not even been added to the roadmap, as we have the most negligible visibility of that milestone as of now. Also, note that we will also release some collaboration-related functionalities during the third milestone of the mobile app launch, which is acceptable to release things as we develop. But our focus should be the launch of mobile apps during this milestone. We will cover the topics of different releases and ongoing development in the following few chapters in detail.

As you can see, capabilities to add educators and some of the content creation will get implemented in **Q1**. Hence, to start early usage of the platform, we can do a beta release or prelaunch release for a few selected educators, who can start creating content. This will get us a head start in the content generation so that when the platform is rolled out to students, there is already some content to engage them. Additionally, we will get early feedback from the educators on critical features and capabilities, which can be addressed before the general release.

This concludes the roadmap creation for our Escola platform, including its end-to-end user journey and the MVP. In the next chapter, we will discuss how to launch our platform.

Summary

This was the first chapter that covered the execution part of the platform product management. We started by understanding the platform roadmap and its relationship with the business and platform strategy. Then, we looked at different roadmap elements and how the platform roadmap is different from the linear product roadmap.

While exploring how to create the roadmap, we understood that platform roadmap creation consists of three phases: defining platform capabilities, defining the platform MVP, and creating the platform roadmap. Each of these phases has its own steps and sub-steps. For example, defining platform capabilities includes mapping an end-to-end user journey and extracting capabilities from that journey.

Similarly, defining the MVP involves the prioritization of capabilities and touchpoints. And, lastly, roadmap creation involves the definition of milestones and organizing capabilities against milestones. We also noticed how each of these steps is different for a platform compared to that of a linear product. For example, the mapping of a user journey must align with the growth focus of the platform strategy, or the MVP must accomplish the minimum tasks for all the entities of the platform, or how the platform roadmap is a combination of functional capabilities, technical capabilities, and experiences.

In the next chapter, we'll learn how to launch the platform. We'll learn about different elements of the launch that can give us a solid entry into the market. We'll learn how to create a marketing plan and understand different factors that must be considered for the timing of the launch. This chapter will help us understand the different tactics and nuances of introducing our platform to the market.

6
Launching the Platform

In the previous chapter, we started with the execution part of platform product management and we understood how to translate the business and platform strategy into a platform roadmap. While understanding the creation of a platform roadmap, we looked at mapping the **End-to-End (E2E)** platform user journey and carving out a **Minimum Viable Product (MVP)** from that journey.

To slice the MVP from the user journey, identifying capabilities is a must. Platform capabilities can be categorized into two types: technical capabilities and functional capabilities. Roadmaps for functional and technical capabilities, combined with a roadmap for touchpoints, form the platform roadmap. Technical capabilities represent the infrastructure layer of the platform, whereas functional capabilities and touchpoints represent the business and the customer experience layers, respectively.

In this chapter, we will understand how to launch the platform. While the development team is working on implementing the platform MVP, product managers should start preparing for the launch. Some vital elements must be planned and agreed upon before the launch, such as the specific market to enter, channels of communication, price point, trial period, support structure, and so on. Hence, to understand all the elements of the launch and learn to prepare for the launch of the platform, we will discuss the following topics in this chapter:

- Executing the launch strategy
- Exploring the marketing plan
- Factors impacting launch timing
- Case study

By the end of this chapter, we will be prepared for the launch of our platform and will be able to create a strong marketing plan that will help us grow at the right pace. Launching the platform will be the first step toward exposing our platform to the outside world; hence, a strong entry into the market is very important. The success of the platform will depend on how successful the launch is. Therefore, creating a robust marketing plan and a solid entry into the market is crucial.

Executing the launch strategy

In *Chapter 4, Building a Platform Strategy*, we looked at go-to-market, revenue and pricing, and onboarding strategies as different components of a comprehensive platform strategy. These three components together form a launch strategy. The following diagram highlights the components of a launch strategy that are part of the overall platform strategy:

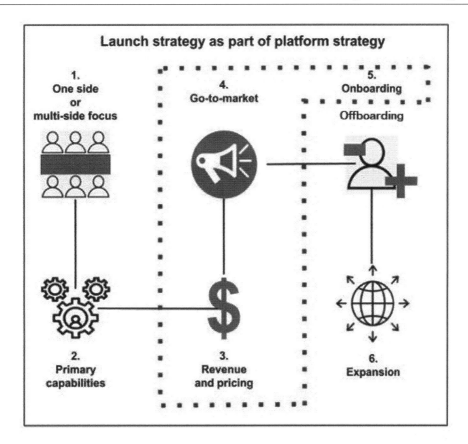

Figure 6.1 – Launch strategy

In the preceding diagram, we can see all the components of a platform strategy, out of which the components that make up the launch strategy are highlighted within the dotted polygon. We have already discussed these elements in detail as part of the overall platform strategy.

In this chapter, we will go a step further—that is, the execution of a launch strategy. During the strategy phase, we specify certain goals that we should target as part of our launch, whereas during execution, we should decide which specific actions need to be taken to achieve those goals. For example, the launch strategy will help us identify the revenue goal for the first few years, whereas in the execution phase, we should decide on the actions that will help us achieve our revenue goal.

To implement and execute a launch strategy, it is essential to understand the critical elements in the launch and the different components that must be planned and prepared for the launch.

Elements of the launch

Elements of the launch of any platform, or any product for that matter, usually answer the specifics of the strategy and help in its execution. Let's dive deeper into different elements of the launch, as follows:

- **Marketing and communications**: A go-to-market strategy answers questions such as when we should launch, where we should launch, and how we should launch the platform, but the specific details of these answers are covered in the execution phase. For example, if the go-to-market strategy tells us that we should launch the platform in the second quarter in one specific city through social media, then before the launch, we should decide on the details, such as whether the launch will be on X date with special invites through email and whether the second release will be on Y date in the same city but through targeted advertising on Facebook.

  We can also plan for a beta release to a specific user group with an invite through email to gather feedback, and iterate and improve upon it before releasing it to a broader audience. In the beta release, we should include users from both sides of the platform in the right proportion. Producers and consumers must be in the right balance depending on the type of platform; otherwise, the beta test results will not be effective.

  The following table illustrates a sample set of all the details that must be included in the launch plan:

Release	Date	Producer target audience	Consumer target audience	Channel
Beta release	July 15, 2021	30 to 50 years age group in Northeast region	25 to 30 years age group in **New York City (NYC)**	Email
General availability	August 5, 2021	30 to 60 years age group on the East coast	25 to 45 years age group in NYC	Email and targeted Facebook message
Big bang	August 31, 2021	30 to 60 years age group across the **United States (US)**	25 to 45 years age group in NYC, **Los Angeles (LA), San Francisco (SFO)**, and Chicago	Targeted Facebook ads

All these details are required for a well-crafted incremental and gradual launch of the platform. These specific details help in creating marketing communications and setting up the operations and support teams. The format and representation of these details can be decided with the help of the marketing team, but including these details is a must for any launch plan. Apart from the target audience and the channel, the launch plan should also include creating assets and other marketing communications. These details are eventually fed into the broader marketing plan.

- **Onboarding**: Onboarding or acquiring users on the platform is very tricky and more challenging than with linear products. As the multi-sided nature of platforms provides the benefits of the network effect simultaneously, this makes onboarding difficult. For instance, if there are no sellers on the e-commerce marketplace, buyers will not be attracted to the platform in the same way if there are limited or no buyers, then it won't be beneficial for sellers to join the platform.

  Hence, it is crucial that the launch plan tactfully rolls out the platform to producers and consumers in an order that attracts them both toward the platform. The onboarding should be based on the focus growth and the type of platform—for example, the producers of the content-sharing platform must be attracted to join the platform and onboarded first. Once a decent amount of content is generated, consumers can be onboarded. Another important thing that a launch plan should include is onboarding incentives such as early-bird pricing, free trial periods, no transaction fees, and so on. The cost of these discounts and free periods should then be factored into the pricing and revenue calculations.

- **Pricing and revenue**: We have learned and understood to define a pricing strategy as part of the overall platform strategy, and we can now discuss the implementation of that strategy. The pricing and revenue plan should include details of which actions must be taken to achieve the goals set during the strategy phase. While creating a pricing strategy, we will have decided the revenue model and revenue projection.

  During the execution, we should decide on different price points, discounts and promotions, and free trial periods, if any. The pricing model must be profitable or incentivized for the producers from the start; otherwise, it will be challenging to attract them to the platform. As a result of that, there won't be any network effect to get all the benefits of a platform. The price point should also be viable for the platform owners in the long run.

Initially, the platform may not profit, but the projection should be able to break even in a few years and then start making a profit. A financial analyst or a stakeholder from the finance team should be the core participant in these discussions. The pricing details will be fed into the broader financial planning and modeling of the business. I found this guide very useful for the financial modeling of a start-up: `https://www.ey.com/en_nl/finance-navigator/the-ultimate-guide-to-financial-modeling-for-startups`. It is a good starting point for financial planning that can be applied to any start-up and then modified for a platform business model. The finance experts do the comprehensive financial modeling and planning, with inputs from product managers on the price point, discounts, offers, promotions, and so on.

The multi-sided nature of platforms heavily impacts the pricing decisions for platform business models. The price point should be competitive, attractive to consumers, profitable to producers, and viable for the platform owners.

- **Support**: Support is another essential element of the launch. We should finalize the support structure and plan for the support before launching the platform. The support plan should include things such as what happens when a user finds an issue or when they cannot proceed, a **Service-Level Agreement** (**SLA**) for resolution, an escalation path, different levels of support, and so on.

  There are different options on how to help users and handle their issues—for example, a help section, a user guide inside the application, a feedback form, a support email, a support phone number, or a chat message that can be replied to by a support team member. Do not overcomplicate the support structure. Keep it very lightweight, especially during the launch. The support method will also depend on the type of platform. For example, transactional platforms need immediate resolution; hence, a live chat or a phone line are recommended as support approaches.

  But for a non-transactional platform, it is fine to have a support email that can be replied to within an acceptable SLA. As always, for the platform support, do not forget to plan for the support of all the entities of the platform. If there are support executives on chat or phone, they must be trained to support consumers and producers. User manuals, help documents, **Frequently Asked Questions** (**FAQs**), and feedback forms should cover issues and questions for both producers and consumers. A detailed support structure and plan are included in the operations plan, which we will touch upon in *Chapter 7, Creating a Platform Operating Model*.

The first two elements of the launch, marketing and communications and onboarding, are part of a broader marketing plan. All the marketing and onboarding activities related to the launch are captured and tracked with the overall marketing plan. The pricing and revenue element goes into the comprehensive financial plan. The support plan and structure are part of the operations plan or are sometimes divided between customer support and technical support, and become part of the operations and development team's plan. We will discuss details about the marketing plan in the later sections of this chapter. We will not get into detailed financial modeling and planning in this book as this is not a day-to-day activity for product managers.

Though these elements are part of different broadscale plans, it is essential that they are decided and planned before the launch. We, as product managers, should ensure that all these elements have been considered, taken care of, and added to their respective plans. Some will need our active participation and heavy involvement, whereas some will need just our input. Irrespective of the product managers' level of involvement, these are the most crucial components of the launch that must be thoroughly planned.

As we discussed earlier, the marketing and communication elements of the launch are part of the bigger marketing plan. Let's go deeper into understanding the marketing plan and how to represent it.

Exploring the marketing plan

The marketing plan deals with creating awareness about the platform, sending communications, customer acquisition, onboarding, engaging the users, and so on. It is not restricted to only launch, but it is an ongoing activity that needs a bigger plan. Some organizations and teams call the launch plan a subset of a comprehensive marketing plan.

The marketing plan comprises marketing activities from pre-launch, launch, and post-launch periods, and these continue for all future releases and launches. For example, we will have pre-launch, launch, and post-launch activities for an alpha release, then for the beta release, followed by a general availability release. Similarly, we can have pre-launch, launch, and post-launch activities for releases on different channels such as the web, Android, and iOS. Let's dive deeper into the marketing activities at different phases of the launch.

Pre-launch activities

For launching any product or platform, most of the heavy lifting is done during the pre-launch phase. This phase is the defining moment for the success or failure of the platform. Mistakes during this phase can have a ripple effect on the entry of the platform into the market—for example, selecting the wrong channel for the launch of your platform, such as using social media when our target audience is not very active on social media; this might lead to an unsuccessful launch and will lead us in the wrong direction. There are some essential activities that must be carried out to set up for a successful launch. Here are some vital pre-launch activities that product managers should do themselves or get them done by other teams such as marketing, communications, business development, or pre-sales, depending on the structure of your organization:

- **Define the target audience**: Before sending out the pre-launch and launch communications, you must define the audience for the launch. You would have known at a high level the target users for your platform, such as riders in LA or designers from NYC. But at this stage, you must be very specific—for example, working professionals in LA who commute daily for work, or shoes and handbag designers from NYC with an average cost of the item ranging from **US Dollars** (**USD**) $120 to $175. Also, remember to define the audience on both the producer and consumer sides of the platform.

- **Select channels**: After defining the audience, you must select a channel to promote and launch the platform. This could be via social media, emails, or even your own website. The channel selection depends on the type of release—for example, if it is a beta release and invites only selected people, you can launch via email. For general availability with a specific group of people, you can launch via targeted ads on social media.

- **Build a distribution list**: Once you have selected a target audience and a channel, the next step is to gather the user information and create a distribution list. Depending on the channel, you can extract the data from social media or external agencies that can provide targeted user data. Some well-established organizations will already have the contact information of users from their ongoing businesses. You will have to distill and filter the available list. For the platform's launch, make sure that you have two distribution lists—one for producers and another for consumers.

- **Pre-launch engagement and communication**: Depending on the type of platform, you should start sending out pre-launch communications to the target users and creating a buzz about your platform. For example, for an infrastructure platform, the developer community and technology executives who make the decisions about the choice of the platform must be aware of this new platform. Some platforms need more initial marketing than others. The more awareness you create before the launch, the more anticipation will be built among the users.

  Pre-launch communications must be different for producers and consumers. Each should highlight the benefits and advantages for their respective side of the platform. You can use multiple channels for pre-launch communications and not just restrict it to the channel of launch. Strike a balance in sending the number of communications and be mindful of users' privacy, especially if you are sending emails.

- **Trials, pre-orders, and early-bird offers**: If you are giving some free trials, early-bird offers, or starting to take pre-orders, before sending out communications, ensure that infrastructure and operations are set for these pre-orders and free trials. Your pre-launch communications should also include details of complimentary trials and pre-orders, if any.

- **Define metrics and Key Performance Indicators (KPIs)**: One of the essential purposes of the launch of the MVP to a smaller group is to collect usage data, accumulate some trends, gather some feedback, and improve on this if needed. Hence, defining key metrics that you want to capture is an important task that you should do as a product manager. The metrics that need to be defined to measure a platform's success is a vast topic, and we have a dedicated chapter (*Chapter 8, Metrics to Measure the Platform Outcome*) on metrics and KPIs to measure platform outcome. But before the launch, your job is to ensure that metrics are defined.

These are some of the essential pre-launch marketing activities. There could be more depending on the type of the platform, growth strategy, region of the launch, and so on, which you should discuss and define with the marketing team.

Launch activities

As with pre-launch activities, there are few launch activities carried out on the launch day or a couple of days before the launch. These are a limited set of tasks as the time window is small, which means mistakes here can be fatal, with limited-to-no time to recover. Here are some critical activities for the launch day:

- **Verify the launch checklist**: All your platform readiness and pre-launch activities should become part of a checklist. Before you launch or open the platform, verify that all the tasks and activities in the checklist are completed.

- **Open the platform**: Turn on any flags or toggles that the platform might have to open the traffic and its usage. Before turning the toggle on, please verify that it is configured with all the correct settings. For example, if we expect traffic from a specific location or region, the platform should restrict all the requests from outside that region.

- **Launch posts, emails, and other communications**: Launch emails, social media posts, and other communications to notify the target audience that the platform is open should go out now. You can also update your corporate website or the marketing page to show that the platform is ready for use. As with pre-launch communications, you can have two types of launch notification posts or emails, one for producers and another for consumers, with specific details on how to join the platform for their respective usage.

  These emails and posts are sometimes configured in advance and scheduled to be sent out at a specific time on the launch day. If you have a scheduler, verify that all the details and settings in the scheduler are configured accurately. Depending on the size and structure of the organization, some or all of these activities might be undertaken by the marketing or communications team, with inputs from product managers.

- **Monitor the platform**: After you have sent the launch communications for a few days, closely monitor if all the metrics and data you have tagged to be gathered are accurately tagged and collected. Report and fix any discrepancy between what is expected and what is being collected. You should also monitor and report any technical abnormality that you observe in the system.

These are some of the important launch-related activities that would apply to most platforms, but there could be more specific activities for your platforms that you should discuss and define with various teams.

Post-launch activities

The launch of the platform is not restricted to the day of the launch—some crucial tasks must be performed after the launch. The actual measurement happens post-launch. The results from this phase define the future of the platform. Most post-launch activities are ongoing marketing functions that must be carried throughout the platform journey. Here are some critical post-launch activities and ongoing marketing activities:

- **Gather feedback and collect data**: Start collecting metrics and KPIs. For a few weeks or even a month, closely monitor all the critical metrics associated with the launch. Make sure that data for all the important KPIs for the specific launch/release is getting collected. For example, if an iOS app is released, make sure that the app downloads and visits for the app are getting tracked.

  Also, any other associated metrics must be closely monitored. For example, was there any significant increase or decrease in the conversion rate after the launch of the iOS app? Apart from the metrics and KPIs, also focus on the number of bugs found and customer queries. Bugs can either be reported by the customer or caught through the logs. After launch, make sure another vital data collection mechanism is collecting customer feedback, by either sending out customer surveys or providing a link on the platform to submit feedback. If you send an email survey, include all the entities involved in the platform and have separate surveys designed for each of them.

- **Analyze KPI data**: After you have collected data from all the sources, you should analyze the data, identify significant trends and patterns from the data, and compare the expected and actual results. Also, you should analyze and list down possible reasons for a substantial deviation in the actual results from expectations, and highlight any outliers and abnormal behaviors.

- **KPI improvement plan**: Based on the analysis, you should come up with an improvement plan. This plan could be either adding new features or making existing features more intuitive, reaching out to a different segment of users, increasing marketing reach, or adding operational steps, and so on. It would depend on which metrics you are lagging on and what you want to improve.

- **Add feedback to the roadmap**: After the improvement plan is finalized, add bugs, features, and enhancements to the platform roadmap. Any marketing-related tasks or activities must be added to the marketing plan, and any other operational task must be added to the individual plan.

We will discuss all the metrics-tracking and KPI-related activities in detail in *Chapter 8, Metrics to Measure the Platform Outcome*, to measure the performance of the platform, metrics, and KPIs for ascertaining the platform outcome.

- **Continue email, posts, and other communications**: After the launch of one release/milestone and before the next, ensure that users are continuously getting updates and hearing about the brand. There shouldn't be a period of silence between releases. If there are any promotions or offers, keep advertising them on different channels. Creating brand awareness and keeping users engaged throughout is one of the most crucial marketing activities.

Most of these post-launch activities are ongoing and long-running, and some of them will overlap with pre-launch activities of the next launch or the release. Separating them into different phases helps in creating a visual for easy tracking and reporting.

Now that we have understood what a marketing plan is and the different activities for different phases of the launch, let's understand how to create a visualization of the marketing plan.

Creating a marketing plan visualization

As mentioned earlier, marketing is not just restricted to launch but is an ongoing operation crucial in building the brand. Most of the marketing time, resources, and effort go into building the brand image. Along with the launch and ongoing brand-awareness activities, marketing research is another important category of activity that becomes a crucial part of the overall marketing plan. These three types of marketing activities— research, brand awareness, and launch—are associated with timelines and tied to marketing goals.

To better track these different categories of activities, it is essential to create a marketing plan and represent this information in an easily consumable format. The marketing plan is usually represented in a Gantt chart format and prepared mainly by the marketing team, with inputs from product managers. Some of the critical components of the marketing plan or the Gantt chart are activities, timeline, dependencies (if any), and marketing milestones such as *X* number of producers and *Y* number of consumers, or *X* number of page visits, and so on.

The following diagram illustrates a sample marketing plan in a Gantt chart format that includes different phases and activities within those phases:

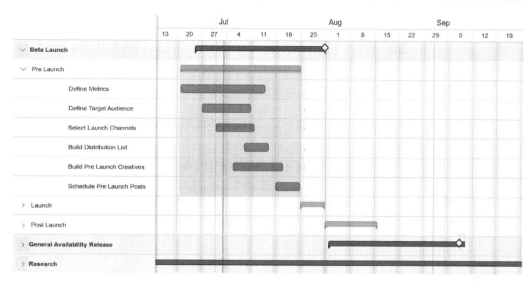

Figure 6.2 – Sample marketing plan

This sample marketing plan shows different releases such as **Beta Launch** and **General Availability Release**. There are different phases such as **Pre Launch**, **Launch**, and **Post Launch** within these releases, with the respective activities inside each phase. If you notice, some or most of the activities are overlapping with each other.

For example, selecting the launch channels begins before the definition of a target audience is completed. Building creatives starts before creating a distribution list and coincides with a couple of activities, as this requires more time to complete. If you want to create an even more granular plan, you can further break down the activities into smaller tasks—for example, building creatives can be broken down into images, videos, and so on. Also, if you notice, research is an ongoing operation that can have different milestones such as researching the most-trending promotions and offers, researching the next-best city for launch, and so on. It is a very simplistic example of a marketing plan. Some teams also add milestones on this Gantt chart; for example, if there is an Android app launch, after the Android app is released, there will be a milestone of X number of downloads of the app.

Now that we have understood all the elements and activities related to the launch, it is important to look at some of the factors that might impact the launch. Even after all the essential elements of the launch are taken care of, some critical factors must be considered to decide the launch time. Some of these factors could be external to our organization, but they play a crucial role in determining the most suitable timing for the launch.

Factors impacting launch timing

One of the most important questions that arise before the launch is about the right time for the launch. There is no right or perfect time to launch your platform, but there are some factors that you should consider when deciding the timing of the launch. These factors are not restricted to a first-time launch but should be considered for all the major releases and milestones.

These factors are not mandatory, and some of them will not even apply all the time. Still, when contemplated, they are valuable and can reduce the chances of your platform getting off to a slower start. Hence, it is advisable to consider these factors while deciding the launch date for your platform. Let's discuss these factors in detail, as follows:

- **Readiness of the platform**: The first—and most crucial—factor to consider for the launch is when the platform will be ready. The readiness of the platform is not just the development of the MVP. It also includes other production readiness factors such as failure recovery and backup plans, logging and monitoring, analytics and tagging, customer and technical support setup, marketing circulars and communications readiness, and so on. It is advisable to decide the launch date after we have a projected completion date for all these items. Some of these items can be merged into a checklist that can be referred to throughout the launch process.

- **Time of the year**: Apart from the platform readiness, another important factor that needs to be considered for the launch is the season or the time of the year. Depending on the type of platform, the launch season must be decided—for example, an e-commerce platform might not be launched during the year-end holiday season. Instead, it can be rolled out mid-year, and by the time the holiday season arrives, the platform will be ready to take up the volume and load of the holiday season. Similarly, an entertainment content platform can be launched during winter when people are not outdoors and looking for indoor entertainment and activities.

- **Day of the week**: As with the time of the year, another critical factor is the day of the week. The launch day must be decided based on the type of platform—for example, a social media platform might be released at the weekend, whereas a development or infrastructure platform might be released on a weekday. It is also recommended for some types of platforms to avoid Mondays and Fridays as people are too busy on Mondays and too burned out on Fridays to check something new. Hence, it is advisable to launch midweek to attract more users and get their full attention.

- **Competitor events**: For deciding the launch timing, it is also essential to pay attention to competitors' events. For example, do not launch an e-commerce marketplace close to the Amazon Prime day or a ridesharing platform near free-ride day on Uber. Apart from popular events, the ongoing promotions must also be carefully scanned before deciding on the platform's launch. One important thing to keep in mind here is that these promotion watches should not be restricted to the consumer side. Many platforms offer huge discounts and perks to the producers. For example, Uber has many promotional programs for drivers that must be considered if you are launching a ridesharing platform.

Now that we have understood how to execute a launch strategy, understood marketing activities required for different phases of the launch, and explored some of the factors that must be considered for the platform's launch, it is time to apply all this knowledge to an example. Let's continue with our case study from the previous chapters and understand what needs to be done to launch our platform.

Case study

In the previous chapter, we defined the MVP and created a roadmap for our educational content-sharing platform, **Escola**. In this chapter, we will create a launch plan for the Escola MVP, and a marketing plan that will cover all the launch activities and some of the ongoing marketing tasks.

To create a launch plan, we will have to look at the launch strategy that we have defined as part of the platform strategy. The launch strategy comprises go-to-market, pricing and revenue, and onboarding components from the platform strategy. Let's quickly revise these three components from the overall Escola platform strategy, as follows:

- **Growth focus**: Both sides (students and educators).
- **Go-to-market strategy**: Escola will be rolled out across the US, but the focus will be only on seven cities with Ivy League colleges and a high number of preparatory schools.
- **Onboarding strategy**: We can offer special incentives and prices for educators to join and share content on the Escola platform. Also, we can run heavy marketing campaigns on campuses for students to join Escola.

- **Pricing and revenue strategy**: There will be no revenue stream for the first year; our focus will only be on capturing the market. The platform will start with an advertising model in the second year. As we discussed in *Chapter 4, Building a Platform Strategy*, projected starting revenue from ads is 25% of the platform development and operating cost of the first year, with 10% growth in revenue every month.

Now that we have revised the summary of our launch strategy for Escola, we should work on translating this launch strategy into a plan.

Escola launch plan

To create a launch plan for Escola, we will have to discuss and plan for all the elements of the launch in detail, which are marketing and communications, onboarding, pricing, and support. Let's look at these in more detail here:

- **Marketing and communications**: Our go-to-market strategy is to focus on seven cities with Ivy League colleges and top schools. Our target audience for the launch is students and educators from these cities, hence our pre-launch and launch announcements must be targeted to these groups. For students, we should focus mainly on juniors and seniors from high schools and undergraduates from colleges. The best channel through which to reach them is social media. We can specifically advertise to the student group of the specific cities via Facebook and Instagram.

  For educators, the focus should be on high-school teachers and college professors with age groups ranging from 30 to 45 years. The rationale behind choosing this target group of educators is that research has shown that this age group is active on social media, likes to connect with people, and is interested in sharing knowledge and valuable content for educational purposes.

  The platform will not be restricted to anyone, but the marketing focus will be on this specific group of educators. To target educators, we must be a little more personal; hence, we can gather information about the specific targeted educator group from data-curating agencies and reach out to the educators via email. Social media platforms such as Facebook and LinkedIn should also be used for posting promotions and launching communications to educators.

- **Onboarding**: The growth focus of Escola is to create a significant user base by growing both educators and students. Hence, we should equally focus on adding students and educators. But the question is: how to attract them to join the platform? As this platform is a hybrid of content sharing and social media, gathering quality content is key to attracting students, and to collect quality content, we should draw and onboard educators on the platform. We should tackle this problem of onboarding educators in two steps, as outlined here:

- **Promotion and testimony from influencing educators**: We should reach out to prominent educators and explain to them the benefits of the platform, request them to support the platform over different channels, and create an official affiliation and associate them with the platform. We can also ask them to share content in advance. This might involve some financial component, which should be carved out from the marketing budget. We should affiliate at least five leading educators with our platform from different fields such as **Science, Technology, Engineering, and Mathematics (STEM)**, literature, art, history, economics, and so on.

- **Contests and incentives for sharing content**: The second step is to roll out different contests for educators to share the content—for example, the most inspirational or informative content, the amount of engagement generated on the content, an educator with the highest content shared, and so on. The quality of the content will be judged by prominent educators that are affiliated with the platform. Winners will be rewarded with gifts and prizes to help and motivate them to engage with the platform further.

We should start marketing and advertising the affiliation of the influencing educators with the platform and the educators' contests well before the launch. All the pre-launch communications should create a buzz about how leading educators relate to our platform and all the rewards that will be given to educators for sharing quality content. These promotions will motivate the educators and attract students because of the influence of the educators and the quality of the content.

Apart from social media, some of these promotions will also run on campus. With the help of the affiliated educators, we will reach out to schools and colleges to place physical banners and hoardings on campuses and digital banners on intranet sites. Colleges are open to promoting collaborative platforms that can help their students learn and their educators grow. Colleges and schools will charge a fee for the placement of these physical and digital promotions, added to the marketing budget.

- **Pricing and revenue**: The pricing and revenue strategy for Escola suggests that there won't be any revenue stream for the first year. We should focus on increasing the user base on both the student and educator sides of the platform. But after year 1, we should start with targeted advertising, where educational institutes, private tutors, and coaches can advertise and share promotional posts and updates.

Hence, we should begin to communicate to targeted advertisers a few months after the launch and start offering them free placements before the end of year 1 so that we are ready to start with a small revenue from the beginning of the second year. Right from the pre-launch communications, we will reach out to these targeted advertisers without pitching in any paid promotions initially but only informing and creating awareness about the platform. Hence, we should include them in all the pre-launch and launch communications. Once the platform is established and we have significant traffic, we should pitch the paid promotions.

- **Support**: As our platform is non-transactional and does not involve processes that require real-time support, we can keep our support structure simple and light. We can have a support form from within the application for users to ask queries or send an issue. Submission of the form will trigger an email to the team. A team member will be assigned to respond to questions and get urgent and critical defects fixed by the development team.

  If a defect is not urgent, it will be added to the backlog. If a query results in any new feature or enhancement, it will be added to the backlog with appropriate priority. If the platform is entirely down and users can't even access the support form, the error page will display the support email address with a message informing the users to send the escalation to a given email address.

Along with this, there will be an email alert set with the technical monitoring of the platform. As soon as a critical error is encountered in the system, an email will be sent out to the team with all the details of the error. Someone from the team will be assigned on a rotational basis to monitor and resolve such production issues. It is an overview of the support structure added to the launch summary that different stakeholders will refer to at different times and that will help make the final go-no-go decision on the day before the launch. The support structure and the plan will be covered in *Chapter 7, Creating a Platform Operating Model.*

We have discussed all the elements for the launch of our platform. Now, let's create a summary report of this information that can be sent to all the stakeholders and can become an easy reference for critical discussions and decision-making points, as follows:

Launch element	Role	Details
Release date		October 1, 2021
Target audience	Students	Juniors and seniors from high schools, and undergraduates from colleges from seven cities
	Educators	High-school teachers and college professors with age groups ranging from 30 to 45 years
Pre-launch communication channel	Students	Facebook, Instagram, and college intranet
	Educators	Facebook, LinkedIn, and personal emails
Launch channel	Students	Facebook and Instagram
	Educators	Facebook, LinkedIn, and personal emails
Specifics onboarding	Students	Announcements and ads on college intranet and campuses
	Educators	Affiliation with influencing and prominent educators
Onboarding offers	Students	Not applicable
	Educators	Contests for sharing quality content, a high volume of content, and creating the most engaging content
Price		Not applicable for launch
Support model		Support form/email in the system. Dedicated team to reply and resolve queries. Automated monitoring and email alerts for technical errors and service downtimes.

Summary

In this chapter, we covered the aspects of launching the platform. We understood that the overall process or the steps to launch a platform are like for any other product, but the execution of each step is different. For example, during the platform's launch, the price point of the product or the service should be attractive to both consumers and producers, which is not the case for linear products. Hence, if there are any free trial periods, they must be offered to both producers and consumers.

We should think creatively about what the trial period for producers means. Apart from the price point and offers, there are other aspects where product managers must think differently and creatively when launching a platform versus a linear product. For example, the target audience for the launch, the city and region of the launch, pre-launch communications, and so on should all be decided and designed for the multidimensional nature of the platform.

While discussing the launch elements, we learned that the most critical and challenging aspect of a platform launch is the onboarding order. To reap all the benefits of the platform's network effect, the onboarding order must be very carefully planned. Based on the platform growth strategy, you should focus on attracting one side by offering heavy discounts, incentives, free goodies, and so on.

Once a significant user base is created for one side, the other side will be motivated and attracted. In some cases, discounts must be offered to both sides simultaneously to grow them on the platform proportionally—for example, offering free rides on a ridesharing platform for riders and not taking any transaction fees or commissions from the drivers. In some cases, the platform must be launched targeting only one side, and after getting good traffic from one side, the other side can be onboarded. We, as product managers, should think creatively about how to onboard both producers and consumers on the platform to create a strong network effect and yield a win-win situation for the parties involved.

We also understood the marketing plan and how to create a marketing plan that can be easily tracked and consumed by different stakeholders. We also discussed factors that should be considered for the launch timing. At a surface level, these factors might sound the same as those affecting the launch of any product, not just the platform. This is true, but while considering these factors, there are small details that would be different for platforms. For example, the time of the year must be considered for all the platform entities and not just consumers. Similarly, when researching competitor events, events impacting the whole platform must be considered, not just one side of the platform.

In the next chapter, we will explore the platform operating model. We will understand and learn the most efficient and effective team structure for the platform and the platform's ways of working, and we will discuss and learn how to create a robust governance model for the platform's effective functioning and operation.

7
Creating a Platform Operating Model

In the last chapter, we looked at executing a launch strategy and the different elements of launching a platform. The trickiest part about launching a platform is to solve the sequence on how the platform is launched between producers and consumers. The onboarding of producers and consumers must be planned based on the growth strategy of the platform to create a strong network effect, such as onboarding renowned producers first or offering free trial periods to consumers to attract more of them to the platform. In the previous chapter, we also explored the overarching marketing plan that should be used for launch and beyond. We also discussed the factors that must be considered for the timing of the launch.

In this chapter, we will start with understanding the operating model and learning the differences between the **platform operating model** and the **linear product operating model**. We will understand the different components of a solid and robust operating model to set us up for success. We must have a team structure that can work efficiently, adapt to change, and quickly iterate over feedback.

We will discuss platform ways of working, and how to create an effective platform governance model that can strive toward delivering value and empowering teams. We will understand how all the pillars of the platform operating model can together help in building a platform that is feasible and viable in the short term and profitable in the long term, by discussing and exploring the following topics:

- What is an operating model?
- The differences between the platform operating model and the linear product operating model
- Platform team structure
- Platform governance model
- Platform ways of working
- Case study

By the end of this chapter, we will know how to create a platform operating model that is well structured and coherent. We will understand the roles and responsibilities of different teams and know how to embed a value-driven, customer-centric culture at all levels. We will also learn about designing a strong and powerful governance model for operating a successful platform.

What is an operating model?

An **operating model** is something that explains how companies or teams operate to create value. The operating model helps companies structure their teams and create an environment suitable for delivering value efficiently. Different companies and organizations have different ways of working, which is reflected through their operating model.

An operating model defines the path of execution and, when done right, can yield astonishing results, but it can also lead to failures when implemented poorly. Sometimes, brilliant ideas collapse because they are not executed right. Hence, organizations must spend time and effort defining the operating model that works best for their teams and business. It must focus on delivering value with minimum overheads and must be flexible. An operating model must be evolutionary, and it should adapt based on the changing priorities and nature of the business.

The key to building an operating model that can provide results and add value is to break silos and create a collaborative culture at all levels. Team structure should be such that it promotes working together rather than individually and creating knowledge pockets. And everyone should work toward creating value and achieving goals. Each team should have its own goals, but it should align with and roll up to the organizational goals and objectives.

To summarize, an operating model is an organization's structure and Way of Working to deliver value. An effective operating model is flexible, promotes collaboration, and focuses on delivering value as an individual team and as an organization.

Now that we have understood what an operating model is, we can dive deeper and explore some of the key components or the pillars of a good and robust operating model.

The components of an operating model

The components of the operating model are like pieces of a puzzle: they are dependent on each other to fit together and create a big picture. They are spread across different functions and aspects of the organization, such as architecture, culture, teams, and so on.

These components are applicable for any organization or business transforming from a traditional organization to a modern-age digital business that believes in customer satisfaction by delivering high-quality products or services faster. The construction and design of these pillars differ between platforms, which we will cover in the later sections of this chapter. Let's first start with understanding what the essential components of a strong operating model are:

- **Autonomous and cross-functional teams**: High-functioning teams are critical to the successful operation of any organization. Building high-functioning teams requires giving them full ownership to manage a feature/product/service and organize themselves. A self-managed team that can operate on its own is often more productive and delivers higher quality than teams that are dependent and lack ownership.

  Each team should be empowered to run their experiments, make their own decisions, create value, and contribute to the overall objectives and goals of the business. Creating autonomous teams means reducing the dependencies between teams as much as possible.

Hence, it is essential to design a cross-functional team that can own the product or the service end to end. For example, a team should be responsible for creating their backlogs, implementing the capabilities, and deploying and supporting their respective product or service. We will discuss platform-specific team structures in detail in the *Platform team structure* section in this chapter.

- **Value-driven agile culture**: Rolling out functionalities faster and learning and iterating over them to maximize the value is crucial in today's world, where things change so rapidly. It is essential to keep up with the changing technologies, increasing customer expectations, and evolving behavior.

  While maintaining pace with the dynamic nature of the business, agility plays a crucial role. Delivering a perfectly implemented feature is more important than quickly adding a capability that creates value faster. Hence, adding value with agility must be instilled in the organization's culture at all levels.

  Every initiative, every feature, and every capability must be designed toward delivering value quickly, iterating over it, and changing as necessary. This agile way of working with the goal of creating value must be implemented across the organization.

- **Organization structure with direction**: As we discussed that each cross-functional team should create value and contribute to the overall objectives of the business, it is essential that the management defines the objectives and goals for the organization. For the successful functioning of any operating model, it is critical that the leaders define the goals and strategies, and clearly communicate them to the teams.

  The organizational goals must be broken down into objectives for individual teams and translated into metrics that can be tracked. Leaders should empower teams to work toward achieving their objectives and providing timely feedback. Creating an organizational structure with an open communication channel, giving direction, and creating a feedback culture are vital aspects of a robust operating model.

- **Modular architecture**: Building cross-functional teams and delivering value in an agile environment depends highly on how flexible and modular your architecture is. For example, to deliver value faster and iterate on feedback, your architecture must support modular development and deployment.

You should be able to make a change to one component and individually test and deploy it without impacting other modules. Creating capabilities that can be shared across multiple use cases accelerates developing functionalities to deliver value. Modular architecture with flexible and reusable components is a foundation for creating an operating model that can rapidly deliver value, quickly iterate, and adapt to changes if needed.

Establishing an operating model with these components and pillars is not a one-time task; it is an iterative exercise. We cannot get it perfect in the first iteration. It is a continuous improvement cycle that must be tested and modified to mature with a growing business, changing behaviors, and expectations.

As mentioned earlier, these pillars or components are not restricted just to the platforms but can apply to any digital operating model. Each of these components should be specifically designed and implemented from the platform's perspective to make platforms function highly efficiently and deliver value for all the parties involved. We will cover each of these components in detail from the platform perspective.

We will explore platform team structure, where we will understand how to build autonomous cross-functional teams. Platform ways of working will teach us how to build a value-driven culture. Similarly, the platform governance model will educate us about the organizational structure suitable for platforms that can help the teams work through the feedback and continuously add value. We will cover some bits about the modular architecture while discussing platform team structure, but we will not go deeper into it, as designing and architecting the platform is primarily done by the technical team with input from the product managers.

Before moving on to discussing each component of an operating model from the platform's perspective, let's first look at some of the differences between the platform operating model and the operating model for linear products.

The differences between platform and linear product operating models

The key differences between the platform operating model and the linear product model are because of the multidimensional nature of the platform, which focuses on creating value across all the entities involved in the platform. Because of this difference, the way value is created and progress is governed in the landscape drastically varies.

The following are some of the key differences between the two operating models that are the byproduct of the multidimensional nature of the platform:

- **Feature teams versus capabilities teams**: Platform teams work toward creating capabilities; hence, they are organized around capabilities. In linear products, teams are focused on delivering features; thus their operating model consists of feature teams. Feature teams are responsible for delivering end-to-end features to add value for the end users. In contrast, capabilities teams are responsible for adding reusable and shared capabilities that can be consumed to provide value for end users.

  For example, searching for products is a capability that can be used by any channel and any feature, such as placing an order, reading reviews, comparing two products, and so on. Hence, the search team will be responsible for implementing the search capability that can be consumed by any channel for any feature. This team will be responsible for any enhancements to the search capability such as keyword search, natural language search, voice search, optimizing the search algorithm, and so on.

- **Projects versus products**: The governance in the linear product is at the project or the program level, but in the platform model, it is at the product level. Here, projects or programs are the end-to-end features or the initiatives that include multiple features. For example, improving the customer onboarding experience will be treated as a program, consisting of few features that would improve the user onboarding. The project or program manager will be responsible for governing the delivery of this end-to-end program and will move on to a different project after this one ends.

  However, in the platform world, capabilities are organized within the service boundaries and each service is treated as a product. Along with the services, every channel is also a product. Product teams are responsible for the end-to-end ownership of their respective products. Product owners and technical leads from each team are responsible for governing their respective products.

- **Consumer versus ecosystem**: In the linear product world, teams are focused on delivering value for single-sided users, who are the consumers for most of the products. But the platform teams are focused on providing value across the platform ecosystem, such as producers, consumers, intermediaries, and internal and external teams that consume capabilities added by the platform teams.

Understanding these differences is crucial while setting up the platform operating model and governing it daily. You will notice these differences influencing almost all the functioning and decision-making of the platform, from big decisions such as prioritizations to smaller tasks such as doing a capability demo.

Now that we know what the key differences that can impact the creation and governance of the platform operating model are, let's dive deeper into each component or pillar of an operating model from the platform's perspective.

Platform team structure

Team structure plays a vital role in the success and failure of any organization. It is essential to structure the organization so that it doesn't create bottlenecks and enables smooth functioning at all levels. This principle of having a less dependent organization is true for platform businesses as well.

Platform teams must be structured so that each team can independently operate but deliver value that is aligned to the overall platform and is beneficial for all the parties involved. I like to divide platform teams into two broad categories:

- The first one is digital teams that comprise lean cross-functional teams that own a digital product or service.

- The second category is business or operation teams, such as marketing, finance, sales, and so on. These teams complement the digital teams by providing them with operational support.

Let's look at these two categories of teams in detail.

Digital teams

Platform **digital teams** can be further divided into three teams, namely infrastructure, functional, and experience teams. Infrastructure teams can own the infrastructure layer of the platform, functional teams own the core/business layer of the platform, and experience teams can own the experience layer of the platform. These teams will have multiple teams or pods within them, depending on the size of the platform and the organization. Let's look at these teams and their responsibilities in detail:

- **Infrastructure teams**: Infrastructure teams deliver the technical capabilities required for the development, deployment, and operation of the platform. The infrastructure team is responsible for providing foundational infrastructure, automating various processes, and creating reusable infrastructural components.

The automated tasks and reusable components enable the functional and experience teams to develop, deploy, and deliver quickly and efficiently. For example, automating environment creation can allow any team to spin up an environment as they need. Creating templates for reference apps helps teams to bootstrap an application to start development. The automation and reusable infrastructure components bring consistency to the foundation and increase the efficiency of all the teams across the organization.

Apart from automation and reusable component creation, infrastructure teams also add technical capabilities and frameworks that are consumed by other teams, such as observability (logging and monitoring), security, analytics, configuration management, A/B testing, and so on. Please note that infrastructure teams are responsible for providing the framework, but individual teams are responsible for consuming the frameworks as per their needs.

For example, the infrastructure team will create the framework for analytics, but the experience teams must use the framework for capturing the analytics data. Initially, we can have one infrastructure team providing technical capabilities, but as the platform grows and scales, infrastructure teams can be divided based on the capabilities and frameworks.

- **Functional teams**: These teams are responsible for creating functional capabilities within a service boundary, which can be used by different experiences/channels, internal and external. Functional teams develop capabilities that can be used across different channels and different use cases. For example, the capability to search for a product is possible via a website, mobile apps, and sometimes even external partner applications.

Similarly, personalized recommendations are shown while browsing the products and sent in emails. Both these use cases consume the same capability of showing recommendations based on user preference. Hence, one capability that is developed within the boundaries of the personalization service and is exposed via an API can be consumed for both use cases. The functional team that owns the personalization service is responsible for adding that capability.

The boundaries and ownership of these services are designed around functional capabilities. One team can own multiple services depending on the size of the platform and the number of services. But the service cannot have multiple owners. For example, one team can own the search service and the personalization service, but two teams cannot own one search service. Functional teams are responsible for adding capabilities to their services, their deployment, support, and enhancements.

- **Experience teams**: Experience teams own the end-to-end development and deployment of channels or experiences, such as mobile apps, websites, TV apps, apps on connected devices, and so on. Experience teams are responsible for creating intuitive user experiences and focusing on serving the requirements of end users. Experience teams consume the capabilities created by functional teams and deliver end-to-end user journeys.

  One team can own one channel or experience, but if the platform size is small and there are fewer channels, one team can own multiple channels provided they have the required skills. For example, iOS and Android apps can be owned by one team, given that the team has Android and iOS developers.

  But like functional teams, one channel should not be owned by multiple teams. Irrespective of the number of channels or experiences the team owns, each channel must be architected to be independently developed and deployed. For example, if there is a change needed on one of the channels, the team should be able to implement and deploy that change without impacting or having to deploy the other channels.

Digital team structure reflects the modular architecture; each team is a cross-functional team that can operate independently. These teams own their modules from end to end, from backlog management to deployment and support. Hence, these teams consist of product managers, testers, and developers that are also skilled in deployment.

Business and other operations teams

The non-digital teams are often referred to by different names like **business teams**, **operations teams**, or **Business Operations (BizOps)**. Some of the examples of these teams are sales, marketing, customer support, and finance. These teams work adjacent to digital teams and often use inputs from digital teams. For example, the marketing team works in collaboration with product managers for launches and releases. Similarly, the finance team works with product managers for product pricing and revenue streams, and the customer support team collaborates with technical leads on the resolution of technical issues.

The number of these teams would depend on the nature of the business and the type of platform. For example, for specific platforms, one team can own both sales and marketing. Similarly, a dedicated customer support team might not be needed in certain platforms where the support channel is emailing. In such cases, someone from the governance team or the head of product, who is responsible for customer communications, receives the email with the customer issue and assigns it to the appropriate capability or experience team. These are some of the options that can help us keep the operations cost at a minimum in the initial phases. These teams can be added as the platform scales, and we might end up with a dedicated customer support team.

Like digital teams, business operations teams must also be self-organized, autonomous, and operate independently. For the smooth functioning of these teams, there must be a governance body that can help these teams to track their progress and remove impediments. We will understand the governance model needed for the platform teams, their role, and the key actions in the following section.

Platform governance model

Any operating model requires governance to track if it is functioning as desired and take corrective measures if needed. The platform operating model is no different. The governance structure should reflect the platform team structure. For example, each team should have a leader who can guide and mentor the team. Apart from the individual team leaders, there must be a lean governance team consisting of a technical head or architect, head of products, and head of BizOps. As the business and the size of the platform grows, we can add the head of the customer experience, head of the infrastructure, and head of the functional capabilities to the governance team. But be careful in creating redundant roles and unnecessary hierarchy.

Apart from the governance team, there are executives and leaders who define the business objectives and strategies. Executives are responsible for setting organizational goals, and they work closely with the governance team to track the progress of those goals. Executives and leaders must try to keep the organization structure as lean as possible, constantly evaluate, and adapt based on the changing size and nature of the business.

The following diagram illustrates a sample platform team structure along with the governance and executive teams:

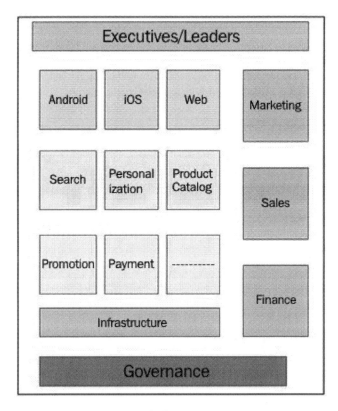

Figure 7.1 – Platform team structure

This is a team structure for a sample e-commerce platform. The top three boxes are the experience or the channel teams for website and mobile apps. If the platform is small with fewer features, we can have one team for multiple experiences, provided that the team has the right skills for development in all the technologies.

The next set of teams are functional teams that will add capabilities within the service boundaries, as represented in the diagram. For example, all the capabilities related to the search will be implemented by the **Search** team, and the **Payment** team will develop any capability within the boundaries of payments. These are some sample services; there are many other services, such as transaction, fulfillment, and so on, that will also be part of the platform.

During the initial phases, one team can own multiple services, and as the platform scales and the number of capabilities increases, we can separate the teams. Similarly, the infrastructure team can consist of one team or multiple teams, depending on the size of the platform and the number of technical capabilities. Apart from the digital team, BizOps teams such as finance, marketing, and sales work closely with digital teams. And finally, there is the governance team that enables the functioning of all the teams and the executives driving the business goals strategies.

The governance team must be small, and it is not meant to create a reporting structure in the organization. The governance team is responsible for providing guidance, tracking performance, and giving feedback to teams. The governance team is also responsible for assigning priorities and balancing resources between teams in case of a conflict.

One thing to note here is that your governance model or the size of the governance team will depend on the phase and size of your business. For example, in the start-up phase, the governance team will be the same as founders and executives, who may also be the architect or product manager. People will have to wear multiple *hats* during the initial stages, and as the business and teams grow, these roles can be separated.

The following are some of the measures that the platform governance team should take to set up a successful governance model:

- **Defining objectives and key results**: Defining objectives for teams and tying them to key results can provide direction to individual teams and help the governance team track each team's progress and the platform as a whole. The **Objectives and Key Results (OKRs)** for each team must align with the overall platform goals.

  For example, the objective for the web experience/channel team for the ridesharing platform can be to *improve the driver onboarding experience*, and the key result for this objective can be *the time to onboard the driver must be reduced by X number of minutes*. This objective must be aligned with the overall platform goal of increasing the number of drivers onboard.

  The OKRs must be aimed at creating value and continuously tracked and measured by the governance team. OKRs play a vital role in creating a value-driven culture across all teams and all levels.

- **Providing feedback**: After defining OKRs and tracking the team's progress against those OKRs, the governance team should provide feedback to the team on how they are performing and how they can improve. Along with the individual team's performance, the governance team should also reflect on the platform's performance as a whole and implement corrective measures if needed.

Hence, the governance team needs to provide performance feedback to leaders and executives along with the team. The governance team can discuss with the leaders any changes or modifications required at the organizational level. This helps in creating and maintaining an open channel of communication from executives to individual teams. It encourages teams to work toward an objective, gather feedback, and iterate over the feedback.

- **Resolving dependencies**: The governance team should work on resolving dependencies between the teams. These dependencies could be around the availability of the sharable components and frameworks or providing input and feedback. For example, the timely availability of an A/B testing framework from the infrastructure or experience teams consuming an API and giving feedback to functional teams could sometimes delay the end-to-end value creation.

  Hence, the governance team should proactively try to resolve these dependencies before they become bottlenecks. Along with resolving dependencies, the governance team should balance the conflicting priorities between teams. For example, suppose one team needs automated provisioning of the environment and another team needs a monitoring framework from the infrastructure team. In that case, the governance team should decide on the priority based on the overall business value and objective.

  The roadmap for each team should be defined and prioritized in advance by the team's product owners and technical leads in agreement with the governance team. Other teams should plan their dependencies according to the roadmaps published by other teams. But in some exceptional cases, last-minute priority conflicts can occur, which should be resolved by the governance team.

The governance team should work closely with individual teams, especially the team leaders, for implementing these measures. Please remember that the role of the governance team is to help and enable teams to add value. It is not a commanding force or a reporting hierarchy. The governance team should empower the teams to make their own decisions and create an environment where teams feel safe while experimenting and trying new things.

The main responsibility of the governance team is to provide direction and goals to individual teams, track those goals, provide feedback to teams, and guide them to succeed. Another crucial role of the governance team is to report the progress of the overall platform to the executives and leaders, work with them in taking corrective measures, and implement changes if needed at the organizational level.

After understanding the platform team structure and the governance model needed for the smooth functioning of the platform, let's look at the platform ways of working.

Platform Ways of Working

Platform ways of working means that people and teams at all levels in the organization use their skills, knowledge, and resources efficiently to create value for the entire platform ecosystem irrespective of their roles or designations. I like to classify the ways of working framework into three elements: culture, skills and knowledge development, and roles and responsibilities. These elements may not be effective individually, but they can create high-functioning and self-reliant teams that can independently deliver value while working toward a common goal when combined.

Culture

As we saw that a robust and successful operating model requires a value-driven agile culture, and teams that continuously deliver value for their customers. But the customers are different for different teams operating in the platform model. Customers for the experience teams are the end users of the platforms, such as producers, consumers, and intermediaries.

Hence, the experience teams should focus on adding value for users on all sides. At the same time, customers for functional teams are the members of the experience teams. For example, capabilities created by the functional teams are consumed by the members of the experience teams. Similarly, the functional and experience teams are the consumers of the infrastructure teams. Technical capabilities added by the infrastructure teams are used by the functional and the experience teams, and eventually, all the teams are working toward adding value to the entire platform ecosystem.

Apart from this customer-centric mindset that is focused on creating value, platform teams must adopt flexibility and agility. It is important to continuously deliver value, modify, and improve the experience based on customers' direct and indirect feedback and behaviors. Executives and leaders should encourage teams to work in shorter iterations of delivery, gather feedback and change.

Teams should not be afraid of experimenting and failing. Gathering customer feedback and iterating over it should become part of the culture for all the teams. Feedback from the functional and infrastructure teams' customers is equally important as that of the platform end users, such as producers and consumers. Hence, this customer-centric, value-driven culture that is iterative and agile must be adopted by all teams and at all levels.

Skills and knowledge development

Value-driven culture and skill development go hand in hand. To create value for customers that is meaningful in the current time and has a competitive advantage, it is essential that teams are skilled and can work with the latest technologies. Hence, a good operating model should always keep room for the skill development of the team members.

Skill development is necessary even in linear products, but it gets multiplied in the case of platforms because of the multiple entities involved. For example, a payment processing platform has buyers, merchants, and financial institutes as its customers. To create value for all of them, teams must keep up with the latest technology in the financial industry, automation in accounts payable and invoicing, and the latest trends in e-commerce. Hence, the operating model must be designed in such a way that teams can learn new technologies, grow their skills, and apply those skills and knowledge to create value for the customers.

Another aspect of knowledge gathering and skill development that is different for the platforms is that the platform team's structure is modular. It is important that people share knowledge and the latest trends across teams to deliver consistent value. For example, suppose one team is adding capabilities that are aligned with the latest trends and are useful for users, but another team is lagging in catching up with the latest technologies and trends. In that case, it will create an inconsistent experience for users. Hence, teams must keep up with the latest trends and technologies, continuously grow their skills, and share knowledge.

Roles and responsibilities

An effective operating model always assigns clear roles and responsibilities among each team and team member. Teams should work in close collaboration, but there should be a distinction in the roles and responsibilities of each team. For example, the infrastructure team will create the framework for automating the deployment, but the individual teams must own the deployment of each service or channel. Similarly, product managers from each team will provide input for the marketing plan, but the marketing team should own it.

When working on a platform with multiple teams, I have always found the **RACI matrix** is useful when assigning responsibilities. It describes the roles for each team/team member when working on a specific task. It identifies the team that is **responsible**, **accountable**, **consulted**, and **informed** for a particular task. It can be done at the team level, department level, or organization level. You can find more details about the RACI matrix here: `https://www.tacticalprojectmanager.com/raci-chart-explanation-with-example`.

As described in this article, the RACI matrix is most useful when responsibilities overlap and many people are involved. Hence, it is helpful and effective for the platform team structure where multiple teams work toward one end goal by accomplishing different tasks.

To sum up, creating an efficient and powerful operating requires the following:

- Clearly defined roles and responsibilities for the teams

- Opportunities to experiment, learn, and grow skills

- A collaborative culture that focuses on delivering value for the internal and external customers

This brings us to the end of the platform operating model. The key here is to create a team structure that can deliver value with fewer dependencies and a governance model that can help and empower teams. Defining ways of working can help in giving recommendations and guidance to teams and enable fluent functioning.

Now that we have understood what goes into creating a platform operating model that can build efficient teams focused on delivering value, and the governance model that can enable smooth functioning of that operating model, we can apply these learnings to an example. Let's continue with our case study and create an operating model and the governance structure for our platform.

Case study

In the previous chapter, we created the launch plan for our educational content sharing platform, **Escola**. In this chapter, we will create an operating model and the governance structure for our platform.

Escola team structure and governance model

For creating an operating model, we will start by defining the team structures for our platform. Let's recap the capabilities identified during roadmap creation and MVP definition to identify the service/product/frameworks boundaries and create teams around those boundaries:

Functional capabilities

The following are the functional capabilities that we have identified for the Escola platform:

Must	Should	Could	Won't
Create educator	Invite students	Show followed educators	Show recommendations
Create students	Send notification	Add reviews	Connect with students
Search educators	View notification	View reviews	Connect with educators
Follow educators			Create groups
Add videos			Reshare content
Add photos			
Add articles			
Post updates			
View newsfeed			
Add likes			
Add comments			
View likes			
View comments			

The *must, should, could,* and *won't* priorities are with respect to the MVP, which means all the capabilities in the *Must* column are needed for the MVP. Similarly, everything in the *Won't* column is not prioritized for the MVP but will be added later. The preceding capabilities can be grouped in the following service boundaries:

- **Profile**: Create educator and create students

- **Connections**: Search educators, follow educators, invite students, show followed educators, connect with educators, connect with students, and create groups

- **Newsfeed**: Add videos, add photos, add articles, post updates, view newsfeed, add likes, add comments, view likes, view comments, and reshare content

- **Notifications**: Send notifications and view notifications

- **Reviews**: Add reviews and view reviews

- **Recommendations**: Show recommendations

These boundaries are defined with the help of architects and technical leads, based on how they will modularize the architecture. As product managers, we should provide input on the logical grouping of the capabilities based on the user flow and user interactions. For example, all the capabilities related to user creation are under the Profile service.

Similarly, anything concerning posting the content and engaging with it is in the Newsfeed boundary. There could be a few differences in how granular these boundaries are, based on how they are architected. For example, someone might add reviews under Profile, as reviews are for educators.

But always remember that it is crucial to keep the services small with as few responsibilities as possible to keep the architecture scalable and maintainable. Hence, if we go with the services mentioned earlier, then Profile, Connections, and Newsfeed are a must for the MVP. The Notifications service should be added in the MVP, the Reviews service could be added in the MVP, and Recommendations won't be added in the MVP but will be needed later.

But if we add five functional teams for the MVP and keep adding teams as the capabilities and services grow, it won't be efficient and optimal. Hence, we can follow the guidelines where one team can own multiple services, but one service cannot have multiple owners.

Hence, we can assign the Profile, Connections, and Reviews services to one team as the capabilities in these services are all user-related. Then, we can have a second functional team that can own the Newsfeed and Notifications services as these capabilities are adjacent in the user flow. The Recommendations service can be added to one of these teams or a third team, depending on how we scale our teams. Hence, the functional team structure and the service distribution for Escola should look as follows:

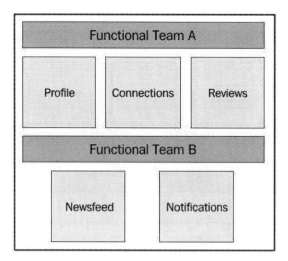

Figure 7.2 – Escola functional teams

The preceding diagram illustrates two teams with ownership of different services for the MVP of the Escola platform. Now, similar to functional teams, let's look at the infrastructure teams based on the technical capabilities.

Technical capabilities

The following are the functional capabilities that we have identified for the Escola platform:

Must	Should	Could	Won't
Authentication	Load balancing		Configuration management
Authorization			
Encryption			
API management			
Provisioning and hosting			
Logging and monitoring			
Analytics			

Like functional capabilities, technical capabilities are also prioritized based on the MVP. These capabilities can be classified into the following groups, based on the reusable components or frameworks that they are providing:

- **Access management and security**: Authorization, Authentication, and Encryption

- **Observability**: Logging and monitoring

- **Frameworks and templates**: API management, Analytics, and Configuration management

- **Environment and automation**: Provisioning and hosting and Load balancing

Similar to service definitions for functional capabilities, this classification should also be done with the help of architects and technical leads. This classification would also vary slightly on how the platform is architected and how technical leads differentiate between these capabilities.

For example, some technical leads might group Authentication and Authorization under Frameworks and Templates as it provides an access management framework. The crucial thing to remember here is the guiding principle, which is that multiple teams should not own one framework. Since the size of these frameworks and templates will be reasonably small initially, we can have one infrastructure team for the MVP that can own these frameworks, templates, or automation tasks. And as we scale, we can divide the teams based on different frameworks and templates.

Like the infrastructure team, we can have one team for the experience/channel as our MVP's scope is the only responsive website that can be accessed on mobile phones and tablets. Our mobile app launches are slated for later releases. Hence, we can add the Android and the iOS teams later as we grow.

The following diagram illustrates the digital team structure for the Escola platform:

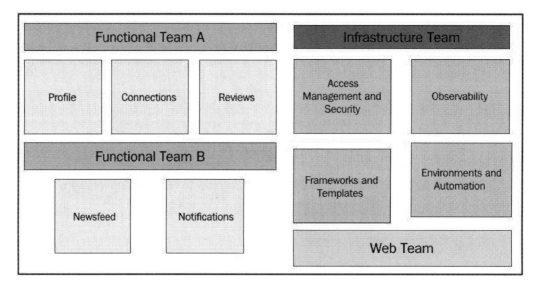

Figure 7.3 – Escola's digital teams

The preceding diagram shows the digital teams for Escola MVP and the services, components, or frameworks they own. Each team should have a product manager and at least two developers. Testers are optional and testing should be the team's responsibility. Developers and product managers should test and assure the quality of what they are delivering. Along with the individual team members, we should have an architect and a product head for the platform. In the starting phase, these roles can be filled by the executives or founders if they have the required skills and background. For example, if one of the founders is from a technical or product background, they should play the architect or head-of-product role respectively.

Apart from the digital teams, two other BizOps teams that are crucial for the Escola platform are marketing and finance. As we saw in *Chapter 6, Launching the Platform*, we need some heavy marketing and buzz creation for our platform. Hence, the marketing team will be a crucial part of the MVP launch and later releases. Similarly, the finance team is needed for budgeting and financial modeling before and after the MVP.

The marketing team should also carry out some of the sales-related tasks. Initially, we don't have any direct sales activities and brand awareness will be the central part of lead generation. We don't need a separate customer support team during the MVP as the support mechanism is email. Our digital team will own issue resolution and support. Dedicated customer support will come in later. Marketing and finance teams will be lean teams with one or two members each and can be scaled as we grow. We should have a head of BizOps, who can overlook marketing and finance. As heads of our digital teams, one of the executives should also take the head of BizOps' responsibilities.

As we discussed, during the initial start-up phase, we should not have a separate governance team, and executives should take up the responsibilities of the governance team. They should play the external-facing role as executives and the internal-facing role as the governance team. And as the platform grows, the number of teams increases, and the business scales, we will have a separate architect, head of product, and head of BizOps representing the governance team.

Here is a diagram of Escola's team structure:

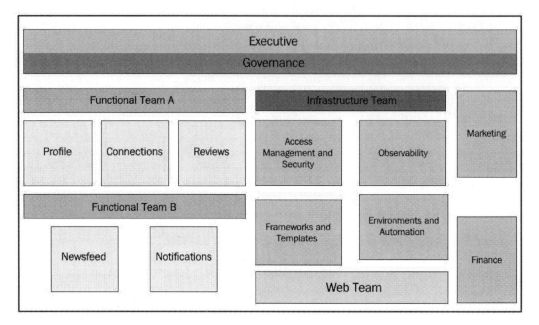

Figure 7.4 – Escola team structure

This diagram illustrates the team structure and the governance model for Escola MVP. Post-MVP, as the platform grows, more functional teams can be added based on the ownership of the services. The infrastructure team can be broken down, and more channel and experience teams can be added with the launch of more channels. Similarly, the BizOps structure is very lean at the start, and as we grow and scale, the BizOps teams can be separated, and new teams can be added based on their responsibilities.

This brings us to the end of the Escola operating model, with team structure and the governance model. The next chapter will explore how to measure the performance of our platform and what the right metrics are that must be tracked for that measurement.

Summary

In this chapter, we understood what an operating model is and the critical components of a strong and robust operating model. We learned that for an operating model to be effective, it must be flexible, able to create a collaborative environment for teams, and focus on creating value. We looked at the difference between the platform operating model and the linear product operating model.

We then dived deeper into each of the components of the operating model from the platform's perspective. We looked at the platform team structure and the different teams within the digital and non-digital space. We learned that the digital team structure should reflect the modular architecture, and each module (framework, service, or channel) must have a single owner. Non-digital teams are mostly business operations teams, such as sales, finance, marketing, and customer support. In the initial phases, when the platform and the overall business size are small, one team can own multiple operations. For example, there is one team for sales and marketing.

We also looked at the governance structure for the platform operating model, which usually consists of a governance team with representation from tech, product, and BizOps. We learned that the governance team is not an authoritative figure but a helping body to guide and enable the teams. The prominent role of the governance team is to define goals for the teams that are aligned to organizational goals, track them, and provide feedback to the teams on improvement.

They also report on the performance of the teams and the overall platform to the executives and leaders. Apart from the platform team structure and the governance structure, we also explored platform ways of working. We discussed that value-driven culture focused on customers is essential at all levels for platforms to be successful as an ecosystem.

In the next chapter, we will learn how to measure the success of a platform. We will look at the different metrics that need to be collected for measuring a platform's performance and how to gather the data for those metrics.

Section 3: Measuring the Performance of the Platform

This section helps you to measure the outcome of the platform business model. Developing something is not beneficial if you cannot measure the result. Hence, the last section of the book will focus on measuring the success or failure of your platform. It will also cover the ongoing prioritization of features for a platform based on the outcome and results. This section comprises the following chapters:

- *Chapter 8, Metrics to Measure the Platform Outcome*
- *Chapter 9, Ongoing Backlog Prioritization*
- *Chapter 10, Moving from Linear Products to Platforms*

8
Metrics to Measure the Platform Outcome

In the previous chapter, we understood that an operating model explains the way and structure in which organizations create value for their customers. We also looked at the various components of the operating model. We learned that the most significant difference between the operating model for a linear product and the platform is the structure that focuses on creating value for one dimension of customers versus the entire ecosystem. We discussed the team structure that is effective for platforms and we also learned about the governance model needed for the smooth functioning of those teams. We also discussed the elements of the **Platform Ways of Working**, including culture, skill development, and roles and responsibilities.

In this chapter, we will understand how to measure the performance of a platform. Here, performance refers to how successful or unsuccessful the platform is as a whole. Also, you will notice that measuring the performance and measuring the outcome of the platform are used interchangeably in this chapter.

We will start this chapter by understanding the different steps involved in measuring the outcome of the platform. We will learn how each characteristic of a platform can be measured. For example, the platform's network effect can be measured by tracking how successful the platform is in creating connections. We will then go deeper into each step of outcome measurement, from the goal definition to the analysis of the results. Hence, we will explore and discuss the following topics:

- Measuring platform outcome
- Defining goals
- Identifying metrics
- Defining targets
- Analyzing results
- Case study

By the end of this chapter, we will understand the importance of tracking goals for each platform characteristic to measure the overall platform performance. We will know the right metrics that must be tracked for different types of platforms, define targets for those metrics, and measure and analyze them.

Measuring platform outcome

Measuring the outcome is crucial for the growth and success of anything built, which is valid for platforms too. Success would be different for each product or platform, and it would also change based on the phase in which your platform finds itself. Hence, measuring the right things that would define the success of your platform is vital.

Measuring the performance starts with defining the success criteria or the goals of your business, identifying the metrics that can track those goals, defining targets for the identified metrics, collecting the data, and finally analyzing and comparing the results against the success criteria. The following diagram demonstrates these steps:

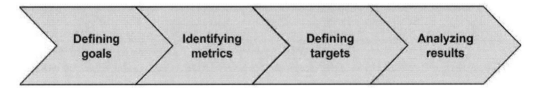

Figure 8.1 – Outcome measurement steps

The preceding diagram illustrates various steps of the performance tracking process. It is an iterative process, as the goals would be different in the different phases of the business. For example, the goals during the start up phase would be completely different from those in the growth and maturity phase. Hence, it is essential to define the goals for a specific time, identify relevant metrics, and track them.

The steps involved in measuring the outcome of the linear product are like that of the platform, but the most significant difference is in the metrics definition step. The metrics that are used for tracking the performance or success of the linear products cannot be applied to platforms because of the nature of the platform business model.

The flow in linear products is one-directional; hence, tracking the metrics at different stages of that flow should suffice. For example, in a standalone retail website, various metrics are tracked throughout the retail funnel, such as visits to the website, website visits to the product searches, product searches to the shopping basket, and finally shopping basket to conversion. But in the case of a platform, these metrics will only provide data on the consumer side, whereas to track the platform's performance, we must track the creation of value on both sides. The platform's success depends on how well it can connect different entities and not how well it can sell. Hence, the metrics should track the ability of a platform to create that connection.

In *Chapter 1, Fundamentals of Platform Business Models*, we looked at three characteristics of a platform business model: multidimensional, network effect, and the plug-and-play mechanism. However, the success of a platform depends on how effective these characteristics are for a given platform. For example, a successful platform will serve the users from all directions. It will create a strong network effect and enable easy plug-and-play for its users. Hence, to track the platform's success, it is essential to measure the success of these characteristics. So, to measure the success of these three aspects of the platform, the metrics that need to be tracked for the platform are broadly classified into the following three categories:

- **Accumulation**: Accumulation here means the accumulation of users on the platform. The plug-and-play characteristic of the platform enables easy onboarding of users. Hence, the success of this characteristic can be measured based on how easy it is for users to join the platform, which can be tracked by the number of users onboarded. People might think that tracking the total number of users is the standard metric for any product.

The difference in the platform business is tracking the number of producers and consumers separately and measuring if they are increasing in the right proportion based on the type of platform. The number of registered users will tell us if the platform enables easy onboarding for all the parties involved in the platform ecosystem and thereby successfully creates a plug-and-play mechanism for all its users.

- **Connection**: The success of the multidimensional characteristics of the platform can be measured by tracking how well it is connecting its producers to consumers and vice versa. Answering the following questions will help us track the connection between producers and consumers: *Are the producers and consumers present on the platform in the right proportion? Can they find each other on the platform?* For example, on a ridesharing platform, *are riders finding the drivers at an acceptable radius of distance?*

If there aren't enough drivers on the platform, riders will have a longer waiting time, and hence, they will not be willing to continue with the ride. Therefore, tracking metrics such as the percentage of riders who did not get the driver, and the maximum and average wait time between the booking and the start of the trip, will help us measure the success of the connection. Also, as connection requires two parties, it is essential to measure its performance from the producer side as well. In the same example of a ridesharing platform, to measure whether drivers are finding the riders, the right metrics that must be tracked would be the drivers' idle time between trips.

- **Interaction**: The next characteristic of the platform that can help measure its success is the network effect. As seen earlier, the stronger the network effect, the more successful the platform is. But the question here is: *how to measure it?*

The network effect can be measured by tracking the successful interaction between producers and consumers. Metrics such as conversion on an e-commerce platform, posts shared and engagement on a post for a social media platform, and messages sent on a communication platform can help us track the successful interactions between producers and consumers. Successfully completed interactions, such as a payment processed or a ride completed, mean revenue for producers. Hence, the higher the number of interactions, the higher the revenue for producers, which thereby attracts more producers to the platform. This will lead to various competitive options for consumers, motivating more of them to use the platform and, therefore, creating a strong network effect.

These factors individually track and measure different aspects and characteristics of the platform, but measuring all three is essential to measure the holistic performance of the platform. The individual success of these metrics will not determine the success of the platform. For example, if the number of rides completed on a ridesharing platform is tracking very high, but if drivers' idle time between trips is also high, it is not beneficial to drivers. Hence, the platform as a whole is not creating value for all its users. This particular trend suggests that there are not enough riders on the platform, and hence optimization is required to increase the number of riders. Accumulation, connection, and interaction are tied to each other. Therefore, they must be tracked and measured in combination to calculate the overall performance of the platform.

Accumulation, connection, and interaction are categories to measure the success of different platform characteristics and the platform as a whole when measured in combination with each other. The exact metrics that must be tracked will be different for different platform types and depend on the platform goals and strategy. And these precise metrics will then fall under one of the categories as we saw in some of the examples, such as tracking the number of producers and consumers onboarded, which falls under accumulation, and the number of completed transactions falls under the interaction category. Let's go through each of the steps of platform outcome measurement and discuss the categories and metrics associated with them for different platforms.

Defining goals

The goals here are the same as the business goals, but broken down into smaller time frames. For example, the goal for the first quarter after the platform's launch could be to have x number of visits; in the second quarter, it could be x number of registered users, and so on. But these goals should be tied to the long-term business goals such as x amount of total revenue, x number of recurring users, or $x\%$ of posts shared. The goals that must be measured would also depend on the phase of the business.

In the start up phase, the goals are used to create awareness, increase the footprint, and grab the market; for example, increasing producer and consumer onboarding, or increasing the number of transactions. In the growth phase, goals are focused on expanding the business, such as increasing the rate of recurring consumers, increasing the longevity of producers on the platform, and increasing the value per transaction. In the maturity phase, the goals revolve around sustainability, such as reducing the consumer and producer onboarding cost and increasing the earnings per transaction.

Part of the goal definition would come from the growth focus of the platform strategy. As seen in *Chapter 4*, *Building a Platform Strategy*, the growth focus of the platform strategy is either on the consumer side or the producer side, or the total user base is increased by focusing equally on both sides. Hence, the goal to measure the success of accumulation should be defined based on the growth focus of the platform strategy.

Defining goals to measure how effectively the platform is connecting its producers and consumers is the trickiest. The goals here should be around the recurrence of consumers, the longevity of active producers, and the engagement of users; for example, buyers, riders, or guests returning to buy, book a ride, or book home accommodation on e-commerce, ridesharing, and vacation home-booking platforms. Their recurrence means they can find and connect to sellers, drivers, and homeowners on the platform. Similarly, if sellers, drivers, and homeowners are actively staying with the platform for long, they can connect and sell through the platform.

The goal to measure interaction is simple. It is the core of the business, for example, increasing the number of transactions on an e-commerce platform or the number of videos shared on a content-sharing platform. The specifics of the goal would differ based on the stage, for example, the number of transactions, the value per transaction, the profit per transaction, or the ratio of completion of the transaction to the earlier step, but it would revolve around the completion of the interaction that is the platform's core offering.

In abstraction, the goals to measure the platform's performance must be defined based on the growth focus of the platform, the enablement of the core offering of the platform, and the completion of the core offering. To measure each goal, it is essential to define metrics for each of them to be tracked. Each goal might have multiple corresponding metrics, and, in some cases, there would be one-to-one mapping between the goal and metrics.

For example, if the goal is to reach a certain number of active users, then the corresponding metrics will involve tracking the number of active users, whereas if the goal is to increase the ratio of producers and consumers by a certain percentage, then the corresponding metrics would be the total number of producers, the total number of consumers, their ratio, and the increase in the ratio from the previous period (month/ quarter). Let's now go deeper and understand how to define and track corresponding metrics to measure the goals of different platform types.

Identifying metrics

After defining the goals, we need a way to track those goals, which is when the metrics come in. Each goal should have metrics tied to it so that it can be tracked and measured. Different types of platforms should track different metrics in various phases of their life cycles. The following are some of the metrics that are applicable to different platform types:

- **Producers and consumers**: The number of active producers and consumers broken down by day and month is the essential metric that must be tracked for any platform during the start up phase. The total number of users is a more appropriate metric for platforms such as social media or information sharing, where producers and consumers are the same.

  For marketplace and service-oriented platforms such as Amazon, Uber, and Airbnb, it is essential to track the producer to consumer ratio. These metrics are useful for the start up phase and will help measure the platform's accumulation goals. Total active users can be broken down into daily and monthly active users to track the growth trend. In the growth phase, accumulation metrics must be tracked in terms of the growth percentage every month or every quarter. In the maturity phase, similar metrics should be tracked with the focus of building loyalty and creating longevity of users on the platform; for example, daily recurring consumers and average active time (month/year) of producers on the platform.

  Another important metric to track with respect to users (producers and consumers) would be the churn rate. The **churn rate** can help us track the number of users who stopped using the platform. This metric is crucial for the platform with a subscription model. It will enable us to know how many users are unsubscribing from the platform and after what period.

- **Search-to-cart ratio**: The search-to-booking ratio is a key metric for measuring the connection between producers and consumers on service-oriented and marketplace platforms. This metric is measured by tracking how many consumers proceeded to the next phase of the booking after the search, such as the product or service offering added to the cart.

  Consumers proceeding to the next phase is an indicator that they found what they were looking for. If this metric is tracking low, it means either the number of producers is limited, or the product and service on the platform do not match consumer needs. In either case, the downward trend of this metric indicates that the platform cannot create a connection between producers and consumers. Hence, tracking the search-to-cart ratio is crucial for marketplace and service-oriented platforms.

- **Producer idle time**: To attract more producers to service-oriented platforms including Uber, Airbnb, and DoorDash, it is essential to track and reduce the idle time of existing producers. This is a critical metric to track the connection goal for the service platforms. Producer idle time indicates that there aren't enough consumers to utilize the services offered by producers, such as rides, home rentals, and deliveries. This particular metric is specific to platforms and optimizing this metric is crucial for the platform's success.

  The idle time is usually calculated as a percentage of the time spent outside of the trip while signed into the app, and it is averaged out for the day and the drivers for every city. Calculating the average for the day and the drivers helps in factoring the peak and non-peak hours and any outliers, such as drivers signing in for 12 hours. It is also advisable to refer to the trend of this metric as the numbers would differ exponentially based on the day of the week and the hour of the day.

- **Average connection per user**: To measure the connection-specific goals for social media and information-sharing platforms such as Facebook, LinkedIn, Twitter, Quora, and Reddit, the suitable metric for tracking is the average number of connections or followers per user. Most of these platforms do not have separate producers and consumers. Users join these platforms to grow their network and follow each other to share and learn. Hence, one of the key aspects of the success of these platforms is how well each user has built their network. Therefore, tracking the average number of connections per user will enable the connection goals of such platforms to be measured.

- **Number of transactions**: Measuring the number of successfully completed transactions is one of the core metrics for marketplace and service-oriented platforms, as well as payment processing platforms. Completing a transaction such as ride booking, a processed payment, or a sale is central to these platforms; hence, tracking the number of transactions is one of the key metrics for measuring the success of the interaction goals. The specifics, such as the number of transactions per day, the month-on-month increase in the number of transactions, or the growth percentage over a period of time, should be decided based on the phase of the business. Another variation of this metric, which is important to track, is the average number of transactions per producer. This will help us measure if the number of transactions is increasing in the same proportion as the producers and whether the platform is adding value for its producers.

- **Transaction value**: Similar to the number of transactions, the average value per transaction is tracked for marketplace and service-oriented platforms, as well as payment processing platforms. The difference between the previous metric and this one is that measuring the number of transactions is appropriate for the platforms where the earning is a fixed value per transaction, whereas tracking the average value of the transaction is more appropriate when the earning is the percentage of the transaction value. Like the number of transactions, the average value of a transaction must also be tracked per producer. It will help to measure and optimize the value generated for the producers.

- **Content creation**: The amount of content created on social media, information sharing, content, and entertainment platforms such as Facebook, YouTube, Spotify, and Yelp is one of the crucial metrics for measuring the interaction goal. For example, the number of posts shared, videos uploaded, songs uploaded, or reviews added are essential metrics to track. Similar to other metrics, this metric should also be altered based on the phase of the platform; for example, the total number in the initial phase and the percentage increase in the growth phase.

- **Content consumptions and engagement**: For end-to-end measuring of the interaction goals of social media, information sharing, content, and entertainment platforms, it is important to track the consumption of content along with its creation. Metrics such as the hours of video consumption, the number of views on the posts, the number of downloads of a song, and engagement, such as comments, reshare, or likes on the content, are key metrics to track for measuring the performance of these platforms. Tracking content creation indicates that users are using the platform as producers, but content consumption indicates that they are also using it as consumers, thereby creating a network effect on the platform and improving its overall performance.

- **Development platform metrics**: The success of development platforms such as Apple's App Store or the Google Play Store can be measured by tracking the number of apps developed, the number of apps downloaded, and the ratio of the two. Some other variations of these metrics that must be tracked at different stages are the ratio of developers to apps developed, the percent increase in the number of apps, and so on.

Apart from the operating systems, the platform that exposes their data and capabilities via APIs for integration with other systems is also classified under the development platforms. The right metrics to measure the performance of such platforms are API adoption rate (number of unique consuming systems), daily requests, requests per minute, and API retention rate. Most of these APIs serve internal and external consumers simultaneously. It is important to track the total number of consumers, but the breakup between internal and external consumption must also be tracked so that the adoption can be optimized accordingly if either of them is trending down.

- **Infrastructure platform metrics**: Infrastructure platforms provide hardware and computing resources to organizations. The appropriate metrics for tracking the performance of the infrastructure platforms are the number of consumers, the total utilization of each resource, the average utilization of each resource per consumer, the cost of each resource per consumer, the average time to onboard a consumer on a particular service, and so on. Tracking these metrics enables the measurement of the adoption of the services and the resources provided by the infrastructure platforms; for example, how many consumers are opting for cloud storage services, what is their storage utilization, and the cost of that storage.

- **Revenue metrics**: Apart from all the aforementioned metrics, some revenue-specific metrics must be tracked to measure the revenue targets and profitability of the platform. Some of the key revenue metrics are total revenue, the month-on-month increase in revenue, the revenue-to-earnings ratio, the percentage growth in earnings, and so on.

Some of the revenue-related metrics are specific to the revenue model; for example, the number of subscribed users, earnings per subscription, total advertising revenue, and the revenue per advertised listing. When to start tracking these metrics will depend on the business and platform strategy. For example, tracking these metrics is not critical in the initial few months if the focus is to create brand awareness and build the user base without starting any specific revenue stream.

All the metrics that track the number of producers or consumers, any increase or decrease in their numbers, and so on correspond to accumulation-related goals. Everything that can track the link and relationship between the producer and consumer, such as the search-to-cart ratio and the average connection per user, helps in measuring connection goals. And finally, metrics that track the completion of actions and communication, such as the number of transactions, transaction value, and content creation, correspond to interaction goals. All these metrics can be modified and tracked in different variations based on the specific needs of the business.

Also, remember that tracking everything is not necessary; you should select metrics based on the business objectives, the type of the platform, platform strategy, and the phase of the business. But make sure you select at least one metric from each category of accumulation, connection, and interaction to measure the holistic performance of the platform.

Defining the metrics alone cannot help in measuring the goals. Each metric must have a target that it should be measured against. These metrics' targets are the breakdown of the goals. Let's go deeper into understanding how that can be achieved.

Defining targets

After defining the metrics, it is important to assign targets to each metric so that they can be measured against those targets. Defining targets for any metrics is a two-step process, let's look at those steps in detail:

1. **Determining the end result**: First, start by defining the desired result for the platform. Here, the desired result could be a mid-to-long-term business outcome, for example, reaching the break-even point in 3 years or achieving 10% gross profit by the end of year 2. Once we know the outcome we want to reach, identify the associated metrics, such as X number of consumers in 3 years with an average Y number of transactions each year, with a Z amount of value per transaction. To serve the X number of consumers, we should onboard the $\frac{X}{P}$ number of producers. Ascertaining the associated metrics also helps us define the desired results of each metric, such as in this example, X number of consumers and $\frac{X}{P}$ number of producers in 3 years.

2. **Working backward**: Once the desired result for each metric is identified, work backward from that result to calculate the short-term goals. For example, X number of consumers in three years means $\frac{X}{3}$ in 1 year and $\frac{(X/3)}{12}$ every month. But the catch here is that the increase in the number of users will not, and should not, be the same month on month.

   Hence, plan for a specific growth rate in the number of consumers each month. For example, if we have to onboard 12,000 consumers in the first year, do not simply target 1,000 consumers each month, but target 600 users in the first month, with 10% growth every month, which will give 660 users in month two, 726 users in month three, and so on, with a total slightly over 12,000 in 12 months. This will require doing some math, but will give us more realistic targets for our metrics.

Another critical aspect to note here is that the target for the growth rate would increase as the platform grows. So, keeping the same growth rate for all 3 years might not be sustainable; hence, the target must be set for a relatively shorter timeframe, such as 6 months or a year, and then re-evaluated and reassigned. Also, as mentioned earlier, the goals are different in different phases of the business, and these differences would impact the target calculations.

For example, the goal for a start-up would be to increase the number of users, but for a mature business, it would be to reduce the user onboarding cost. Hence, the target for calculating the number of users to be onboarded would be different in both scenarios, such as onboarding X number of users daily to achieve the monthly goal, versus onboarding Y number of users to bring down the per-user cost of onboarding.

After defining the monthly or even weekly targets for all the metrics, start tracking them. In *Chapter 6*, *Launching the Platform*, we discussed the fact that, as part of the pre-launch activities, we should identify the key metrics and KPIs for the platform; these are the metrics that must be added to that list for tracking. And post platform launch, we should ensure that all these metrics are getting tracked appropriately and the data is being collected.

Analyzing results

After collecting the data for all the metrics, we should analyze the results. Analysis of these results mainly involves comparing the actual result with the expected target. The outcome must be examined for each metric individually and frequently. Initially, the trends must be observed daily and thoroughly analyzed weekly. Product managers should do this analysis with support from others, such as technical leads and customer support.

Analyzing the deviation in the result and finding the root cause is an essential part of this step. Sometimes, the root cause of the variation could be straightforward, for example, the number of new consumers was low in a particular week because many people were on holiday due to extended weekends. But sometimes, it can be complex and tricky.

For example, the number of transactions at a particular time on a certain day went down significantly due to latency in response from a major credit card provider. This might not be very quickly identifiable, and it would take collaboration between different teams, the monitoring of logs, the reviewing of customer queries, and so on to arrive at the conclusion of the latency at the credit card provider. These events skew the data; hence, it is crucial to analyze the trend (weekly/daily) and remove these outliers from the final analysis. The outliers could be impacting the data positively or negatively, for example, a strike in the public transport sector may result in a surge in demand for ridesharing services, but that increase in demand would be temporary and should be excluded from the average calculation.

The analysis report must be shared and presented to all the stakeholders and executives along with the proposed action items to optimize the metrics that are trending downward. Each action item must be discussed, brainstormed, and added to their respective plans. For example, if the action item is to increase marketing via email, this task or activity must be added to the marketing plan. Similarly, if the action item is to simplify the onboarding by removing a step in the flow, then changes to the feature must be added to the backlog. Let us apply our understanding about defining the metrics and measuring the performance of the platform to an example and continue with our case study.

Case study

To track the metrics for measuring the performance of our educational content-sharing platform, Escola, we will start by defining the short to the mid-term goal that we want to measure. Then, we will identify all the metrics required to measure that goal. And finally, we will explain the target for all the specified metrics. But before that, let's recap a few things that we had identified and discussed in relation to our platform:

- **Business strategy**: We need to target uncharted producers and consumers by increasing the total user base.

- **Growth strategy focus**: We should focus on both the student and educator sides.

- **Onboarding strategy**: We should offer special incentives and prices for educators to join and share content on the Escola platform. We should also run heavy marketing campaigns on campuses for students to join Escola.

- **Onboarding plan target**: This means an aggressive growth and increase in the user base. The targeted increase in the number of users every month is 30 to 40%.

- **Pricing and revenue strategy**: We'll have no revenue stream for the first year; our focus will only be on capturing the market. The platform will start with an advertising model in the second year. The projected starting revenue is 25% of the platform development and operating cost of the first year, with a 10% growth in revenue every month.

- **Revenue target**: We'll need to break even in 3 years (based on initial revenue projections).

Defining goals for Escola

As our business strategy is to increase the total user base, we should define our measurable medium-term goal around creating a user base. And because the focus of our growth strategy is on both sides, we should aim at increasing both educators and consumers simultaneously. Based on the initial research and competitor analysis, we defined a target growth figure of a 30 to 40% increase in the number of users every month.

This growth projection was based on the initial growth rate of some of the established social media platforms, which was 50% to 70%. So, let's go with the same goal of a 30% to 40% increase in users every month. Since we are just starting, we do not have a baseline to base our growth percentage on, so we should define the target for the first few months in the actual numbers.

Additionally, our revenue strategy suggests focusing on increasing the user base for the first year so that we can attract potential advertisers when we have a significant number of users on the platform. But the number of users alone does not define the platform's usage to attract advertisers in the future. Users must be actively using the platform. Hence, we should target active users instead of just the total number of users. Our goal for the first 6 months that we want to measure for our platform should be to increase the number of active educators and students. We will discuss calculating the actual target numbers for the first few months in a later section of the case study.

Identifying metrics to measure goals for Escola

Now that we have identified the goal for the first 6 months of our platform, the next step is to identify all the metrics that we should track to measure our identified goal. As our goal is to increase the number of active educators and students on the platform, which falls under the accumulation category, our highest priority should be to track the following accumulation metrics:

- Total number of educators
- Total number of students

- Monthly active educators

- Monthly active students

- The monthly increase in the number of educators (as a percentage)

- The monthly increase in the number of students (as a percentage)

- The ratio between active educators and students

Although our goal is toward accumulation, we cannot improve accumulation in isolation from connection and interaction. Unless students are not following educators and educators are not sharing content, the platform creates no value. Existing users must benefit and stay on the platform to attract new educators and students to the platform. Hence, it is essential that they connect with one another, share content, consume it, and engage on the platform. Therefore, along with the accumulation metrics, we should also be tracking the connection and interaction metrics that would enhance the platform's overall value, thereby leading to more accumulation.

The following are some of the valuable connection metrics that we must track:

- The average number of followers per educator

- The average number of educators each student follows

These metrics will enable us to find the trend in the connection between our users and help us optimize it. Like connection metrics, we should also track the following interaction metrics to measure overall platform performance:

- The average number of posts shared by educators

- Average engagement per post

These interaction metrics will help us understand the overall value that the platform is creating for its existing users and how to improve them to attract new users to the platform.

Now that we know what metrics we want to track for measuring the platform's performance, we should assign the targets for these metrics.

Defining targets for the metrics

As we had identified in previous chapters and did a recap of at the start of this section, our revenue target is to break even in 3 years. And to achieve this revenue target, our projection was a starting revenue of 25% of the platform development and operating costs in the first year with 10% growth. Hence, achieving 25% of the first year's costs in advertising revenue is our short-term result. We should work backward from this end result to define the target for different metrics.

Advertisers pay based on the daily and monthly active users on the platform and some of the well-established social media platforms charge somewhere between $6 and $9 per 1,000 active users. Hence, we can assume that we can charge somewhere around $4 per 1,000 active users. You can find more details about current advertising charges with different platforms in this blog: `https://www.topdraw.com/insights/is-online-advertising-expensive/`.

Based on our revenue target and the cost that our advertisers will pay for every 1,000 active users, we can calculate the number of active users we want to achieve in the first year and arrive at the monthly growth rate for that year.

For the connection and interaction metrics for the first few months, we should create a baseline from the tracked data and then set the target to improve the numbers on those metrics every month by a certain percentage. The percentage should be decided based on the platform's performance and overall tracking of our goals; for example, how we are tracking our total number of target users.

Please remember, defining these metrics and their targets is not a one-time activity. All the metrics will be continuously monitored, and the targets will be adjusted based on the progress and other factors that might impact our business.

Now that we have discussed essential metrics for our platform, we will cover the metrics-driven, ongoing backlog prioritization of features and capabilities for our platform in the next chapter.

Summary

In this chapter, we learned that, like everything else, measuring the outcome of a platform is crucial to determine its performance. To know whether the platform is successful, we must know how the platform is performing for each of its characteristics: being multi-dimensional, creating network effects, and enabling easy plug-and-play. To measure these characteristics, we should track how easily the platform is accumulating its users, how good it is in connecting its producers and consumers, and how well it enables interaction between them. Tracking the goals concerning accumulation, connection, and interaction will help measure the platform's holistic performance.

We explored different steps required to measure the outcome of the platform. While discussing these steps, we looked at various metrics that must be tracked for different types of platforms under accumulation, connection, and interaction categories. Most of the goals and metrics that fall under the accumulation category are defined based on the growth focus of the platform strategy. Connection- and interaction-related goals and metrics mostly depend on the type of platform and the phase of the business.

We also looked at the two-step process of defining targets for metrics. Finally, we discussed analyzing the results and the next steps after measuring the outcome.

In the next chapter, we will understand the ongoing backlog prioritization for the platform. We will explore various techniques of prioritization. We will look at some of the differences between prioritization for linear products versus platforms. We will also discuss the common mistakes to avoid while prioritizing.

9
Ongoing Backlog Prioritization

In the previous chapter, we explored how to measure the performance of the platform. We understood how each characteristic of the platform business could be tracked using different metrics to determine the overall success of the platform. We also discussed different steps involved in the outcome measurement process of any product and how each of those steps is different for platforms. The biggest differentiator is the metrics that we collect and analyze for linear products cannot be applied to measure the platform's performance. The success of the platform depends on connecting its producers with consumers and creating a network effect. Hence, all the metrics are aimed at measuring the network effect.

In this chapter, we will understand how to prioritize the features and capabilities of the platform. We will explore metrics-driven prioritization and understand how to utilize the data from the metrics discussed in the last chapter. We will apply metrics-driven prioritization to an example using a simple framework. As platform backlog prioritization requires a different approach and thinking because of the nature of platform business, this different approach entails certain challenges. These challenges also lead to some mistakes that product managers make during the prioritization process. To uncover all these details, we will discuss the following topics in this chapter:

- What is platform backlog prioritization?
- Metrics-driven prioritization
- Prioritization framework
- Challenges of platform backlog prioritization
- Mistakes to avoid during platform backlog prioritization

By the end of this chapter, we will know the difference between linear product and platform backlog prioritization to apply different techniques and approaches to manage the platform backlog. We will also learn the essential aspects or factors that product managers should be familiar with for effective platform backlog prioritization.

What is platform backlog prioritization?

Even before a product is launched, it has a significant backlog of features. There is a list of features and functionalities that we want to add to the product. This list is usually created from user research, competitive analysis, product managers' experience, and so on. A minimum set of features is selected from this list to launch a viable product, which becomes our **Minimum Viable Product** (**MVP**).

The rest of the features are added to the backlog. Over time, there is the continuous addition of features to the backlog from user feedback, product analytics, market research, business needs, and so on. The challenge that every product manager faces is prioritizing that backlog and developing features that bring maximum benefit.

There are several frameworks and techniques available that product managers use to prioritize their backlog based on their business and organizational needs. There are also some guiding principles that product managers follow when prioritizing the backlog, including user-first thinking and value versus effort. These techniques and directions have been tested and used by millions of products.

However, these techniques that have proven successful for linear products cannot be applied to the platforms as-is. For example, if applying user-first thinking, a platform has users on multiple sides, so which side gets priority? *Or, when we want to use the value versus effort technique, are we creating value for consumers, producers, or platform owners?* Therefore, to prioritize the platform backlog, product managers must think differently and apply different methods.

Let's discuss in detail the difference between the prioritization of linear products and platforms.

Difference between linear product and platform prioritization

As we have seen multiple times, the multi-dimensional nature of platform business makes its execution very different from linear products. And this fundamental variance applies to backlog prioritization as well. The following are some of the differences that elaborate the distinction between the backlog prioritization for a one-dimensional user flow versus an ecosystem:

- **Moving away from the funnel**: In the previous chapter, regarding metrics for measuring the platform, we saw that linear products have a single flow, and the metrics are collected to track the performance across that flow. Similarly, the prioritization of features for linear products is based on optimizing that one-directional flow, usually referred to as a **funnel**.

  In the platform world, user actions do not flow in a single predetermined flow. Hence, we cannot prioritize the enhancements or optimizations around that unidirectional flow. For prioritizing the improvements and selecting features for enhancing the platform experience, product managers should move away from the funnel thinking and treat the platform as a mesh. Platforms should optimize with a view to creating connections and facilitating exchanges between producers and consumers.

  Capabilities and features that improve the platform network effect or strengthen the mesh must be prioritized over improving the flow for a single user or optimizing the funnel.

- **Creating an equilibrium of experience**: Moving away from funnel optimization will lead us to create enhancements for users on all sides of the platform. But the challenge here is to strike a balance. An enhancement for one side should not become an obstacle for the other side. For example, improving the delivery experience for buyers should not increase the logistical operations for sellers on the e-commerce platform. Similarly, enhancing the product merchandising flow for sellers should not negatively impact the product search for buyers. As linear products have users on one side, their feature prioritization doesn't face this challenge.

  The two examples given here apply to a standalone retail website as well, but as there is only one seller, the impact of the logistical changes or having an average flow for adding merchandise is not very high. And these challenges and risks can be mitigated by training and other internal process changes. However, in a platform where the number of sellers is enormous, the impact of these challenges is intense and cannot be easily mitigated. Additionally, there is a risk of losing sellers from the platform if they cannot get an efficient and beneficial experience. Hence, while prioritizing the capabilities for a platform, it is crucial to create an experience that is equally optimized for both sides.

- **Dependency management**: Dependency management for the platform prioritization is at a broader level than dependency management for linear products. It is at the initiative level. And it involves managing conflicting priorities and resolving dependencies for capabilities directed toward users on different sides of the platform. This also ties back to the point of creating an equilibrium of experience.

  For example, if adding a new capability for producers requires changes to the consumer experience, then product managers should first understand the impact on the consumer side. Suppose it is positive and will improve the consumer experience. In that case, the changes for both the users must be planned and sequenced so that it does not create a spiral of dependencies but incrementally enhances both the producer and consumer user experience.

  Similar dependency management exists for linear products, but it is at a very tactical level, and the scale and magnitude are not as significant as platforms. Different types of users, smaller cross-functional teams, and one initiative spreading across various capabilities teams bring the platform's dependency management at a more strategic level and earlier in the process than linear products.

- **No internal customer**: Most linear products have one user role that is an external customer and others are treated as internal customers. For example, for a standalone hotel booking website, guests are external customers, and hotel staff, content managers, and so on are internal customers. Traditionally, to develop new features or enhance the experience, external customers were always given priority over internal customers. Some linear products did not even create the experience for internal customers and focused solely on end users or external customers.

  But that is not the case with platforms. The traditional internal customers are all external users on the platform because of its multi-dimensional nature. Producers, consumers, and intermediaries are all end users, and we cannot compromise on experience for any of them. Hence, the capabilities cannot be prioritized simply based on internal versus external users but must be decided on the needs of the business and which user type requires more optimization.

One additional thing to remember here is that even the capabilities developed to cater to the internal team must not be treated differently from those developed for end users. We have discussed this in *Chapter 7, Creating a Platform Operating Model,* that customers for capabilities teams are the developers from the experience teams, and for infrastructure teams, it is developers from capabilities and experience teams. Although these may be internal teams initially but as the platform scales, these capabilities will be exposed to external partners and other users.

Therefore, treating them differently will hinder future growth potential. AWS is a classic example in this category, where the infrastructure platform was initially developed for Amazon but later exposed to external users. Similarly, Google, Uber, Netflix, and several other platforms have APIs that were initially developed for internal consumption but were later exposed to the outside world. Therefore, it is essential to treat every customer as an external customer and build features and capabilities that can cater to any user at any time.

Understanding these differences in backlog prioritization for linear products and platforms is crucial for effectively managing the platform backlog. Treating platform backlog the same as the linear products is a fundamental mistake that most platform managers make, which obstructs the growth and sustainability of platforms in the long run. Apart from understanding these differences, there are some essential factors that product managers should be aware of for the efficient management of their platform backlog.

Let's look at those factors in detail.

Factors to know before platform backlog prioritization

Every product manager should know the ins and outs of their business, for example, the exact type of users they are catering to, their product offering, or their pricing stream. Platforms are no different, but knowing the answers to these questions is not straightforward. For example, a ridesharing platform is not offering rides but enabling riders to find and connect with drivers.

The following are the factors that product managers should know precisely in terms of managing and prioritizing their backlog effectively:

- **Know your ecosystem**: As we have discussed multiple times, that platform does not cater to one user role or user type; it serves numerous customer types and creates a platform ecosystem. Hence, to prioritize features and capabilities for a platform, it is critical to understand who is part of the platform ecosystem. It is not just producers, consumers, and intermediaries but also partners and affiliates in some cases, internal developers, developers from external partners, and so on.

  For example, in a B2B payment processing platform, buyers, merchants, banks, credit card processors (Master and Visa), ERP partners, developers from internal teams, and external partners will form the platform ecosystem. Therefore, the capabilities and features must be developed in a way that is beneficial for all the parties involved. Hence, product managers need to understand the different participants of their platform and what role each one plays so that they can prioritize capabilities to enhance the experience of all the user types and improve the platform's entire ecosystem.

- **Know your product/service**: For product managers to prioritize capabilities, it is essential to know the product or service they are offering. But it is tricky in the case of platforms to understand what your platform is offering. For example, the marketplace platform is not selling products but providing an avenue for sellers to showcase their products and offering buyers the service to easily search between various products by multiple vendors.

  Similarly, social media platforms offer people the opportunity to connect and build a network. Hence, the prioritization of capabilities should focus on, and revolve around, the core service your platform is offering. For example, recommending products based on the user's browsing or shopping history leads to the easy searching of products for buyers and friends; suggestions on social media improve network building. These features offer unique capabilities to users, but they are ultimately improving the core offering of the platform.

- **Know your price**: Nothing is free in this world. Every business is expecting something in return from its users. For example, platforms such as Facebook and YouTube provide content in exchange for users' time and attention. And they are trading this time and attention with advertisers to generate revenue. Hence, these platforms are constantly trying to keep users engaged on the platform. Their features are primarily aimed at users spending more and more time on the platform.

  Every business wants to increase their revenue and maximize profits; hence, they build capabilities and features that can help them do that. The same must be valid for platforms, but the difference here is understanding what your users are paying and prioritizing features according to that price is not straightforward. Platform product managers must understand the price their users are paying for using the platform, which is not the cost of goods or services. The cost of goods goes to producers. But by using the platforms, both producers and consumers are paying something extra.

  For example, when users use services offered by platforms such as Uber or Airbnb, they trust these platforms. Otherwise, who would imagine renting their homes to total strangers, staying in a room of strangers, even sharing a cab ride with other people, or giving a lift to a hitchhiker. There were some exceptions where people were using similar services, but platforms brought it to the mainstream. Now, services such as Uber and Airbnb are the norm.

  When users are using these services, they trust these platforms, which is the price they are paying for using the platform. Hence, it is the platform's responsibility to build features and capabilities such as reviews and ratings on both sides to strengthen producers' and consumers' trust. As more and more users trust the platform, the usage of the platform increases, thereby leading to more revenue for producers and the platforms.

- **Know your sustainability model**: One of the reasons for prioritizing the right features at the right time is the growth and long-term sustainability of the business, and the sustainability of any business depends on its recurring consumers repeatedly buying or using the products or services. But for the platform, sustainability depends on creating a strong network effect that requires the usage of platforms by both producers and consumers.

Hence, the longevity of producers is as important as the loyalty of consumers for the growth and long-term sustainability of platforms. Before prioritizing capabilities for growth and a sustainable platform, product managers must understand the sustainability model of their platform. For example, product managers should know whether their platform needs upfront producer engagement or usage by consumers or proportionally engaging both parties and prioritizing capabilities accordingly. Striking the right balance between use by producers and consumers is essential and that balance should be maintained in the backlog prioritization.

Now that we understand the difference between backlog prioritization for linear products and platforms and we have also seen the aspects that product managers must know for effectively managing platform backlog, we can go deeper in exploring how to prioritize the platform backlog.

Metrics-driven prioritization

One of the critical reasons for collecting metrics and gathering data around trends is to track the performance in different aspects and make any necessary improvements if required. Therefore, the most appropriate and effective prioritization mechanism is prioritizing and implementing capabilities and features based on the metrics. In the previous chapter, regarding metrics for measuring the platform, we discussed the fact that the platform goals and metrics are classified mainly into three categories – accumulation, connection, and interaction.

Hence, if we prioritize features based on the metrics, we must add and prioritize features that would optimize and improve **accumulation**, **connection**, and **interaction**. Some features and capabilities can be added to each of these categories and when they all perform in conjunction with each other, the platform generates value, as depicted in the following diagram:

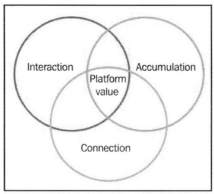

Figure 9.1 – Platform value generation

As illustrated in the diagram, **Platform value** is created when it can accumulate, connect, and enable interaction between its producers and consumers. Hence, each of these categories must perform well individually and in conjunction to generate value. Let's now discuss how to optimize each of these categories and what features and capabilities must be added to improve them.

Accumulation

If the data from our metrics suggests that adding the users is not on track or trending below our expectations, then we should take steps to improve the accumulation of users on the platform. Let's discuss different features and approaches that can be taken to increase producers, consumers, or the total user base when producers and consumers are the same on the platform:

- **Producer**: *So how do we prioritize features and capabilities if our metrics are trending downward in terms of getting producers on the platform or other relevant data shows that we need more producers on the platform?* First, you must understand your producers, their motivation for joining the platform, and their incentives. Once you know this, plan features to incentivize producers, for example, reputation and ranking on information-sharing platforms such as Stack Overflow and Quora.

  There are monetary incentives, such as no commission or fees for a few transactions, but these incentives must go through the cost and benefit analysis and require buy-in from the finance team. But once the decision has been made to offer those incentives, product managers must prioritize features around those offers and promotions. For example, using promotion codes for the first X number of transactions to be commission-free, and so on. Another aspect of getting more producers is simplifying their onboarding process, reducing the number of online and offline steps, and automating the process as much as possible. Once we have the data suggesting an increase needed in the number of producers on the platform, we should analyze why producers do not join the platform.

  Is the joining or onboarding process too complicated and cumbersome, or is there no motivation for producers to join the platform? Answers to these questions should determine which features to prioritize to increase the number of producers on the platform.

- **Consumer**: Like producers, if our metrics suggest increasing the number of consumers on the platform, capabilities to increase consumer participation must be prioritized. Consumers join the platform to consume goods, services, or content; hence, the first step in the analysis process here would be to know whether there is enough content, goods, and service providers on the platform, whether the quality is good, and whether the price is affordable.

  The first aspect of this problem can be solved by onboarding more producers, but if the problem is around price and quality, then we should prioritize capabilities specifically for consumers, addressing these problems. For example, if the data suggests that people are not sure about the quality, ask for reviews and ratings from those who have used the product or service.

  For knowledge- and content-sharing platforms, onboarding influencing and expert producers who can generate quality content and motivate consumers to join the platform can improve the quality of content. If the problem is with the price point, then offers for producers, discounts, promotions, and free trials for consumers must be analyzed for cost and value proportion. Then, features and capabilities must be implemented to offer those promotions accordingly.

- **Producers and consumers**: For platforms where producers and consumers are the same, such as social media or information-sharing platforms, capabilities directed to increase the overall user base would differ slightly. The best or the most tried and tested approach is to integrate with other platforms, letting people share and post from other platforms to your platform and vice versa. This capability helped Instagram build their initial user base when they let people share photos from Instagram on Facebook even before Facebook owned Instagram. This started the trend, and now many websites and platforms allow users to share content on different social media platforms, such as Twitter, Facebook, and LinkedIn. This cross-platform posting and sharing opens your platform to users of other platforms, leading to a more extensive user base. It also motivates them to join and sign up to take full advantage of this cross-platform sharing experience.

Connection

If the user accumulation is on target, but the metrics for the connection are tracking low, then the capabilities to improve the connection between producers and consumers must be prioritized. The following are some of the optimizations for improving the connection:

- **Search, match, and recommendation algorithm**: If we have a decent number of producers and consumers on the platform and they are also present in the right proportion, but cannot connect with or find one another, and metrics such as producer idle time, the average number of connections per user, or the search to cart ratio are trending down, then the capabilities and features that improve the connection between producers and consumers must be prioritized. Improving the search logic for the marketplace, where users can search for and find the right products.

  Enhancing the matching algorithm for service-oriented platforms such as ride-sharing are some of the features that must be enhanced to improve consumers' search and find experiences and boost connection metrics. Refining the search and match logic helps consumers to find the products, services, content, or people that they are looking for, but capabilities such as recommendations and suggestions can further raise the connection on the platform. Features such as recommendations work best for a marketplace where recommending products based on users' preferences, their browsing and shopping history, and current trends can motivate shoppers to check out more products.

  Similarly, suggestions and recommendations are excellent capabilities for improving the connection ratio on social media platforms where platforms can suggest and recommend people to connect based on their mutual connections/friends, common interests, and so on. If the recommendation feature already exists on the platform and still the connection metrics are below target, we should revamp or refine the recommendation algorithm. Too many recommendations can also prove ineffective. Therefore, it is crucial to recommend the right product or person rather than recommending everything or everyone.

- **Privacy and reducing noise**: As we discussed, it is crucial to recommend the right products and people instead of recommending everything, and this point of reducing noise ties in with that. Reducing noise is not just applicable to recommendations, but also when people connect; everyone's privacy must be respected.

When there is too much noise, people tend to ignore and slowly reduce the usage and activity on the platform. Hence, it is important to add features that do not hinder people's privacy and reduce noise. In fact, an intentional effort must be made to ensure that users don't abuse each other's space. LinkedIn, for example, has got this part right: people cannot send connection requests to anyone or send a direct message to non-connections unless they have a premium account.

This minimizes the noise, rather than letting anyone send a connection request or a message to anyone. This restricts the usage by mutual connection or the premium service that only a few people will opt for. Increasing connections on the platform is essential, but not at the expense of users' privacy. If we don't strike a balance here, it could prove counterproductive and encourage people to leave the platform rather than build connections on it. Hence, to improve connections, we, as product managers, should ensure that none of the features are creating unnecessary noise for users or abusing their privacy.

Interaction

We have well-connected producers and consumers in the right proportions present on the platform, yet the overall transactions on the platform are still low, so the focus of our prioritization and feature improvement must be on improving the level of interaction on the platform. The following are some of the approaches that can assist in improving platform interaction:

- **Optimizing overall interaction steps**: Users shy away from using any product if it is too cumbersome to use. Hence, to improve the usage of a product, it is essential to make it easy, in particular, the core transaction of the product must be simple and as short as possible. Imagine if creating a post or sharing content on a social media platform was a 20-step-long process; users would not be interested in creating those posts.

  Therefore, to improve interactions on the platform, it is important to optimize the overall interaction process. Capabilities that reduce users' time and make the process efficient must be prioritized and implemented. For example, getting rid of the sign-up process during transactions, removing the need to add a credit card and address for every purchase, allowing users to browse without logging in, or one-click sharing or similar capabilities that make the interaction faster and easier must be prioritized to increase the number of transactions or the overall level of interaction on the platform.

- **Optimizing the cost of transactions**: This is applicable for marketplaces, service-oriented, or any other payment-based platforms. Reducing the overall transaction cost will benefit producers, consumers, and the platform businesses in the long run. Consumers will not use the platform if the overall price of goods and services increases because of commissions and fees. Similarly, producers will not opt for the platform if they pay a significant amount for every transaction. Hence, optimizing the cost per transaction is crucial to increasing the number of transactions on the platform.

  Therefore, capabilities to automate manual steps and improve process efficiencies to reduce the cost must be added. Similarly, features that reduce costs in exchange for consumer convenience can be added. For example, picking up the food at the restaurant rather than getting it delivered to save delivery fees, or sharing a ride with other passengers rather than going alone to reduce the trip cost, can help reduce transaction costs and the price for consumers.

- **Quality over quantity**: We briefly touched upon this point in accumulation-related features. We discussed improving the quality of content by onboarding experts to generate content or asking existing users to review the product or the service so that others can trust the quality and be motivated to join the platform. Good quality is not just restricted to the people joining the platform, but it encourages them to interact and transact on the platform. Imagine that we got users on the platform by some other means, such as partners or promotions, but they will not interact, meaning they will not consume the content or buy the product if the quality is average.

  Hence, quality is not just needed to get users on the platform, but it is also critical for the purpose of interaction. Therefore, adding features that will inform users of the quality and build trust in the platform and products is necessary to increase interaction on the platform. Capabilities such as ratings for producers or rewarding and giving discounts to the best-rated producers are examples that can ensure the quality of the content, products, or services on the platform.

- **Partners, affiliations, and external platforms**: Using partners and a network of affiliates rapidly augments user connections on the platform. This capability is best suited for payment processing platforms such as PayPal, Stripe, and Marqeta, where they integrate with other platforms and websites that accept payment and need to transfer money.

Integrating with partners and affiliates gives access to the user base of the established brand and guarantees the connection or completion of transactions. The capabilities to connect with and integrate with partners is most appropriate for a B2B payment processing platform where it can integrate with accounting systems, invoicing, and other ERPs. Hence, prioritizing and adding capabilities to integrate with other platforms, partners and affiliates increases the number of transactions on the platform, while increasing the level of interaction overall.

These are approaches and examples of features and capabilities that can be added to the backlog based on the metric results in three categories that help track the goals and measure the performance of the platform. *The bottom line here is to prioritize and focus on the metrics that are tracking low*. However, features or capabilities cannot be purely added or implemented based on the metrics. Metrics will give us a list of potential features and focus areas, but there are a few other factors, such as the cost of development, that must be considered on top of the metrics data while picking up the features for implementation. Let's look at the prioritization mechanism that can help us sequence the capabilities and features of our platform in the right order.

Prioritization framework

Once we have a list of capabilities or features identified based on the metrics results, we can use any prioritization techniques and frameworks, such as the **trade-off slider**, **KANO model**, or **RICE prioritization** to rank and sequence our features and capabilities. You can read more details on the different prioritization techniques in this article: `https://roadmunk.com/guides/product-prioritization-techniques-product-managers/`. I like to follow my own platform backlog prioritization technique, which combines a few methods that already exist.

Let's go deeper and understand the different steps of that technique in detail:

- **Sorting based on metrics**: We have already covered part of this step in the metrics-based prioritization section, where I emphasized adding capabilities to optimize the metrics that are tracking low. So that is the first part of compiling the feature list based on the results of our metrics. Then, sort this list in the order of metrics that are tracking high or doing well and assign a number from 1 to the end of the list. For instance, if we are at or above target in terms of accumulation, then the features that improve accumulation will be at the top of the sort order. This is just a first pass in sorting the feature list. There might be a lot of tie in this step.

For example, two features belonging to the same metric that is trending low would be tied at the same position, or the features belonging to two different metrics that are both tracking low will also be tied at the same place. This is acceptable as we will further categorize and rank all the features and capabilities. Let's look at an example, assuming we have a local business search and review aggregator platform such as Yelp, where we have already launched the MVP and a few more releases post MVP. Our metrics results from initial releases suggest that we are getting users on the platform, but they cannot always find what they are looking for.

They get blank results, and after a few tries with different keywords, they drop. The next concern is that the number of reviews added to the platform is very low compared to our targets. So, the conclusion here is that we have good accumulation, but our connection and interaction are low. We added some features to our backlog based on this analysis and some features were already present in the backlog following initial research and analysis. Assume that we have the following list in the backlog and based on the metrics results, we sorted the list. After sorting this, the feature list would look like this:

Feature	Description	Goal/Metric	Sort order
Social media share	This feature allows users to share reviews and details of local businesses on social media, opening the possibility to more users. This feature helps in the accumulation goal. Because our accumulation metric is trending high, this is on top of the list.	Accumulation	1
Claim or add your business	This feature lets the business owners add or claim their business. It will bring more users (producers) but can also increase the search result options, thereby facilitating accumulation and connection to some extent. Therefore, it is next in order.	Accumulation	2

Side panel advertisement postings	This feature mainly focuses on revenue with a slight improvement in connection if users find the advertisements relevant to what they are searching for. This might help with connection improvements, but not significantly and not immediately. As we want to improve our connection metrics, this feature is after the features associated with improving accumulation.	Connection (less probability)	3
Recommend sponsored listing	This feature is like advertisement postings. The only difference here is that the sponsored listing will be on top of the search results for the specific local business that the user has searched. So, the chances of users selecting these listings (connecting) are a little higher than side panel advertisements. Hence, this comes after the ad posting feature in the sort order.	Connection (less probability)	4
Voice search	This feature will improve connections for people who are more comfortable with voice commands, either because of the tech savviness or physical challenges. This may improve the chances of connection, but the probability is low. Hence, it is sorted at the same level as the recommended sponsored listing.	Connection (less probability)	4
Show featured reviews on the top	This feature increases the level of interaction on the platform. If the review at the top of the list is interesting, more people tend to read it, share it, and engage with it. This feature is in the list after the less likely features to improve connection as we want to improve the level of interaction on the platform.	Interaction	5

Filter search results and reviews	This feature also improves interaction, and if users can filter out the results and eliminate the noise, they are more likely to proceed with the interaction. Hence, this feature is tied to the other similar features that will optimize the interaction metric.	Interaction	5
Nudge to write reviews	This feature would send notifications and reminders to people to write reviews if they had searched for a particular business after asking them if they visited it. This can be combined with some monetary incentives, such as coupons or gift cards, for some extra motivation. This feature improves our interaction goal, hence it is at the same level as other features aimed at interaction.	Interaction	5
Search Engine Optimization (SEO)	This feature improves our ranking on search engines such as Google. Especially if people have searched for a specific local business type, such as *the kids' craft shop near me*, then a link to our results page with shops selling kids' craft items is shown. This feature improves the level of connection and interaction on the platform. Hence, it is last in the list as we want to optimize for these two metrics.	Connection and interaction	6
Search algorithm enhancement	This feature will improve the relevancy and accuracy of search results. This is the most critical need of the hour. It will enhance the connection and lead to better interaction, the two metrics that we want to improve. Hence, it is tied to the SEO feature that leads to a similar outcome.	Connection and interaction	6

The preceding list is sorted in order of the highest trending metrics or the least required feature on the top, with a score of 1, and the most needed feature at the bottom with the highest score.

- **Categorizing impact**: Once we have a sorted list of features and capabilities based on the metrics data, we should categorize them based on the impact. I like to classify impact in three categories – revenue, competitive advantage, and customer convenience. For example, if we add a feature to sort and filter the reviews on a review aggregator platform, it should be categorized as customer convenience.

  Feature to display a sponsored business listing based on the reviews that the user has searched will fall under revenue. A feature such as voice search might fall under competitive advantage. This categorization helps assign the right impact value based on the business priorities and phases of the business. You cannot assign the same impact to these features at different points of your business. Hence, it is important to categorize the impact. Continuing with the example from the first step, this is how the feature list would look after classification in different impact categories:

Feature	Goal/Metric	Impact	Sort order
Social media share	Accumulation	Competitive advantage	1
Claim or add your business	Accumulation	Customer convenience	2
Side panel advertisement postings	Connection (less probability)	Revenue	3
Recommend sponsored listing	Connection (less probability)	Revenue	4
Voice search	Connection (less probability)	Competitive advantage	4
Show featured reviews on top	Interaction	Customer convenience	5
Filter search results and reviews	Interaction	Customer convenience	5
Nudge to write reviews	Interaction	Competitive advantage	5

| Search Engine Optimization | Connection and interaction | Customer convenience | 6 |
| Search algorithm enhancement | Connection and interaction | Customer convenience | 6 |

Please note that some of the features might fit under two categories, such as customer convenience and revenue, or competitive advantage and customer convenience. In such cases, apply your best judgment and categorize it in the bucket that it most resonates with.

- **Assigning impact value and final scoring**: After categorizing the feature list in different buckets of impact, it is time to assign the impact value and score the features. We categorize features with different impacts to assign value based on the needs of the hour. For example, if the business priority is to increase revenue, all the features categorized under revenue will get a higher value.

Let's continue with our example and assume that the highest business priority for our review aggregator platform is to improve customer convenience as we are in the start up phase; competitive advantage is second; and revenue generation is the last priority. Then, we should assign 3 for customer convenience, 2 for competitive advantage, and 1 for revenue generation. These impact values must then be multiplied by the original ranking to calculate the final score. After the final scoring, this is what our feature list would look like:

Feature	Goal/Metric	Impact	Impact value	Sort order	Final score
Social media share	Accumulation	Competitive advantage	2	1	2
Claim or add your business	Accumulation	Customer convenience	3	2	6
Side panel advertisement postings	Connection (less probability)	Revenue	1	3	3
Recommend sponsored listing	Connection (less probability)	Revenue	1	4	4

Voice search	Connection (less probability)	Competitive advantage	2	4	8
Show featured reviews on top	Interaction	Customer convenience	3	5	15
Filter search results and reviews	Interaction	Customer convenience	3	5	15
Nudge to write reviews	Interaction	Competitive advantage	2	5	10
Search Engine Optimization	Connection and interaction	Competitive advantage	2	6	12
Search algorithm enhancement	Connection and interaction	Customer convenience	3	6	18

The feature with the highest final scoring will be at the top of the priority list. This is how the finally prioritized feature list would appear:

Feature	Final score
Search algorithm enhancement	18
Filter search results and reviews	15
Show featured reviews on top	15
Search Engine Optimization	12
Nudge to write reviews	10
Voice search	8
Claim or add your business	6
Recommend sponsored listing	4
Side panel advertisement postings	3
Social media share	2

This method gives you the prioritized list of features and capabilities sorted in order of impact and value based on metrics and business priorities of the hour. You can add this list in the same prioritized order to your backlog or further sort it based on the effort required to develop the features using the value and effort matrix method mentioned in the article.

The value versus effort method will help you in further prioritizing and sorting your features and capabilities based on the effort and complexities. It will also provide you with the cost estimates and the time that each feature will take to be released. These details will aid us in our prioritization decisions.

In the initial phases, I would recommend keeping it simple and prioritizing the features that add maximum value and impact. Also, please note that the feature or capabilities shared as an example did not have any technical capabilities, but there will be a few technical capabilities that would be added to the backlog list from the metrics results and monitoring data, and some would be the effect of adding functional capabilities. Technical features and capabilities must be part of the same list and must be prioritized according to the same criteria as what metrics they are optimizing and what business impact they are creating.

Now that we have understood the platform backlog prioritization approach and technique, let's discuss some of the challenges that product managers face during platform backlog prioritization.

Challenges of platform backlog prioritization

Platform backlog prioritization is tricky and challenging because of the network effect with the web of users interacting with each other. As discussed earlier, user interaction on platforms is not a one-directional funnel, but it is a mesh. And this mesh of interaction brings a few challenges with it when we are planning and prioritizing features or enhancing the experience of our platform. The following are some of the challenges encountered while prioritizing features for the platforms:

- **Striking a balance between connection and noise**: As we discussed earlier, to increase accumulation and connection, we must be careful not to increase the noise and to respect everyone's privacy. Striking this balance is a challenge while prioritizing capabilities that will increase the number of users on the platform and enable them to connect.

We must intentionally plan the features that do not let users invade each other's privacy, as we saw in the LinkedIn example, where users cannot send connection requests to far-off acquaintances. Similarly, some platforms ask users their preference on who should be able to send them connection requests. These features and capabilities are designed to reduce noise and maintain the reliability of the platform.

Reducing noise and considering privacy also applies to the communications and suggestions given from the platform; for example, asking users what kinds of notifications they want to get or reducing the number of promotional emails. Similarly, while recommending products to buy or people to connect with, recommendation engines make suggestions strategically. For example, do not recommend a big piece of furniture like the one the user just bought; no one frequently buys durable items.

Adding capabilities that seem like they will increase the connection metrics is easy, but striking a balance, so it doesn't become detrimental, is difficult. Product managers must make prudent decisions in planning such features.

- **Regulations, checks, and balances**: The concept of the platform works because of its open use policy. For example, anyone can share information, anyone can answer the question, anyone can drive a cab, or anyone can offer their room for rent. This approach of less or no regulations makes platform usage easy and successful, but it comes at a cost.

For example, homeowners on Airbnb don't have to comply with the same regulations as hotels, and Uber drivers don't have to follow the same licensing and badging process as the other cab drivers. Some countries have banned the use of these platforms for these reasons. I am not saying that what Uber and Airbnb are doing is illegal, but because they do not fall under a particular category of business-like hotels or cab services, they don't have to comply with the regional and local laws and regulations applicable to those services. And this brings specific challenges, including safety concerns, consumer protection, human rights violation, and holding businesses accountable.

A similar concern is faced by information-sharing and social media platforms where the authenticity of content is not verified. For example, information added on Wikipedia is not always verified, and in some cases, it is not accurate as it is added by regular users and non-experts. But because of the popularity and universal adoption of the platform, people trust the information shared on it.

The challenge for product managers is to make sure that we are not adding features that exponentially increase this problem and take it beyond our control. In addition, we should ensure that we have some verifications or checks and balances in place to avoid platform misuse and protect every participant's rights and safety without compromising the freedom of the platform.

- **Social responsibility**: If we extend the regulations and compliance point a little further, platforms also face challenges around meeting social and ethical requirements. It isn't easy to control what people share and ensure that everything complies with social and ethical standards. For example, pirated content shared on YouTube, communal hatred spread through Facebook, or spreading disinformation about a product or a person through Quora or Reddit are genuine problems these platforms face. There is nothing illegal about this, but it is unethical and harmful for society.

One video chat platform had to shut down after users turned it into an inappropriate, lewd chatroom. I am sure this was never the platform's intent; freedom to share anything led to this mishap. This is the challenge that the openness of the platforms brings with itself. There is no easy solution to this problem. As product managers, we must be careful not to introduce anything that adds to this existing problem. We can add some process changes and automated verifications that would trigger based on certain keywords or a specific type of image and video files to reduce the spread of this problem.

- **Keeping users engaged**: The success of the platform depends on how strong it is in connecting users and creating the network effects that can happen if users are continuously engaged on the platform. But it becomes a challenge after a while to keep users engaged. This challenge is more significant on some platforms than others.

For example, marketplaces and service-oriented platforms don't face this challenge if there is enough demand and supply in the market. But for knowledge- and information-sharing platforms and social media, it is a considerable challenge to keep users engaged and active on the platform without compromising the quality of the information and the reputation of the platform.

It is not just about encouraging people to connect and share, but also keeping the platform beneficial for all entities. Therefore, product managers must plan for capabilities and features that will keep users engaged and create value for them. This links back to the point I made earlier that product managers should know what motivates their producers and consumers to use the platform. And then, use that motivation factor to enhance their experience. It is challenging to add features and capabilities that will drive user engagement constantly, but it will become slightly more manageable if we know what inspires our users and their incentive to use the platform.

There are more challenges that product managers might face depending on the type of platform, the phase of their business, their experience working with platforms, and so on. These are some of the common ones. Making a conscious effort to resolve these will help product managers in the long run while prioritizing platform backlog.

Mistakes to avoid during platform backlog prioritization

As we looked at some of the challenges that product managers face while prioritizing capabilities for platforms, they also make inevitable mistakes during this process. Most of it is the result or outcome of our approaches that we take for linear products. Because of the multifaceted and multilayered design and nature of platform business, we cannot apply the same methods and techniques for feature prioritization that we use for linear products. And while undertaking prioritization with this new way of thinking, there are some mistakes that we should be mindful about. Let's discuss these in detail:

- **Building Uber for something**: In the last few years, you have probably heard the phrase that *company X is Uber for something*. Following the initial success of Uber, entrepreneurs started believing that if we pick up any service and create a crowdsourced platform for that service, we will have the same success as Uber. The catch here is that not every service is in the same demand as ridesharing or has a similar supply as car owners in the form of drivers. The fact is that even Uber cannot blindly replicate its model for another service. Before creating Uber for any other service, we should know the inner workings of that service, understand its demand and supply mechanism, its revenue and pricing model, its regulatory requirements, and so on. It will need its own research, analysis, and validation.

If we take this concept one level down, we cannot blindly copy capabilities from similar platforms. Product managers get stuck in the trap of competitor parity without adequately analyzing the competition, such as if the competitor is a direct competitor or how a particular feature from the competitor will impact our unique selling point. It is essential to stay on par or, in some cases, ahead of the competition, but do your own research and analysis for adding features and capabilities to your platform.

- **Not focusing on the ecosystem**: As mentioned multiple times in this book, that platform is not serving and catering to one user type or user role, but it has an entire ecosystem that must be considered for any additions or changes to the platform. And this is one common mistake that platform managers make. While deciding the capabilities to add to the experience to enhance, they prioritize the consumer side over everyone else. This happens because traditionally, that's how we are trained and have been operating by creating value for consumers. But in the case of platforms, it is essential to treat every user with the same priority, whether consumers or producers, whether internal or external customers, it doesn't matter. The priority should be to create value for the entire ecosystem.

- **Prioritizing the revenue-generating side**: Another similar mistake that product managers make is to focus on the revenue-generating side. In some cases, it is consumers. In some cases, it is producers; for example, in search platforms such as Zillow that charge the producer side for advertisements in the form of sponsored listings and premium spots. In such cases, where one side is using the platform for free and one side is paying a premium, product managers tend to focus on the revenue-generating side, especially if there is pressure from management to increase revenue. The tricky part to understand here is that the so-called revenue-generating side is paying because the other side uses the platform. Therefore, regarding producers as the revenue-generating side, in this case, is misleading. The actual revenue is coming because consumers are using the platform.

Similarly, if a marketplace platform is charging consumers a convenience fee for every transaction and product managers prioritize consumers over producers, assuming that it is the revenue-generating side, then this is a misconception. As consumers can buy from the platform owing to the existence of producers, it is crucial to prioritize the creation of more substantial network effects rather than enhancing one side, which would seem like a revenue-generating side.

- **Analyzing metrics in isolation**: Another mistake that product managers make along similar lines is analyzing the results of metrics in isolation. Three categories of metrics and goals for the platform – accumulation, connection, and interaction, go hand in hand and must be tracked and analyzed together to measure the platform's performance; for example, if the number of users (producers and consumers) is high on a content-sharing platform and the number of posts or articles created is also on target, but the average number of connections or followers that content creators have is very low. Hence, there is no engagement in the content that is shared. This will slowly reduce the content generation and gradually make the users inactive, making the platform stagnant. In this example, accumulation and transaction metrics were on target initially, but because the connection metrics were low, the overall impact and benefit of the platform were not created. Hence, platform usage started declining. Therefore, to plan and prioritize features and capabilities based on metrics, the metrics for all three categories must be analyzed comprehensively. Otherwise, we may not be able to enhance and improve the impact of the platform.

These are some common and acceptable mistakes that we will make while prioritizing our backlog for the platform, especially if we are new to platform product management. The key here is to be aware of them, understand that these mistakes will happen, and, most importantly, pivot and take corrective action as soon as you realize that you are going in the wrong direction.

This brings us to the end of platform backlog prioritization. Let's now apply these learnings to our case study.

Case study

For the backlog prioritization of our educational content-sharing platform, **Escola**, let's list down the features or capabilities that we had identified prior to the launch but were not added in the MVP:

- Show the educators followed
- Recommendations
- Add and read reviews
- Connect with other students
- Connect with other educators
- Create groups

- Reshare content

- Configuration management (technical capability)

For this backlog prioritization exercise, we will assume that our metrics results suggest we are trending low on getting users on the platform. Interaction on the platform is good, which means educators who are on the platform are actively sharing content, and students are engaging with the content. The ratio between users on the platform and content shared is good. Also, the connection ratio is trending OK. Hence, the metric that we want to optimize by way of priority is accumulation, followed by connection and interaction.

To improve accumulation, we should look at different ways to invite and add students and educators to the platform. Encouraging educators to share more quality content will motivate more students to join the platform, improving the accumulation and interaction metrics. Providing more options for connections, such as not restricting connection to just students and educators, but allowing educators to connect with other educators and students to connect with other students will lead them to invite their friends and colleagues onto the platform. As we are expanding the platform and making it more open for people to connect, we should add some privacy settings and security configurations.

So, let's look at the revised list of features with metric/goal classification and the sort order:

Feature	Goal/Metric	Sort order
Show followed educators	Interaction	1
Reshare content	Interaction	1
Add and read reviews	Interaction	2
Create groups	Connection and interaction	3
Show recommendations	Connection and interaction	4
Connect with other students	Connection	5
Connect with other educators	Connection	5
Ranking content from other educators and showing ranked content on top of the newsfeed	Interaction and accumulation	6

Configuration management	Accumulation	7
Invite students and educators by email	Accumulation	7
Invite students and educators from other social media platforms	Accumulation	7
Privacy settings	Accumulation	7

Features optimizing the accumulation metric are sorted with the highest number as we want to improve the number of users on the platform, followed by connection and interaction.

Now that we have this list of features classified and sorted, the next step is to assign the impact category for each feature. Since we are not focusing on any revenue stream for the first six months and none of our current features apply to the revenue impact, we categorize our list only under competitive advantage and customer convenience. Because we want to increase the number of users on our platform, we should attract them to join and spend time on our platform as opposed to those of our competitors.

Hence, we will give more weight to competitive advantage than customer convenience. Features that will make our platform better than, or close to, the platforms of our competitors are classified as a competitive advantage. Features that are improving the experience of users are classified under customer convenience. As mentioned earlier, there might be features that would fall under both categories of impact; we can categorize such features with an impact with a closer association. After adding the impact category, impact value, and final score, our feature list would be as follows:

Feature	Goal/Metric	Impact	Impact value	Sort order	Final score
Show followed educators	Interaction	Customer convenience	1	1	1
Reshare content	Interaction	Customer convenience	1	1	1
Add and read reviews	Interaction	Competitive advantage	2	2	4
Create groups	Connection and interaction	Competitive advantage	2	3	6

Show recommendations	Connection	Customer convenience	1	5	5
Connect with other students	Connection	Competitive advantage	2	6	12
Connect with other educators	Connection	Competitive advantage	2	6	12
Ranking content from other educators and showing ranked content on top of the newsfeed	Interaction and accumulation	Competitive advantage	2	6	12
Configuration management	Accumulation	Customer convenience	1	7	7
Invite students and educators by email	Accumulation	Competitive advantage	2	7	14
Invite students and educators from other social media platforms	Accumulation	Competitive advantage	2	7	14
Privacy settings	Accumulation	Customer convenience	1	7	7

The prioritized list after the final scoring will be as follows:

Feature	Final score
Invite students and educators by email	14
Invite students and educators from other social media platforms	14
Connect with other students	12
Connect with other educators	12
Ranking content from other educators and showing ranked content on top of the newsfeed	12
Configuration management	7
Privacy settings	7
Create groups	6
Show recommendations	5

Add and read reviews	4
Show followed educators	1
Reshare content	1

This feature list is our prioritized backlog. But before we wrap up this backlog prioritization, a few things to note here are the following:

- **Technical capabilities**: This list doesn't have all the technical features or capabilities required to accomplish all the goals and optimize all the metrics. Product managers should work with the technical lead or the architect to identify those features, and they must be prioritized using the same method along with other features.

- **Spread across different teams**: This list contains end-to-end features that might be developed in more than one team. Capabilities and features within each team must also be prioritized in the same order. For example, if one team is working on adding capabilities for connecting with other students and creating groups, then capabilities related to connecting with other students should be a high priority.

- **Ongoing and frequent activity**: Prioritization of backlog is an ongoing activity. It must be revisited after every milestone or release. Priorities must be updated based on the new metrics results, business priorities, and other external factor changes.

This was the concluding part of this case study. We started with the concept of this platform and covered the different stages of its life cycle, from initial research to measuring performance following the launch, along with its ongoing operations.

Summary

In this chapter, we looked at backlog prioritization and how it is different for platforms compared to linear products. We discussed some of the essential factors that product managers should know about the platform for effectively prioritizing their backlog. For example, *what is the platform's core offering or the price that the platform users are paying for its usage?* Understanding these details can help product managers to identify and prioritize capabilities of the platform that are beneficial for the entire platform's ecosystem.

We learned why metrics-driven prioritization is useful and how to utilize the metric results to identify features. We looked at some example features and capabilities to optimize each category of platform metrics: accumulation, connection, and interaction. We also explored a prioritization framework and understood how it could be applied using a few sample features.

We discussed some challenges that product managers face for platform backlog prioritization because of the open and multi-dimensional nature of the platform. While discussing these challenges, we also looked at some of the mitigation approaches for these challenges. And finally, we discussed common mistakes to look for and avoid during platform backlog prioritization.

So far in this book, we have discussed product management aspects, techniques, approaches, and processes for the platforms that are either starting out as a platform or always were a platform business.

But in the next chapter, we will cover the transformation of linear products to platforms. We will explore the detailed steps and dos and don'ts regarding the effective transformation of linear products to platforms.

10
Moving from Linear Products to Platforms

In the previous chapter, we discussed the ongoing backlog prioritization for features and capabilities in a platform. We understood the difference between backlog prioritization for the linear product and the platform. We also learned about the importance of metrics-driven prioritization and understood how to execute it for a platform.
We discussed a new prioritization framework and its implementation. We also discussed some of the common mistakes and challenges that product managers make and face while prioritizing the platform backlog. In the end, we concluded our case study by creating a prioritization framework for the educational content sharing platform **Escola**.

The previous chapter was the last chapter covering the end-to-end platform life cycle. Throughout this book, we have mainly discussed building and designing a new platform from scratch, but there are so many existing linear businesses that are good candidates to be transitioned into a platform model. Hence, in this chapter, we will focus on the transformation of existing linear businesses to a platform model.

Before you decide to transform your linear business model, it is essential to understand whether your business is suitable for the transition, whether your industry is ready for the change, and whether your business will sustain itself in platform mode. After all the research and validation, when you decide to go ahead with the transition, you should know where to start.

There are some preconditions or factors that you should be aware of, for example, what your core offering is or which user role you should add to the transition from a linear business to a platform model, and so on. Similarly, you should also know the tasks and things that must be accomplished before starting the transition and some of the short- and medium-term impacts. Therefore, we will cover the following topics in this chapter:

- The need for transformation
- Validating the viability of the platform model
- Prerequisites to start the transition
- Starting the transition
- Running a hybrid model
- The platform transition at different layers
- Case study

By the end of this chapter, you will know how to validate whether the platform model is viable for your business. You will also have learned the aspects that you should be aware of before starting the transition and the steps involved in the transition from a linear business model to a platform business model.

The need for transformation

In *Chapter 1, Fundamentals of Platform Business Models*, we covered the benefits of the platform business model in detail, such as the variety of choices and lower prices for consumers, increased revenue and profits for producers, and the distribution of responsibilities for all the parties, hence the division of risk between them. These benefits were also applicable to the non-digital platforms that existed until a few years ago and still exist in some cases. For example, real estate agents who connect home buyers and sellers for a commission or a fee have now moved to the digital world, thanks to platforms such as **Realtor.com**. The platform business model supported by technology has disrupted almost all industries, ranging from retail, travel, and hospitality to entertainment, housing, finance, and so on.

The disruption caused by platform businesses is unavoidable and organizations that do not realize this change find it difficult to compete. While some organizations realize that a platform is the way to go, they don't understand the workings of the platform business model. Many organizations misunderstand the curation of products and services with the platform business model.

While curation is an integral part of the platform model, it is not the only thing that makes the business a platform model. The platform allows easy self-onboarding, offboarding, and management of inventory. For example, a mall or a marketplace is a platform business where the mall provides space to each seller, and then sellers are responsible for managing their shops, inventories, and prices.

On the other hand, a department store is a curation business where stores stock up the merchandise and manage the inventory and the prices. Sellers are not free to join and take up the shelf space on their own. They must sign a contract and undergo various processes to add their products to these department stores. In this case, the flow of goods and services is still linear, where sellers sell to the department stores, and then stores sell to end users. To compete with digital platforms, these traditional businesses not only need a robust digital presence but also must change their business model. Along with consumers, they will have to open platforms to producers. The following diagram illustrates the flow of goods and services in a linear product versus a platform:

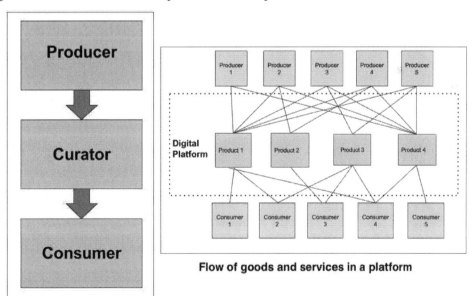

Flow of goods and services in a platform

Flow of goods and services in a linear product

Figure 10.1 – Flow of goods in a linear product and a platform

This diagram illustrates that the goods flow linearly even if there is a **Curator** between the **Producer** and the **Consumer**. The **Curator** decides which goods from which **Producer** will be offered to the consumers.

A few years back, I was working with a client which is a more than 100-year-old luxury department store in the US specializing in the sale of upscale fashion apparel and accessories. For the last few years, they had been struggling to compete with the newer online platforms. Their biggest problem was that they were not able to attract the younger generation. Their solution to this problem was to improve their digital footprint by creating a website built on an advanced tech stack and add some competitive features.

They had collections from some of the world's top designers, but their revenue and market share were constantly declining. And they did not realize that just creating a modern website would not attract millennials or the younger generation. They needed a shift in their business model. They could have transformed their business into a platform model and let designers create their boutiques and independently manage their merchandise.

This model would attract newer designers who would find it challenging to otherwise get shelf space in a physical store or a contract for their website. New and upcoming designers would have choices that are affordable and appealing to younger generations, which established brands and designers would not offer. There would be options for all the different consumer types, from affluent buyers who like to spend on designer brands to millennials who enjoy various options at more affordable prices. It would also give more choices to consumers and increase the competition between designers, bringing the overall prices down. Along with attracting new designers and younger consumers, a growing platform would also bring in benefits such as economies of scale that would help in reducing operating costs and other overheads.

An example of such a company that is making use of platform disruption by leveraging its existing capabilities is Walmart. Walmart Marketplace was started to let sellers add their products and sell on `walmart.com`. They are attracting sellers with their current consumer base of more than 200 million users. They are effectively using their existing capabilities from linear products to expand to the platform model. Recently, Walmart surpassed eBay as the second-largest online retailer in the US because of the combination of its vast existing consumer base and the continuous addition of producers through its Marketplace offering.

For some or most industries, transforming businesses to the platform model is inevitable. Organizations that understand the importance of this change and can pivot accordingly are moving toward success. However, those who don't realize this disruption are struggling to compete and are even getting wiped out. The question that arises here is: *where does your business fall in this transformation era and is it ready for the transformation?* Let's discuss how to answer this question by validating the viability of the platform model for your business.

Validating the viability of the platform model

Transitioning from linear products to platforms is essential, but the nature of each business is different. Every business has its own characteristics and components that may or may not make the platform model viable. It is essential to understand how to validate your business's transformation from a linear model to a platform model. Please remember, this validation is for existing linear businesses willing to transition. A new business validating the viability of the platform was covered in *Chapter 3, Research and Validation*. Let's look at some of the factors that can help us validate the viability of this transition:

- **Which side of the platform do you fall on?**: Most linear businesses are either producers or curators, as seen in the department store example earlier. Producers are manufacturers and suppliers of goods and services who sometimes sell directly to consumers, sometimes go via a curator, or sometimes both. For example, a hotel accepts bookings via their website and also through **Online Travel Agents** (**OTAs**).

  In this example, hotels are producers, and OTAs are curators, and it is advisable for OTAs to transition to the platform model as compared to hotels. Hotels should focus on improving their rooms, enhancing their services, reducing their operating costs, and so on. This will give better options to consumers at a reduced price. Hotels should leave the digital booking and all the technical investments associated with it to the OTAs and focus on their core capability, that is, hospitality.

  On the other hand, OTAs can transition to a platform; instead of individually contacting and contracting with each hotel, they can open a platform where hotels can register themselves, add their room inventory and rates, and so on. For example, Expedia allows hotels to register themselves and add their property. It gives hotels access to close to 18 million daily Expedia visitors and provides an additional choice for Expedia consumers, increasing the number of visitors on Expedia. Hence, in turn, increasing the network effect generated by the platform.

To summarize, it is more viable and suitable for curators to transition to a platform business model and producers to leverage these platforms so that the entire ecosystem can benefit from the platform network effect.

- **The demand and supply proportion**: As we discussed in the previous chapter, if you are planning to launch a platform, building something without research doesn't work. It is crucial to understand whether the demand and supply are in the right proportion for the given service. This is also true when you are planning to transition your existing business; analyzing the ratio of producers and consumers for your particular service is the most critical step of platform viability validation.

For example, say you are a shop selling winter sports gear and equipment from different manufacturers. You are a curator, so the transition to a platform sounds reasonable, but remember this is a very seasonal business and may not be worth the platform investment. Your producers will not go through the pain of onboarding on your platform, adding their merchandise, and managing it for a seasonal business that will generate demand only for a few months. This is true for any niche business; constant demand around the year is crucial to motivate producers to take the effort of onboarding on the new platform. And as a platform owner, it is also essential for you to know the ROI from the platform. If it cannot generate enough revenue to cover the investment and make a profit, then it is not viable to transition to a platform.

Like having a year-round demand for the service, it is also essential to have enough suppliers (producers). Otherwise, it will lead to the similar problem of consumers not finding producers and hence not being attracted to join the platform, leading to low revenue and no profit. In some cases, it is possible that you might find producers in one city but not in all of them. For example, dog walking or veterinary clinics – these services might have enough vets or dog walkers in a few cities but not in all. In such cases, expansion becomes difficult. Hence, the research and analysis that is essential here is: *can your platform be sustained within the cities where the supply levels are high?* If you cannot support your business and get ROI, then transitioning to a platform is not a viable option in this case.

- **Is opening to producers suitable?**: The fundamental functioning of the platform is that it is open and allows unrestricted signing up of producers. But it is important to understand the impact of openness on producers. We touched upon this topic in *Chapter 9, Ongoing Backlog Prioritization*: how producers can misuse the platform and turn it into something unethical and socially irresponsible. Suppose your business falls under one of these categories and you are planning to transition to a platform model. In that case, you would have to take additional measures to ensure that producers don't misuse the platform, for example, a payment processing platform becoming a money laundering source.

  In some cases, you would also have to follow certain rules, regulations, and censorship for the products, services, and content you are offering on the platform. Even though the producer is selling it directly, you must adhere to those rules and censorship. This is one of the reasons that Netflix does not allow content creators to upload their shows or movies directly. They must first submit a proposal and go through an approval process. Therefore, many people argue whether Netflix is a platform business model or not. In my opinion, it is still a platform where content from all over the world can be streamed at any time consumers want, as opposed to a local cinema running one movie for a limited period. They are not as open to producers as other platforms because they must follow different regulations and censorship requirements in different countries.

  The point here is if your business cannot be directly open to producers without adding layers of reviews and regulations, then there is an extra cost and operational overhead that gets added to your overall system. This additional cost and operational effort may make your platform unsustainable and hence not a viable choice to transition.

Increasing the number of businesses transitioning to the platform is unavoidable and it is recommended to create a strong demand and supply ecosystem that can generate value for everyone. But certain industries and business types are not ready yet and have a long way to go before they can transition to the platform model. In some cases, where you are a producer, it makes sense to stick to your area of expertise and leverage other platforms to improve your business. In this case, the industry and the ecosystem, including you, benefit from the platform model, but it is not a viable choice for you to transition.

This is the first step of your research and validation for transitioning to the platform model. But to determine the ultimate viability of transitioning from a linear business model to the platform business model, you should also undertake other validation steps discussed in *Chapter 3, Research and Validation*:

- Gathering feedback from the users on the new side to understand their willingness to use the platform and the products, services, or functionalities they are interested in.

- Doing competitor analysis to know the competition from similar platforms and linear businesses catering to this new side.

- Conducting pricing and cost analysis to understand the financial viability and implications of the transition.

Before starting the transition toward the platform model, you should know the answers to some essential questions. These answers will help you make strategic decisions for this transition. Let's dive deeper into those questions.

Prerequisites to start the transition

Assume that after all the research, analysis, and validation, you have concluded that it is viable for you to transition from a linear business model to a platform model; the question is *how will you execute this transition and where should you start?*

Before you start executing the transition, there are certain details that you should understand and identify, such as which is your stronger side, what your core capabilities are, and so on. Let's go deeper into understanding what the aspects are that you should know and define as the first step in executing the transition to a platform business model:

- **Know your core offering**: When you have a linear business, over the years, you will have developed many offerings for your customers. But when you want to transform to a platform model, you should focus on your core service or offering and start with that rather than platforming multiple services and offerings simultaneously. For example, you have a logistics company that hires and contracts delivery personnel to fulfill orders for consumers taken by various manufacturers.

Over the years, as your business expanded, you also started a standalone e-commerce website to accept orders, source them via different manufacturers, and fulfill them using your logistics expertise. Since you already had logistics expertise, you expanded to be a curator, which is a small part of your business. Most of your business still comes from fulfilling the orders taken by different manufacturers. When you want to transition to a platform model, you should start with logistics and fulfillment, as that is your core. And later, you can expand to be a marketplace that also has end-to-end fulfillment abilities.

- **Know your expansion side**: When you want to transition to a platform model, you should understand which side of the platform spectrum your current users are on and which side you should grow in order to make it a platform and achieve the benefits of the network effect. For example, if your existing business is focused on the consumer side, you should open and grow the producer side and vice versa.

In *Chapter 4, Building a Platform Strategy*, one of the platform strategies discussed was expanding to the opposite side. This strategy is applicable in this scenario when existing linear businesses are willing to transition to the platform model. The strategy here is to use the current user base to attract the other side. For example, if you have a significant user base of consumers, then it is easier to attract producers. Similarly, if there are many producers on the platform, consumers get better choices at competitive prices, which will attract them to the platform.

Remember, this is not about the number of users, but which side is your existing customer base. For example, as we saw earlier in the instance of OTAs and department stores, these businesses are open to consumers, who act as their current customers. They don't allow producers to openly come on board, which means producers are not their customers. Hence, their expansion side should be producers. Similarly, for B2C payment processing companies, their existing customers are sellers. That means they are strong on the producer side and should expand on the consumer side when transitioning to a platform and create a network of buyers and sellers or producers and consumers.

Hence, while transforming from a linear model to a platform model, the strategy is to complete the network by expanding to the opposite side.

- **Know the motivation of your expansion side**: Once you have identified which side of the platform you want to expand to complete the network, the next step is to determine how to attract users from that side. Understanding the motivation or the driver for the users on the opposite side to join the platform can help formulate appropriate plans to expand the user base of that side. For example, if we want to expand the consumer side, then some of the motivational factors could be the variety of choices, reduced prices, good quality because of competition between producers on the platform, and so on. Whereas, if we want to expand the producer side, the motivational factors could be giving them access to the vast consumer base, global reach, low digital investment, and so on.

  When you know the users' motivation on the new side of your business, your focus should be to keep improving and optimizing for the motivation factor. For example, if your producers are attracted because of your existing consumer base, do not let your active consumers decrease – in fact, keep increasing that number. If your producers are attracted by low digital investment, keep it less technical for them to join the platform, such as providing a user interface instead of APIs to integrate. Similarly, if their motivation is global reach, then do not lose sight of your international expansions. In the same way, if you want to expand to the consumer side and their motivation is quality, then make sure that producers on your platform are offering quality products and services. Adding mechanisms to review and rate producers can help get feedback about the quality of products and services.

Once you know the core offering that you'll be using for transitioning to the platform model, know your current customer side along with the side you want to expand, and understand the motivating factors to attract that side of users to the platform.

Starting the transition

After all the research, analysis, and finishing the prerequisite steps, you will have the strategy in place for which customer side to expand, the offering to focus on, and how to motivate the users. The marketing team will start their research by captivating the market share of the new user group, experimenting with different communications, and beginning to create initial awareness about the platform approach.

In this stage, product managers, along with other team members and product stakeholders, will start planning the features and capabilities. This is the introduction phase of the product life cycle that consists of development and launch, but it will be different from the brand-new platform. You will have an established brand, existing users, analytics data from the existing business, and expertise in the domain. You should make use of all your existing resources to transition your linear business to a platform model.

For the development stage of this transitioned model, which is a platform, product managers will go through some similar steps, but the execution of these steps will differ as you are not starting from the ground up. The following diagram illustrates different steps of the development stage and what factors must be considered in each of them:

Figure 10.2 – Steps in the development phase of the transition

This diagram depicts various steps in the development phase that are not different from any other product development, such as identifying the roadmap, defining the MVP, and prioritizing the ongoing backlog. But each of these steps will be executed slightly differently because you are not starting from scratch. Hence, there is a highlighting factor in each of these steps that must be considered during execution; let's understand these factors:

1. **Leveraging existing capabilities**: While creating the roadmap with features and capabilities for the new user group and completing the end-to-end platform flow, remember to leverage as many existing capabilities as possible that you could use. Do not reinvent the wheel unless absolutely necessary. Leveraging existing capabilities implies that capabilities common for both producers and consumers such as authentication, user onboarding, preferences and recommendations, notifications, and so on must be reused for the new user role if you have already built them for the existing one.

You will have to expand and tweak those capabilities to fit the new user role. For example, producers' preferences will be different from consumers', and hence new changes must be accommodated and added to the existing capability. The same goes for technical capabilities and experience; for example, if you have a sign-up form for consumers, do not build it from scratch for producers.

But there is a caveat here. If your existing capabilities are not implemented with a modular architecture, you should plan to re-architect them. Please do not take up your entire current product for re-architecting and identify capabilities that are needed for the new flow and start to modularize them. For example, suppose authentication and recommendations are two capabilities required for this new flow, and you must modify them to fulfill the new use case. In that case, you should plan to redesign these capabilities in a modular architecture.

In your roadmap, you should first define all the capabilities and features in the experience apps and channels needed for onboarding the new user group and platform end-to-end flow. Secondly, divide these capabilities and features into three buckets: first are new capabilities that don't exist, second are the ones that can be reused with modifications, and third are the ones that need an architectural rewrite. Lastly, plot these capabilities and features in the roadmap view discussed in *Chapter 5, Defining the MVP and Creating a Platform Roadmap.*

2. **Starting small on the expansion side**: After the roadmap is created, the next step is to define the MVP. As with any other MVP, you should start small with the new user side. Identify the thinnest user flow that will let the new user group join the platform, match them with the existing user of the other side, and complete the flow.

   Based on the identified end-to-end flow, define the MVP. This flow will cut across different capabilities and features that you have added to the roadmap. Your MVP development work might have capabilities from all three buckets or just one of them. Please remember that you want to test the water here by opening the platform to this new user role and connecting it with the existing user group. Hence, keep the features simple and the flow as optimized as possible.

   Starting small is not just applicable for features and capabilities but also to the launch. Restrict the release to a small test group and gradually increase the size. If possible, pilot the launch in one city or an even smaller locality, collect feedback, improve, and slowly roll it out to different cities.

3.   **Planning around motivations**: For the first few months of the transition phase, the focus should be to accumulate the users from the new side, either producers or consumers. Hence, we should prioritize capabilities around the motivation factors that we would have identified to attract the new user group to the platform.

Along with attracting the new user group to the platform, connecting and matching both types of users – producers and consumers – is extremely critical. And then, finally, enabling the increase in interaction on the platform. Motivational factors are not restricted to accumulation, but they also enable producers and consumers to connect and complete interactions.

You should focus on adding features and capabilities that create the correct ratio of producers and consumers on the platform in the initial stages. And the bigger your existing customer side is, the longer it will take to reach the proper ratio. After a few releases, slowly start to adopt the metrics-driven prioritization that was discussed in *Chapter 9, Ongoing Backlog Prioritization*. Metrics-driven prioritization will help improve accumulation, connection, and interaction, thereby enhancing the overall platform value.

The business will run in a hybrid model during the transition journey, which means it is not entirely transitioned and operates as a linear and platform model. This could be a conscious business decision to continue in this mode for a long time or just for an interim period. We will discuss what a hybrid model looks like in the next section, but as product managers, you should plan and prioritize capabilities to manage both models offered by the business. Do not lose sight of or ignore your current user role and user flow while adding capabilities for the new user group.

After the launch, you will continue with the post-launch activities, gathering metrics, and prioritizing your capabilities and features driven by the result of the metrics. Once you have introduced the platform model for your business, you will run both the platform and the linear model in parallel for some time. Let's go deeper into understanding what that means for the day-to-day functioning of the business.

Running a hybrid model

A critical aspect of the transition to the platform model is that you will be running in a hybrid model for quite some time. Sometimes, it will be your long-term strategy to run the business in a hybrid model as a linear product and as a platform. In some cases, running both in parallel will be a short-to medium-term approach until you transition entirely. Let's look at the logistics business example that we touched upon earlier in detail to understand what that transition will look like.

We discussed in the example that there is an existing logistics business that contracts and hires delivery personnel to fulfill the online orders taken by different manufacturers. Later, the business expands and starts accepting online orders and continues with the fulfillment service for orders taken elsewhere. We discussed in this scenario that when the business decides to transition to a platform model, it should first focus on *platforming* the fulfillment service as that is its core offering.

If we go deeper and break down this transition, then for the fulfillment service the manufacturers will be the existing customers. They will send the order details to this logistics and fulfillment service provider. Delivery personnel will be individually contracted and manually added to the ecosystem. They will be assigned orders to deliver where they will have no selection option. Fulfillment service providers manage the contracting of delivery personnel based on the forecast of the number of orders to be fulfilled in upcoming weeks/months.

If we want to transition this business to a platform model, the first step would be to start open onboarding for the delivery personnel. Delivery personnel will sign up to the platform. They will have their dashboard where they can see all the available orders to choose from. They'll select and fulfill the orders that are convenient for them to deliver. They can also select different legs of the shipment if it is a multi-city shipment, for example, from manufacturer warehouse to loading warehouse, from destination city warehouse to consumer, and so on. During the interim period, when there aren't enough delivery personnel on the platform, the fulfillment service provider will have to continue contracting the additional people to complete the delivery of the orders that manufacturers are continuously sending.

This individual contracting will gradually reduce and ultimately stop until enough delivery personnel are on the platform to fulfill all the orders. I would call this phase *a hybrid approach* because there is no open onboarding for manufacturers. There is an existing partnership between the manufacturers and the logistics company for the fulfillment of the orders. The next step in further *platforming* this business would be to allow manufacturers to sign up for the delivery and fulfillment services. The manufacturers will add orders on the platform with all the necessary details such as the expected date and time of delivery, delivery address, package size and weight, and so on. The platform will create a shipment with all the legs needed for the delivery. The delivery personnel within the closest range of the source and destination of the shipment legs will receive a notification, and they can accept the order and continue with the delivery. If they reject it, other delivery personnel will be assigned.

When any manufacturer and delivery personnel can openly join the platform, and the platform's job is to connect and match them, the platform is completely transitioned. This will be a long journey, and there will be many pivot points based on the internal and external factors impacting the business. For example, a sudden shortage of delivery personnel, changes in regulations, and so on. Further expansion of this platform would be to create an end-to-end marketplace, including fulfillment, where manufacturers are not just sending orders but also adding and managing their inventory, consumers are searching for products and ordering on the platform, and delivery personnel are fulfilling those orders.

As discussed earlier, during the hybrid phase, product managers should add and prioritize capabilities to meet the requirements of both models. But it is crucial to understand whether the hybrid model is a long-term strategy or an interim phase. If it is just a stopgap, then make sure that you strike a balance in adding capabilities that will not be useful or applicable after the transition is completed and the necessity of the system to operate.

So far, what we have seen in this chapter will help us with transitioning an end-to-end business to a platform model. This is a long, iterative journey, with multiple phases, where you will run the model in hybrid mode for quite some time, and it is all about transitioning the entire business to a new model. But there is a completely alternate aspect of the platform transition: transitioning individual layers to a platform. Let's explore this transition of layers to the platform in detail.

The platform transition at different layers

We have discussed multiple times in this book that digital platforms consist of three layers: infrastructure, business, and experience/channels. Each layer can be treated and converted into a platform. Infrastructure and business layers are the most common internal platforms that some organizations have started moving toward as part of their digital transformation journey.

The first phase in this transformation is to modularize the architecture and separate the layers. All the technical and functional capabilities of infrastructure and business layers can be exposed as APIs for consumption by internal channels and other layers. For example, adding a room for a hotel on an OTA portal can be extracted out and exposed as an API that will be consumed by a website or an iOS app accessed via an iPad. Similarly, data encryption can be built out as a framework that any other APIs or channels can use.

This phase of modularizing the architecture is not a sprint but a marathon, and a challenging one. Every feature of the product, be it functional or technical, must be converted to individual APIs or reusable frameworks and libraries. Product managers play a vital role during this phase, in identifying and prioritizing capabilities to be extracted. The essential capabilities of the new features must be prioritized first to be extracted to the platform. Assuming that we have followed metrics-driven prioritization for our features, then our capability extraction to the platform will be prioritized based on metrics indirectly. As the platform grows with technical and functional capabilities, we can structure the teams around those capabilities and build a governance model for those teams, as discussed in *Chapter 7, Creating a Platform Operating Model*.

Once the capabilities are exposed as APIs for consumption by internal channels, they can also be exposed to external channels. In the example mentioned earlier, the capability of adding a room can also be exposed to external channels such as hotels. Hotels can directly integrate using the API and start adding rooms on the platform.

This exposure of APIs to external channels is the starting point of the journey of externalizing the platform. This external consumption is not restricted just to the functional capabilities; the same applies to technical capabilities. Technical capabilities can also be converted to APIs and frameworks, which the internal and external systems can consume. To expose the APIs and frameworks to external channels and partners, we do not have to wait for all the features to be translated to the platform; we can expose them as and when they are ready and even start monetizing them in some cases.

We touched upon this topic in the earlier chapters, that when extracting capabilities into APIs and frameworks, make sure that there is no difference between internal versus external consumption. Every capability must be implemented independently and with the same robustness to be consumed by any other application and system, whether internal or external. This enables us to open our internal APIs and frameworks to the external world without any extra implementation.

There are tons of examples of APIs and frameworks initially built only for internal consumption that were later exposed externally. The most disruptive example in this category is **AWS**. AWS infrastructure was created to support the scale of **Amazon.com**, and it was later launched as an infrastructure platform for other businesses. Currently, around 52% of Amazon's operating income comes from AWS. This explains why there is no restriction on a particular part or module of your application that can be transitioned to a platform. Each layer of the digital platform, if built right, can be treated as a platform of its own.

The following diagram illustrates different layers of the end-to-end digital platform as individual platforms:

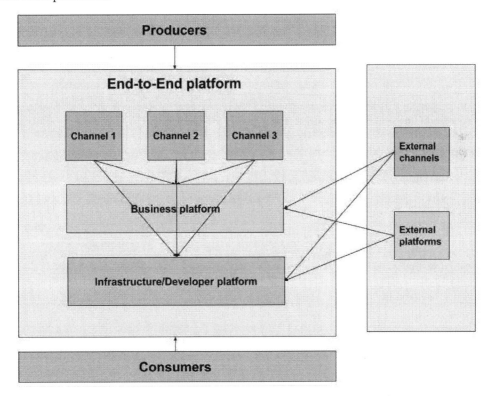

Figure 10.3 – Layers of the platform business acting as individual platforms

The diagram depicts the breakdown of an end-to-end platform into different layers and how each layer can be a platform in itself. **Business** and **Infrastructure** platforms usually start as internal platforms and are later exposed to **External channels** and **External platforms**. It will depend on the platform type for us to know how big, small, heavy, and lightweight our **Business** and **Infrastructure** platforms/layers are going to be.

The bottom line here is if you have a product built on modularized architecture with independent components and if you implement your features with the *platform-first approach*, you can transition any layer or any module of your product to a platform.

Case study

During the course of this book, most of the case studies and examples that we have discussed fell into the B2C category; B2B businesses need the same disruption and transition to the platform model. Many organizations have started to see the need for this transformation and have begun making advances in this direction, but they are even slower than B2C businesses. In particular, the product function is unable to adapt to this change and take everyone forward in this transformation journey. Hence, in this case study, we will cover the transition of a B2B enterprise solution from a linear model to a platform model.

Let's take a common and very popular enterprise solution that helps organizations automate their **Accounts Payable** (**AP**) and pay cycle (also known as payment automation). The flow of this process is that the supplier sends an invoice to buyers, it goes through the approval workflow in the buyer's organization, invoices are added to the accounting system, the payment requests are created in the accounting system, and finally, payment is executed with the agreed-upon method. All the AP and payment automation software mirrors this flow and automates this process. This is what the automated flow looks like:

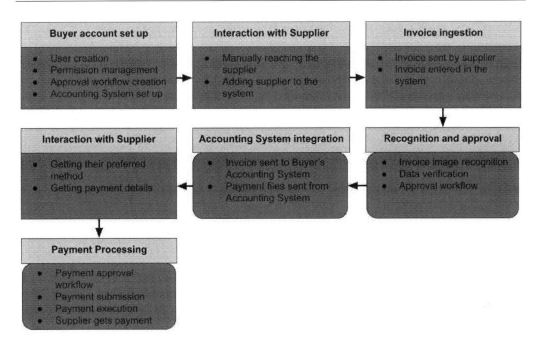

Figure 10.4 – Accounts payable and payment flow

At a high level, all AP automation solutions have the same flow as depicted in the diagram. The steps in *rounded boxes* are automated and the steps in *normal (rectangular) boxes* are either fully manual or semi-automated depending on the maturity level of the solution. For these enterprise solutions, buyers are the end users who pay for the license for the software.

Usually, the sales team reaches out to individual buyers and closes the deal with them. After the solution is sold, the software is customized for each buyer and integrated with their accounting systems. Customization involves adding their users with different roles, setting up their approval process, payment details, and so on. *This whole process takes close to 2 months. This is a tedious process, loaded with manual interventions and operational overheads repeated for each and every buyer.* And this is just the buyers' side.

The automation of the suppliers' side varies in different software as they are not the paying customers; the majority of their process is manual, where associates from the software provider reach out to suppliers during invoice ingestion and payment processing and complete the necessary actions. Some solutions have this flow semi-automated where suppliers are added as the users in the system, and they can upload invoices in the system and add their payment preferences. And this semi-automation only starts after the associates from the software providers have used the system on suppliers' behalf at least once and manually added them.

The first phase in *platforming* this flow is to open it to the new side – the suppliers, in this case. Supplier onboarding should be open, fully automated, and with as few steps as possible. Suppliers joining the platform can manage their workflow. After they have signed up and are onboarded, they can add buyers to their *My Buyers* list. Also, while raising an invoice, they can choose the buyer they want to send the invoice to and select the payment method for that invoice, which will be their regular workflow.

To add suppliers to the platform, we will have to start with the networks of suppliers in business with existing buyers. They should be added to this new system and should be given control of their accounts. New potential suppliers of existing buyers should be reached out to next and encouraged to join the platform. Some of the motivating aspects that would help attract suppliers are a fully automated process that is efficient and fast, giving them complete control of their accounts, the possibility to reach out to new buyers from the platform in the future, and so on.

At this stage, the buyer flow will remain as is. The customization happens manually for each buyer; they receive the invoice after the supplier has raised it, followed by invoice approval, payment creation in accounting systems, and payment processing. This is what the flow will look like after this first phase of transformation:

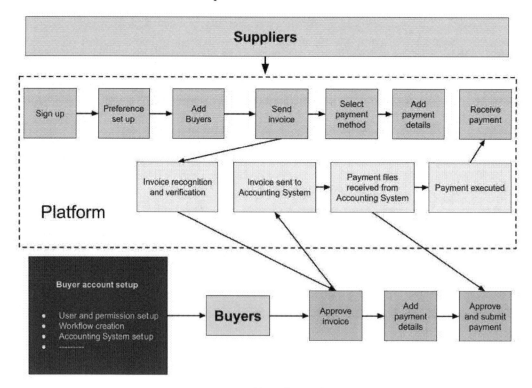

Figure 10.5 – Accounts payable and partial payment platform

This diagram illustrates a partial platform where **Suppliers** can openly onboard the platform and use all the capabilities without any intervention. **Buyers** go through the existing flow of getting the account set up via the platform provider. All the tasks and actions in the *top* row are the supplier flow, the *last* row outside **Platform** is the buyer flow, and the *middle* row is the background processes that happen in the system. The **Buyer account setup** is represented in a big block before the buyer flow starts, which is a semi-automated process undertaken by the platform provider's team. The platform provider repeats this setup for every buyer.

The next phase of this transition would be to let **Buyers** openly sign up and customize their accounts. They can add all their users with different roles, configure their workflows, select their accounting system for integration, add their payment details, and so on. **Buyers** should be able to do all this setup and customization independently without intervention from the platform provider's team.

In this phase, the **Suppliers** outside the network of the existing **Buyers** should also be reached out to join the platform. And this growing supplier network should be used to captivate buyers, thereby improving the platform's network effect. The following diagram depicts the flow after the platform is open to both **Suppliers** and **Buyers**:

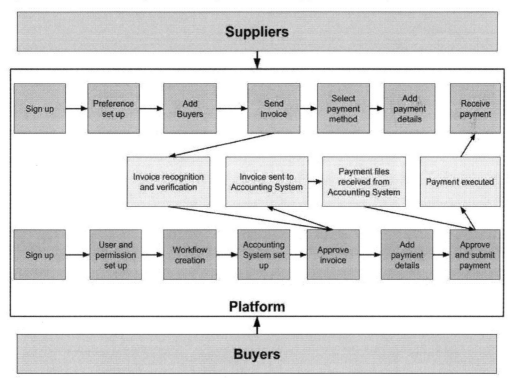

Figure 10.6 – Accounts payable and full payment platform

This diagram illustrates the platform that is open to both **Buyers** and **Suppliers**. There is no intervention from the platform provider's team for any setup. Like *Figure 10.5*, all the tasks and actions in the *top* row belong to the supplier flow, the *lower* row is the buyer flow, and the *middle* row is the background process that happens in the system.

There is another entity in this platform ecosystem, which is the accounting system. Allowing open integrations from an accounting system could be one more phase of this platform. Partnering with accounting systems will open the doors for all the buyers already using that accounting system. With this flow, accounting systems could sign up and integrate with the platform. So, when the buyer signs up to the platform, they do not have to set up the accounting system but only select from the list of already integrated accounting systems.

Summary

In this chapter, we discussed the transition journey of businesses from linear products to the platform. We started by understanding the need for transformation. We discussed how disruption occurring in various industries due to rising platforms is inevitable, and hence transforming linear businesses to the platform model is essential. And this transition to the platform model can benefit the entire ecosystem and not just the platform owners.

We learned how to validate whether transforming to a platform model is a viable option or not. Businesses in certain industries are not yet ready to be changed because of the open nature of the platforms and regulations and misuse opportunities in those industries. In some cases, the platform model is advisable for the system, but it may not be suitable for specific players in the system. For example, in industries such as retail, travel, and service crowdsourcing, where platform businesses have proven themselves, the platform model is the way forward, but it is not suitable for producers. Producers should focus on their core expertise and improve their products and services but leverage the existing platforms to reach and connect with consumers.

We discussed the aspects and factors that you should know about and consider before starting the transition from a linear business to a platform model. We discussed the steps of the transition and the specific execution of those steps by product managers. We looked at a critical facet of the transition: the hybrid model that the business reaches during the transition. Sometimes it is a long-term strategy to run both models in parallel, and sometimes it is just an interim phase that every business will go through as part of this transformation journey.

This was the last chapter of this book. We covered the end-to-end platform life cycle while understanding in detail the different concepts, techniques, frameworks, strategies, and execution plans necessary for effective platform product management. The key to effective platform product management is to understand the difference between traditional linear products and platforms. Platforms are multidimensional; they enable plug-and-play mechanisms and their success depends on creating more substantial network effects. These are three fundamental characteristics of the platform and you will observe these characteristics playing a vital role throughout the platform life cycle.

As product managers, we must ensure that these three characteristics of the platform are factored in and considered at every phase and stage of the platform life cycle – right from ideation to growth and expansion. Remember that these characteristics don't work in isolation; they work together to generate the overall value of the platform.

The platform's success depends on how robust these three characteristics are, which means how good the platform is in the accumulation, connection, and interaction of its users. The definition for the platform strategy and its day-to-day execution should be continuously optimized for accumulating users from all sides (producers, consumers, and intermediaries), connecting them, and enabling their interactions. The core offering of a platform is not selling products and services but connecting its users and enabling their interactions. Hence, as product managers, make sure that this is reflected in all your strategies, plans, and prioritizations.

Other Books You May Enjoy

If you enjoyed this book, you may be interested in these other books by Packt:

Lean Product Management

Mangalam Nandakumar

ISBN: 978-1-78883-117-8

- How do you execute ideas that matter?
- How can you define the right success metrics?
- How can you plan for product success?
- How do you capture qualitative and quantitative insights about the product?
- How do you know whether your product aligns to desired business goals?
- What processes are slowing you down?

Scaling Scrum Across Modern Enterprises

Cecil Rupp

ISBN: 978-1-83921-647-3

- Understand the limitations of traditional Scrum practices
- Explore the roles and responsibilities in a scaled Scrum and Lean-Agile development environment
- Tailor your Scrum approach to support portfolio and large product development needs
- Apply systems thinking to evaluate the impacts of changes in the interdependent parts of a larger development and delivery system
- Scale Scrum practices at both the program and portfolio levels of management
- Understand how DevOps, test automation, and CI/CD capabilities help in scaling Scrum practices

Packt is searching for authors like you

If you're interested in becoming an author for Packt, please visit `authors.packtpub.com` and apply today. We have worked with thousands of developers and tech professionals, just like you, to help them share their insight with the global tech community. You can make a general application, apply for a specific hot topic that we are recruiting an author for, or submit your own idea.

Share your thoughts

Now you've finished *Effective Platform Product Management*, we'd love to hear your thoughts! Scan the QR code below to go straight to the Amazon review page for this book and share your feedback or leave a review on the site that you purchased it from.

https://packt.link/r/1-801-81135-0

Your review is important to us and the tech community and will help us make sure we're delivering excellent quality content.

Index

Made in United States
Orlando, FL
04 June 2022